Source Book of American Presidential Campaign and Election Statistics
1948–1968

Source Book of American Presidential Campaign and Election Statistics

===== 1948–1968 =====

COMPILED AND EDITED BY

John H. Runyon / Jennefer Verdini / Sally S. Runyon

EAGLETON INSTITUTE OF POLITICS
Rutgers University, State University of New Jersey

FOREWORD BY

Hubert H. Humphrey

UNITED STATES SENATE

FREDERICK UNGAR PUBLISHING CO.
NEW YORK

IN MEMORIAM

Miss Harriet Nadine Saks

A FRIEND

CONTENTS

FOREWORD

This handbook is not just a compilation of names, places, vote percentages, and other data on campaigns and campaign practices. It literally should be a book in hand for every practicing politician. It should be available not just during campaigns and elections but throughout the years a man or woman is in office.

The Source Book of American Presidential Campaign and Election Statistics, compiled at Eagleton Institute, is more than raw data and a few lessons drawn from that data—more than a blueprint for victory. It also provides those in office with the know-how to tailor approaches and programs to achieve voter acceptance.

A President, Senator, and Congressman need to know the hopes and fears, likes and dislikes of the people. They are there to represent the people and to give voice to their views and aspirations. Reflecting the opinions of the electorate requires a political leader to know the full spectrum of these opinions in depth. Faithful representation requires this detailed knowledge of the electorate.

How people vote is how they feel and think on the issue or the individual office seeker. But a politician—a representative of the people—is also in office to provide leadership. He is not in office to reflect the electorate's views slavishly. He is there to be educated and made fully aware of the complexities of an almost numberless catalogue of local and national problems. He is there to educate and lead.

We know now that we don't know all the answers. We must look for new ways to solve old problems—not look to solve these same problems with answers that create new problems. Most of our approaches and answers are being questioned. The times demand change, and those who attempt this change must realize the risks involved—both to their ideas and to themselves. But the leader must take these risks—must dare to solve massive problems without losing the human touch or dimension.

The data and insights provided by this volume can be invaluable in helping prepare the voter for these new ideas, new political terrain, new approaches, and new programs. While this is a handbook of victory, it is also a guidebook for leadership.

We have mentioned that political leadership providing fresh ideas and new approaches to solving perennial problems of government can be risky. Before embarking on this path of certain uncertainty, an innovative leader must be sure of his facts. He must have the type of data provided by this source book. He must have the tools to draw up a blueprint not only to personal political victory but to victory in the exercise of constructive and innovative leadership.

That is the way I look on this source book—as a guide to leadership. The Eagleton Institute of Politics at Rutgers University, the authors and editors are to be commended for compiling this one-of-a-kind volume. It is needed and should be used extensively by those who first ask the people for their vote and then ask for a vote of confidence in their leadership and vision.

HUBERT H. HUMPHREY

INTRODUCTION

This book is the only reference volume that is a comprehensive compilation of the data pertaining to American Presidential Campaigns and Elections for the period of 1948–1968. We have tried to edit this information so that it will be useful not only to scholars and political practitioners but also to the general public. Prior to this volume, information on contemporary Presidential Campaigns and Elections was scattered and, in some cases, unobtainable for scholarly or practical application. We believe our work will be of some help in alleviating the research dilemmas of the many who attempt to deal with and understand this subject.

Our rationale in selecting 1948 as the first campaign for inclusion in this volume is straightforward. The campaign of 1948 is the watershed of contemporary presidential campaigning. Presidential Preference Primaries regained considerable importance in that year. The electronic media was beginning to edge into presidential campaigning as an important factor. Public opinion polls were given widespread, though erroneous, credence. Schisms within the Republican and Democratic parties, which were to have their effect for the next twenty years, found their beginning in 1948 as the Roosevelt coalition and the Republican presidential party began to change. For all of these reasons, 1948 seemed a most propitious starting point for our work.

We have arranged the data in this volume in approximately the same sequence as that of an actual presidential campaign, beginning with Presidential Primaries and ending with the General Election returns. Deviations from this pattern occur because of the need to keep the various types of data separate for the sake of clarity. For instance, preconvention and postconvention public opinion polling are included in Part VII. Within each part of the volume the data is arranged by year, beginning with 1948 and ending with 1968. We did not perceive organization of the data into comparative tables as one of our primary functions. To do so would have, at times, imposed our assumptions concerning the nature of the data onto the user.

The several brief essays included represent some of our thoughts on presidential campaigning that have evolved in the course of editing and transcribing the data for this volume. The intent is to trigger greater and more precise analysis of the organization, techniques, and substance of presidential campaigning. Additionally, each part of the volume is preceded by a technical note. This should be read before the data in that part is used.

Part I opens with an essay on Presidential Preference Primaries, followed by the primary results for 1948 through 1968. The vote for major contenders in the various party primaries is reported, as well as the write-in vote for other less important contenders. As is the case with all of the data in this volume, Part I should be approached with some historical perspective. Knowing the winners and losers of specific primaries does not necessarily indicate the importance of those primaries in the campaign as a whole. In the 1968 New Hampshire primary, President Johnson actually won the preference vote of Democrats in that state. Historically, however, the New Hampshire primary was a crucial defeat for President Johnson in his early bid for reelection.

The dates, vote, and officers of the twelve party conventions since 1948 are recorded in Part II. In addition to the voting for nominations, roll call votes for platform and rules committee matters are also included. As the convention essay in this part states, the roll call voting on platform and party rules matters is perhaps of greater interest and importance to students of party conventions than the ballots cast for the presidential nominee. The roll call votes on substantive matters, more often than not, reflect the mood of the party and indicate the strength of the various candidates in the convention before the actual process of nomination begins. It has been on these matters that the great conflicts of opinion beneath the unified face of our parties have been revealed.

The number of people involved in a presidential campaign is enormous, probably totaling several hundred thousand at all levels. Part III lists the major advisors of the party nominees since 1948. These men and women represent the nucleus of the campaign organizations. Though each candidate for President has approached the organization and staffing of his campaign in a different manner, leadership in the hectic pace of presidential campaigning falls on the shoulders of that small cadre of individuals upon whom the candidates have had to depend for previous political successes. Part III is preceded by an overview of presidential campaigns from 1948 to 1968, and it attempts to draw a broad outline of an increasingly complex picture.

The reconstruction of the itineraries of presidential candidates is an illusive task. It is one of the mysteries of American history that no attempt has been made, save for 1960 and the campaigns of incumbent Presidents, to record an accurate record of the course of presidential campaigns. In Part IV we hoped to remedy this situation by reconstructing the campaign routes of the presidential candidates. Since the candidates themselves have no record of their whereabouts during the campaigns, this was no simple task. The itineraries as presented are as complete as all available information would allow. They undoubtedly will be modified somewhat as additional information is uncovered. These itineraries are a key to the campaign strategies of the candidates, and as such, represent an important piece of information on presidential campaigning.

The financing of presidential campaigns is one of the largest can of worms in American political life. Very little attention was paid to the subject until Alexander Heard began his inquiries. Thus, there is little or no information available before 1948. Candidates are required to file reports with the Congress on campaign financing, but their reports probably do not reveal more than fifty percent of the income and expenditures of presidential campaigns. However inaccurate these reports are, they do provide data that demonstrates that the costs incurred in being a candidate are skyrocketing. The cost of the campaigns, as reported, jumped from nine million in 1948 to sixty-two million in 1968. The receipts and expenditures of Republican, Democratic, Labor, and minor party campaign committees are reported in Part V.

The increasing cost of presidential campaigning has been accompanied by the growth in importance of the electronic media in campaigning. The media costs are responsible to a degree for the rapid increase in campaign costs. The campaign of 1952 was the first to see television play a significant role. Unfortunately, it was not until 1956 that an attempt was made to compile the cost and extent of television and radio exposure for the campaign. Thus, Section A of Part VI, on the time and costs of media exposure, begins with data for 1956. In addition, for 1952 through 1968 information is available on the network television programs and announcements of the candidates. This data was compiled by the A. C. Nielsen Company for this book and is included in Section B of Part VI. The entries in that section are the date, network, time, person appearing, sponsor, length of program, and Nielsen ratings for each program or spot announcement of the candidates since 1952.

Public opinion polls are another factor of presidential campaigns that has grown in importance since 1948. Not only are the polls used to test voter preference among or between candidates, but also to sample voter attitudes on major issues and the acceptability of the candidates' stances on those issues. Part VII contains the public opinion polls on candidate preference as reported by Gallup. This part reports the preconvention preference of party members among their party's candidates, the preconvention public preference among major party candidates, and the postconvention public preference between party candidates.

Voting participation in American Presidential Elections has generally been considered low for a Western democracy. For the first time in any volume, comprehensive voting participation data has been compiled. Part VIII includes—by state—the voting age population, the number of registered voters (where registration is required), the number of votes cast, the percentage of voting age population voting, and the percentage of those registered voting for each presidential campaign.

Parts IX and X record the general election results. Part IX presents the popular vote for the Republicans, Democrats, and other candidates; the total vote cast; party percentages; and the plurality and electoral vote allocation for each election. Part X amplifies the vote for other than the Republican and Democratic candidates by including a state-by-state breakdown of minor party voting since 1948.

The selected bibliography that concludes this volume lists other major information sources on the presidential campaigns of 1948 through 1968.

The Eagleton Institute of Politics at Rutgers University provided the resources required for the production of this volume. Without Eagleton's support we could not have attempted this book. Any praise this volume might generate belongs to Eagleton, any criticism should be directed toward the compilers. Donald G. Herzberg, Executive Director of Eagleton, gave us the opportunity and moral support we needed. We thank him for his patience and faith in our endeavor. We also wish to thank those who contributed their insight to our project at the outset. Among them were Alan Rosenthal, Gerald Pomper, and Richard Scammon.

Our appreciation must also be extended to the Eagleton staff—in particular, to Juanda Kirk and Edith Saks—for their encouragement and assistance. Karen Osowski performed the arduous task of typing the manuscript for publication. Her dedication and professional skill is inestimable.

Among the many others we should thank for their assistance and cooperation are Miss Calliope Scumas, Production Manager of Frederick Ungar Publishing Co., Miss Josephine Good of the Republican National Committee, Mrs. Patricia Adams of Gallup Polls, Lou Bracknell of Senator Humphrey's staff, Pat DeCandia, Chris Shaw, and Chickie Charwin of the Eagleton Institute staff, and Henry Plotkin of Livingston College. Finally, but perhaps most importantly, we wish to thank Mr. Frederick Ungar for having enough faith in us to undertake the publication of this volume.

There is one last group of individuals who must merit our attention and praise and they are the Eagleton Fellows of 1968–1969. It was their research on the Presidential Campaigns of 1952–1964 that revealed the paucity of data on the subject and provided the germ from which this volume grew. They are: Betsy Crone, Kim Gilbert, David Harris, Anne Henderson, Susan Olsen McNamee, Beryn Roberts, Gene Robinson, Irwin Stoolmacher, Phyllis Daniel Stoolmacher, Tom Huntington, and Philip Kelsey.

The compilers hope that errors are few, but we shoulder the responsibility for all that is included here. If we have in some way advanced the availability of information concerning Presidential Campaigns and Elections, we are satisfied.

JOHN H. RUNYON
JENNEFER F. VERDINI
SALLY S. RUNYON

December 31, 1970

PART I

Presidential Preference
Primaries

NOTE

In Part I vote totals not attributed to a specific candidate or slate
are scattered and miscellaneous votes. Footnotes appear at the
conclusion of each table.

SOURCES

1948–1964 Presidential Preference Primaries

Davis, James W. PRESIDENTIAL PRIMARIES: ROAD TO THE
WHITE HOUSE. New York: Thomas Y. Crowell Co., 1967.
Copyright 1967 by Thomas Y. Crowell Company.

1968 Presidential Preference Primaries

Compiled from the records of the various Secretaries of State.

PRESIDENTIAL PREFERENCE PRIMARIES

For John F. Kennedy and Hubert Humphrey, there was no other than the primary way to the convention. If they could not at the primaries prove their strength in the hearts of Americans, the Party bosses would cut their hearts out in the back rooms of Los Angeles.[1]

The post-World War II era has been marked by the reemergence of the presidential preference primary as the critical battlefront where candidates for their party's nomination demonstrate their vote-getting abilities. There has been a shift of emphasis from party accountability to public accountability, which means that now candidates must at least demonstrate some strength with the public before the party machinery will choose them. This trend is a result of and has been paralleled by the growth of the electronics media and national public opinion polls. Television and radio transforms localized state primaries into national news; public opinion polls are quick to register the public's response to the candidates and the issues. Due to this phenomenon, presidential primaries since 1948 have been used by candidates for creating a national reputation and a winner image; for challenging rival party candidates for the nomination; or for settling an important issue or limitation surrounding a candidacy. John F. Kennedy and Hubert Humphrey would have had their "hearts cut out" if Kennedy had not settled the Catholic question in the primaries and if Humphrey had not created a national image. As it turned out, Humphrey never survived the primaries, a peril of this route, but the fact remains that he could not have gained the nomination otherwise.

Franklin Roosevelt's radio fireside chats were the first instance of the political use of mass communication, and it was only a matter of time before electronics would affect the nominating process. In 1948 Thomas E. Dewey and Harold Stassen debated coast-to-coast, via 800 radio stations. Since then there has been such extensive use of radio and television by aspiring candidates that contemporary campaign history is written in terms of the making and the selling of the President. A good indication of the extensive impact of the media on campaigning is the costs incurred by the major networks in any given election. It is not uncommon for the networks to spend over a million dollars for the cover-

---

[1] Theodore White, *The Making of the President, 1960* (New York: Atheneum Press, 1961), p. 79.

3

age of just one primary. In the New Hampshire primary of 1964, for example, just the telephone equipment for the networks cost $500,000.[2] Likewise, the increasing use of public opinion polls has resulted from and has been correspondent to the growth of mass communications. Today, an aspiring candidate can not only speak to millions of people at one time, but he can also gauge their response through the use of opinion polls. In 1948, opinion polls were limited to general usage such as news media coverage, but by 1960 polling became a sophisticated tool used by candidates in the construction and design of their campaigns.

Primaries are by no means necessary or sufficient for gaining one's party nomination. Usually primaries are crucial for the "out-party" nomination. Thus, despite Eugene McCarthy's impressive primary victories in 1968 he failed to gain his party's nomination because President Johnson maintained control of his party to the extent that he could choose his successor, Hubert Humphrey. The out-party, not controlling the Presidency, has to search more diligently for a candidate and competition is keener. Primaries become an important vehicle for weeding out and selecting national candidates. In 1968 George Romney was weeded out in New Hampshire while Richard Nixon regained a national reputation through successive primary victories. Primaries, however, remain as just one tactic in the quest for delegate strength at the national party convention. In order to win a party's nomination a candidate must accrue a majority of the delegate votes, and winning every primary will not yield enough delegate votes for victory.

The primary is, like most Twentieth-Century political reforms, an attempt to curtail boss rule. Until 1912, presidential candidates were selected at a national convention whose delegates were selected by party bosses or state party organizations. The primary was a way of cleaning up the convention by allowing for popularly selected delegates. A chronicle of the state convention in Chicago in 1896 is revealing in that it describes the typical delegate that would hopefully be replaced in a primary system:

> Among the 723 delegates, 17 had been tried for homicide, 46 had served terms in the penitentiary for homicide or other felonies, 84 were identified by detectives as having criminal records. Considerably over a third of the delegates were saloon keepers; two kept houses of ill-fame; several kept gambling resorts.[3]

By the time of the 1912 Republican convention twelve states had primary laws, and by 1916 nine more states had passed some kind of presidential primary law. This push for reform, however, came to an

---

[2] See James W. Davis, *Presidential Primaries: Road to the White House* (New York: Crowell, 1967), pp. 7–15.

[3] Quoted in Davis, *op. cit.*, p. 24.

abrupt halt during the roaring twenties, so that by 1935 eight states had abandoned their primary laws altogether. There are many reasons for the initial failure of primaries to become a viable political institution, but the most plausible explanation in retrospect is that primaries were not very functional prior to the growth in mass communication. Primaries have become significant because of their psychological affect on the electorate-at-large, an affect that could not be transmitted without the use of radio and television. By 1968 the American public had come to expect party candidates to come before them. To the public, primaries weren't just a campaign tactic; they were a very real means of voicing public opinion on who should be the candidate. After McCarthy's failure in his quest for the nomination, it became clear that the reality of seeking a presidential nomination does not lie in winning primaries per se. But because of the media coverage of primary candidates, an important part of the process for gaining nomination (the primaries) was now perceived as either the process itself or at least what should be the process. Thus, this misperception of the nominating process caused widespread dissatisfaction with the outcome. The cry that the people had no voice in the selection of the nominee was widespread.

The history of presidential campaigns since 1948 is sprinkled with key primary victories or defeats. Every campaign has been marked by a crucial primary battle. In 1948 the Oregon primary was important for Dewey in his battle with Robert Taft and Harold Stassen for the nomination; in 1952 the Eisenhower victory in Pennsylvania thrust the General into the center of the political limelight; in 1956 Florida was the decisive victory for Stevenson over Kefauver. In 1960 John Kennedy laid the Catholic issue to rest with his victory in the West Virginia primary. Goldwater's defeat of Rockefeller in California in 1964 dispersed the last shread of doubt that Goldwater was to be the nominee. In 1968, a year of political turmoil, New Hampshire was perhaps the most significant primary, although California would have been crucial if Robert Kennedy had not met with tragedy.

Though it is generally agreed that primaries are significant, political analysts differ in their assessment of how significant and desirable primaries are in the nominating process. It is argued that the primary is not very significant because it is an expensive and time-consuming tactic that cannot guarantee victory for a potential candidate. Critics of the primary system maintain further that primaries are not very useful or desirable because, first, presidential candidates are not required to participate in them; second, primary battles create divisions within the party; third, favorite-son candidacies dilute the significance of some state primary contests; fourth, a single primary defeat can eliminate an important and good presidential candidate; fifth, primaries are not really representative because they only involve a few states.

5

Despite the obvious limitations of the system, when assessing the significance of primaries one must take into account the fact that primaries do involve a large audience in the political process and, as such, influence delegates to the national conventions. In those states holding presidential primaries, the total population exceeds ninety million, and four of the most populous states of the union are among this group. While it is true that primary victories will not guarantee a convention victory, no major candidate has survived successive primary defeats to go on to victory. Delegate polls, taken before and after the primaries in any given election year, always indicate a shift on the plus side for the primary victor. Before the West Virginia primary Kennedy had approximately 241 delegates committed to him, but after his victory there and in Oregon, where only 13 delegate votes were at stake, his delegate support rose to 330.[4]

Primaries are useful for a number of reasons. They allow the rank-and-file voter to participate in the nominating process. They provide a forum where any man can come forth as a potential candidate and demonstrate his leadership abilities to the voter and the party leadership. Primaries are also an excellent testing ground where candidates can discuss issues and gauge what the public expects of them. Finally, primaries are useful in the absence of a more efficient and democratic method for detecting presidential timber.

The role of presidential preference primaries in the years ahead is hard to predict, but it seems clear that they will grow in importance and become perhaps the means of nominating rather than the significant, though not crucial, device in the process of nominating candidates for President.

---

[4] *See* Davis, *op. cit.*, pp. 77–98.

State	Truman	Other§	
Alabama			161,629^^
California	811,920		
Florida			92,169
Illinois	16,299	Eisenhower –	1,709
		Lucas –	427
			1,513^^
Massachusetts			51,207^^
Nebraska	67,672		894
New Hampshire			4,409^^
New Jersey	1,100	Wallace –	87
Ohio			271,146^^
Oregon	112,962		7,436
Pennsylvania	328,891	Eisenhower –	4,502
		Wallace –	4,329
		Stassen –	1,301
		MacArthur –	1,220
			2,409
South Dakota		Fellows –	11,193
			8,016
West Virginia			157,102^^
Wisconsin	25,415		4,906

§ Scattered voting unless otherwise allotted throughout
^ Write-in vote
^^ Delegate-at-large vote

PRESIDENTIAL PREFERENCE PRIMARIES
Republican: 1948

State	Dewey	Stassen	Taft	MacArthur	Other	
California					Warren-	769,520
Illinois	953	1,572	705	6,672	Bender-	324,029
						475^
Massachusetts						72,191^^
Nebraska	64,242	80,979	21,608	6,893	Vandenberg-	9,590
					Warren-	1,761
					Martin-	910
						24
New Hampshire						28,854^^
New Jersey	3,714	3,123	495	718	Vandenberg-	516
					Truman-	1,100
					Eisenhower-	288
						211
Ohio						426,767^^
Oregon	117,554	107,946				1,474
Pennsylvania	76,988^	81,242^	15,166^	18,254^	Vandenberg-	8,818
					Martin-	45,072
					Truman-	4,907
					Eisenhower-	4,726
					Wallace-	1,452
						1,537
South Dakota					Hitchcock-	45,463
West Virginia		110,775			Byer-	15,675
					VanderPyl-	6,735
Wisconsin	40,943	64,076		55,302		2,429

^ Write-in vote
^^ Delegate-at-large vote

8

State	Kefauver	Truman	Stevenson	Other	
California	1,155,839			Brown-	485,578
Florida	285,358			Russell-	367,980
				Compton-	11,331
				Shaw	9,965
Illinois	526,301	9,024	54,336	Eisenhower-	6,655
					3,798^
Maryland	137,885				
Massachusetts	29,287	7,256		Eisenhower-	16,007
Minnesota	20,182^	3,634^		Eisenhower-	1,753
				Humphrey-	102,527
Nebraska	64,531			Kerr-	42,467
New Hampshire	19,800	15,927	40	MacArthur-	151
				Farley	77
New Jersey	154,964				
Ohio	305,992			Bulkley-	184,880
Oregon	142,440		20,353	Eisenhower-	4,690^
				Douglas-	29,532
Pennsylvania	93,160^	26,504^	3,678^	Russell-	1,691^
				Eisenhower-	28,660^
				Harriman-	3,745^
				Taft-	8,311
					9,026
South Dakota	22,812			Downs-	11,741
West Virginia					191,471^^
Wisconsin	207,520			Fox-	18,322
				Broughton-	15,683

^ Write-in vote
^^ Delegate-at-large vote

PRESIDENTIAL PREFERENCE PRIMARIES
Republican: 1952

State	Eisenhower	Taft	Stassen	Warren	Other
California				1,029,495	Werdel– 521,110
Illinois	147,518^	935,867	155,041	2,841^	MacArthur– 7,504^ Bender– 22,321 1,229^
Maryland					46,361§
Massachusetts	254,898^	110,188^			
Minnesota	108,692^	24,093^	129,706	5,365^	MacArthur– 1,369^ Slettendahl– 22,712 Kefauver– 386
Nebraska	66,078^	79,357^	53,238	1,872^	MacArthur– 7,478^ Kenny– 10,411 767
New Hampshire	46,661	35,838	6,574		MacArthur– 3,227^ Schneider– 230
New Jersey	390,591	228,916	23,559		
Ohio		663,791^^	178,739^^		
Oregon	172,486	18,009^	6,610	44,034	MacArthur– 18,603 Morse– 7,105 Schneider– 350
Pennsylvania	863,785	178,629^	120,305	3,158	MacArthur– 6,028^ Truman– 267 1,121

PRESIDENTIAL PREFERENCE PRIMARIES
Republican: 1952
(continued)

State	Eisenhower	Taft	Stassen	Warren	Other
South Dakota	63,879	64,695			
West Virginia		139,812	38,251		
Wisconsin		315,541	169,679	262,271	Ritter- 26,208 Stearns- 2,925

PRESIDENTIAL PREFERENCE PRIMARIES
Democratic: 1956

State	Stevenson	Kefauver	Harriman	Other	
Alabama					209,102
California	1,139,964	680,722			
Florida	230,285	216,549			
Illinois	717,742	34,092^	134	Lausche- Symington-	1,146 232 128^
Indiana		242,842			
Maryland		112,768			
Massachusetts	19,024^	4,547		McCormack-	26,128^
Minnesota	186,723	245,885			
Montana		77,228			
Nebraska	3,185	55,265			
New Hampshire	3,806	21,701			139
New Jersey	4,043	117,056		Meyner-	1,129
Ohio					205,733^^
Oregon	98,131^	62,987^	1,887		
Pennsylvania	642,172	36,552	647	Eisenhower- Truman-	4,506 524 1,805
South Dakota		30,940			
West Virginia					112,832^^
Wisconsin		330,665			
Alaska	7,123	4,536			
District of Columbia	17,306	8,837			

^ Write-in vote
^^ Delegate-at-large vote

PRESIDENTIAL PREFERENCE PRIMARIES
Republican: 1956

State	Eisenhower	Knowland	Daly	Other
California	1,354,764			
Illinois	781,710	33,534	8,364	91^
Indiana	351,903		13,320	
Maryland	66,904			
Massachusetts	51,951			Herter - 550 Stevenson - 604
Minnesota	198,111	3,209		
Montana			5,447	Arnold - 73,732
Nebraska	102,576			230^
New Hampshire	56,464			600
New Jersey	357,066	8		
Ohio				478,453^^
Oregon	231,418			
Pennsylvania	951,932	43,508		Kefauver - 359 Stevenson - 349 268
South Dakota				Foss - 59,374
West Virginia				111,883^^
Wisconsin	437,089			Chapple -18,743
Alaska	8,291	488		

---

^ Write-in vote
^^ Delegate-at-large vote

13

PRESIDENTIAL PREFERENCE PRIMARIES
Democratic: 1960

State	Kennedy	Humphrey	Stevenson	Johnson	Other
Alabama					142,762
California					Brown – 1,354,031 McLain – 646,387
Florida					Smathers – 322,235
Illinois	34,332^	4,283^	8,029	422	Symington – 5,744 377
Indiana	353,832				Daly – 40,853 Latham – 42,084
Maryland	201,769				Morse – 49,420 Daly – 7,356 Easter – 3,881 24,350§
Massachusetts	95,914^	946^	4,505^	296^	Symington – 414
Nebraska	80,408	3,202^	1,368^		Symington – 4,083 1,631
New Hampshire	45,568				Fisher – 9,241
New Jersey					217,608^^
Ohio	222,799				
Oregon	146,332	16,319	7,924^	11,101	Morse – 91,715 Symington – 12,496 1,210^
Pennsylvania	183,073^	13,860^	29,660^	2,918^	Symington – 6,791^ Rockefeller – 1,078^ Nixon – 15,136^ 4,207^

PRESIDENTIAL PREFERENCE PRIMARIES
Democratic: 1960
(continued)

State	Kennedy	Humphrey	Stevenson	Johnson	Other
South Dakota		23,287			
West Virginia	236,510	152,187			
Wisconsin	476,024	366,753			
District of Columbia		13,860			Morse – 7,310

^ Write-in vote
^^ Delegate-at-large vote
§ Uninstructed delegation

PRESIDENTIAL PREFERENCE PRIMARIES
Republican: 1960

State	Nixon	Rockefeller	Goldwater	Other	
California	1,517,652				
Florida	51,036				
Illinois	782,849				442
Indiana	408,408			Beckwith –	19,677
Massachusetts	54,438^	4,235^		Lodge –	578
Nebraska	78,356^	2,028^	1,068^		
New Hampshire	65,204				1,805
New Jersey					304,766^^
Ohio					504,072^^
Oregon	211,276	9,307	1,571	Kennedy –	2,864
					2,015^
Pennsylvania	968,538	12,491	286	Kennedy –	3,886
				Stevenson –	428
					1,202
South Dakota				Lloyd –	45,512
West Virginia					123,756^^
Wisconsin	339,383				
District of Columbia					9,468§

^ Write-in vote
^^ Delegate-at-large vote
§ Uninstructed delegation

PRESIDENTIAL PREFERENCE PRIMARIES
Democratic: 1964

State	Johnson	Wallace	Kennedy	Other	
California				Brown -	1,693,813
				Yorty -	798,431
Illinois	82,027^	3,761^	2,894^		841^
Indiana		172,646		Welsh -	376,023
					30,367
Maryland		214,849		Brewster -	267,106
					28,927
Massachusetts	61,035^	565^	15,870^		5,739
Nebraska	54,713^	1,067^	2,099^		3,391
New Hampshire	29,317		487		973
New Jersey	4,863^	491^	431^		124^
Ohio				Porter -	493,619
Oregon	272,099	1,365			
Pennsylvania	209,606	12,104	12,029		19,489
South Dakota					28,142
Wisconsin		266,136		Reynolds -	522,405

^ Write-in vote

17

PRESIDENTIAL PREFERENCE PRIMARIES
Republican: 1964

State	Goldwater	Rockefeller	Lodge	Nixon	Scranton	Other
California	1,120,403	1,052,053				
Illinois	512,840	2,048^	68,122^	30,313^	1,842^	Smith-209,521 3,105^
Indiana	267,935					Stassen-107,157 24,588
Maryland						57,004§ 40,994
Massachusetts	9,338^	2,454^	70,809^	5,460^	1,709^	Smith-426^ 1,938^
Nebraska	68,050	2,333^	22,622^	43,613^	578^	Smith-243^ 1,083^
New Hampshire	20,692	19,504	33,007	15,587	105	Smith-2,120 Stassen-1,373 465
New Jersey	5,309^	612^	7,896^	4,179	633	304^
Ohio						Rhodes-615,754
Oregon	50,105	94,190	79,169	48,274	4,509	Smith-8,087 2,585^
Pennsylvania	38,669	9,123	92,712	44,396	235,222	Smith-1,721 Stassen-280 30,745
South Dakota	27,076					Gubbrud-57,653

State	Goldwater	Rockefeller	Lodge	Nixon	Scranton	Other
Texas§§	104,137	6,207	12,324	5,390	803	Smith-4,816 Stassen-5,273 373
West Virginia		115,680				
Wisconsin						Byrnes-299,612

^ Write-in vote
§ Uninstructed delegation
§§ Sponsored unofficially by Goldwater partisans

PRESIDENTIAL PREFERENCE PRIMARIES
Democratic: 1968

State	McCarthy	Kennedy	Johnson	Humphrey	Other
California	1,329,301	1,472,166			380,286§
Florida	147,216				Smathers – 236,242 128,899§
Illinois	4,646^		162^	2,059^	E. Kennedy – 4,052^ Wallace – 768^ 1,119^
Indiana	209,695	328,118			Branigan – 238,700
Massachusetts	122,697	68,604^	6,890^	44,156^	Rockefeller – 2,275^ Nixon – 575^ Wallace – 1,688^ 2,018^
Nebraska	50,655	84,102	9,187	12,087^	Nixon – 2,731^ Wallace – 1,298^ 1,905^ 646
New Hampshire	23,280	600^	27,243^		Nixon – 2,529^ 1,534^
New Jersey	9,906	8,603^	380^	5,578^	Wallace – 1,399^ Nixon – 1,364^ 216^
Oregon	163,990	141,631	45,174	12,421^	Reagan – 3,082^ Rockefeller – 2,841^ Wallace – 957^ Nixon – 2,974^
Pennsylvania	428,259^	65,430^	21,265^	51,998^	Rockefeller – 1,897^ Nixon – 3,434^ 1,556^

PRESIDENTIAL PREFERENCE PRIMARIES
Democratic: 1968
(continued)

State	McCarthy	Kennedy	Johnson	Humphrey	Other
South Dakota	13,145	31,826	19,316		
Wisconsin	412,160	45,507^	253,696	3,605^	Wallace – 4,031^ 1,142^

^ Write-in vote
§ Uninstructed delegation

PRESIDENTIAL PREFERENCE PRIMARIES
Republican: 1968

State	Nixon	Reagan	Rockefeller	Other	
California	1,525,091				
Florida					51,509§
Illinois	17,490^	1,601^	2,165^		1,141^
Indiana	508,362				
Massachusetts	27,447^	1,770^	31,964	Volpe –	31,465
				Kennedy –	1,184^
				McCarthy –	9,758^
					2,933^
Nebraska	140,076	42,703	10,225^	Liberator –	1,302
				McCarthy –	1,544^
					1,959^
				Stassen –	2,638
New Hampshire	80,666	362^	11,241^	McCarthy –	5,511^
				Johnson –	1,778^
				Romney –	1,743
				Stassen –	429^
					2,999
New Jersey	71,809^	2,737^	11,530^	McCarthy –	1,358^
					1,158^
Oregon	203,037	63,707	36,305^	McCarthy –	7,387^
				Kennedy –	1,723^
Pennsylvania	171,815^	7,934^	52,915^	McCarthy –	18,800^
				Wallace –	13,290^
				Kennedy –	10,431^
				Humphrey –	4,651^
				Johnson –	3,027^
				Shafer –	1,223^
					2,563
South Dakota	68,113				
Wisconsin	391,368	50,727	7,995	Stassen –	28,531
				Romney –	2,087^
					3,362

^ Write-in vote
§ Uninstructed vote

PART II
National Party Conventions

NOTE

For specific analyses of the roll call votes see:

Bain, Richard C. CONVENTION DECISIONS AND VOTING
RECORDS. Washington: Brookings Institution, 1960.
———. CONGRESSIONAL QUARTERLY ALMANACS, Volumes
XX, XXIV. Washington, D.C.: Congressional Quarterly Service,
1965 and 1968.

SOURCES

1948–1964 National Party Conventions

Democratic National Committee. OFFICIAL REPORTS OF THE
PROCEEDINGS OF THE DEMOCRATIC NATIONAL CON-
VENTIONS, 1948–1964. Washington: Democratic National
Committee.
Republican National Committee. OFFICIAL REPORTS OF THE
PROCEEDINGS OF THE REPUBLICAN NATIONAL CON-
VENTIONS, 1948–1964. Washington: Republican National
Committee.

1968 National Party Conventions

Data supplied by the Republican and Democratic National Committees.

CONVENTIONS

The importance of national party conventions has been modified during the post-World War II era. The modern convention has become a more controlled and staged event in the face of the ubiquitous television camera. Since 1956 the nominations have been foregone conclusions. The conventions themselves seem anticlimactical in the process of a party's search for presidential and vice presidential nominees. Today, candidates seeking their party's presidential nomination begin campaigning months, sometimes years, in advance of a convention by wooing state party leaders, by filling party posts with their supporters, and by winning key presidential preference primaries. The convention remains as the mechanism for gaining nomination, but much of the politicking that was once associated with the smoke-filled room image of the convention has become a function of preconvention activity. "Dark horse" candidacies, such as that which led to the selection of Republican James Garfield on the thirty-sixth ballot in 1880, are highly unlikely today.

The national convention is, and always has been, the only national party machinery. It is the one mechanism whereby local and state party organizations converge to select a presidential nominee and to construct a national party platform that ostensibly defines the national needs and the goals of the party. The convention system was instituted in 1832, replacing the congressional caucus as a device for selecting presidential candidates. The early conventions, like the most recent conventions, were characterized by the ratification rather than the selection of candidates. It wasn't until the Democratic convention of 1844, when James K. Polk won the nomination, that the convention evolved into a body where factional and sectional differences were ostensibly ameliorated as the parties attempted to select "compromise candidates." This is not to suggest that contemporary presidential politics is devoid of differences in search of compromise. Since 1956, however, by the time of the convention candidates have been eliminated or elevated to prominence in primaries, the press and news media have found the heroes, and the delegates to the conventions have been carefully selected and romanced by the aspiring candidates and their supporters.

The real decisions that have been made in the modern convention have involved either the party platform or the proceedings and decisions of the credentials committees. Invariably these controversies have been resolved, so they can be characterized as corresponding to the various stances taken by the presidential candidates seeking nomination. In most cases since 1948, the convention has resolved platform and credentials matters in a manner consistent with the views of the man who ultimately obtained the party nomination. The following are some examples.

In 1948, Truman forces defeated the Moody Resolution on States' Rights. Instead, the Biemiller Resolution was adopted commending Truman on his Civil Rights stance. Stevenson, in 1952, backed the seating of the Virginia delegation in the loyalty oath fight. Again in 1952, Eisenhower supporters won the fight on the Brown Amendment involving contested delegations. Goldwater forces, in 1964, defeated the Scott Amendment on Civil Rights. In 1968, Humphrey supporters defeated the minority report on Vietnam as well as the motion to delay the credentials dispute. They also defeated the motion to seat the Georgia Loyal National Democrats and the motion to seat the insurgent Alabama delegation. The motion they supported to seat the regular Texas delegation was adopted. Only once in the 1948–1968 period have these disputes led to a split in the party resulting in the nomination of a third party presidential candidate. That was in 1948 with the nomination of Strom Thurmond representing the States' Rights party.

The convention, in contrast to the primary, has been seriously criticized for its viability as a democratic political institution. Essentially the criticism has focused on three issues: first, the representativeness of conventions; second, the elitist nature of conventions; thirdly, the inadequacy of the convention system to select the "best man" for the job. The Civil Rights movement in this country has been the single most important impetus in raising the issue of convention representativeness. That the two major political parties could, like the rest of the country, systematically ignore or accord only minimal recognition to the needs of approximately twenty-two million people, drastically underscored the question of the responsiveness of the party system. An analysis of the roll call votes in both Democratic and Republican conventions since 1948 attests to this fact. The attack against the "elitist" nature of the convention is closely associated with this question of representativeness. This issue, however, is muted by the fact that the primaries and the influence of the mass media both indicate that the "smoke-filled" room can no longer be impervious to the public. The contemporary party leader, like the modern businessman, is concerned about his public image.

It is difficult to assess the convention's viability in selecting the best man in view of the fact that the alternative mechanism of a national primary does not guarantee protection against the limitations faced by any group attempting to choose a leader; rather, it only expands the level of participation. The national primary may be more democratic, but it is conceivably also more expensive. Given the present state of affairs, where campaign costs are rising indefinitely, a candidate entering a national primary would no doubt incur costs similar to a presidential candidate. This added economic burden might be as much a restraint in the quest for the best man as the more selective, elitist convention system.

26

NATIONAL PARTY CONVENTIONS

DEMOCRATIC: 1948

Dates: July 12-14, 1948
Site: Philadelphia, Pennsylvania

Presidential Nominee
Harry S. Truman of Missouri
(Nominated on first ballot.)

Vice Presidential Nominee
Alben W. Barkley of Kentucky
(Nominated by acclamation.)

Chairman of the National Committee
J. Howard McGrath of Rhode Island

Secretary of the National Committee and of the Convention
Mrs. Dorothy Vredenburgh of Alabama

Temporary Convention Chairman and Keynoter
Alben W. Barkley of Kentucky

Permanent Convention Chairman
Sam Rayburn of Texas

Chairman, Committee on Platform and Resolutions
Francis J. Myers of Pennsylvania

Chairman, Credentials Committee
Mary T. Norton of New Jersey

Chairman, Committee on Rules
Herbert R. O'Connor of Maryland

Chairman, Committee on Permanent Organization
John O. Pastore of Rhode Island

DEMOCRATIC: 1948
Roll Call of the States: Selection of a Presidential Nominee

States, etc.§	Number of Votes	Candidates Truman	Russell	Other	
Alabama	26		26		
Arizona	12	12			
Arkansas	22		22		
California	54	53-1/2			
Colorado	12	12			
Connecticut	20	20			
Delaware	10	10			
Florida	20		19	McNutt	1
Georgia	28		28		
Idaho	12	12			
Illinois	60	60			
Indiana	26	25		McNutt	1
Iowa	20	20			
Kansas	16	16			
Kentucky	26	26			
Louisiana	24		24		
Maine	10	10			
Maryland	20	20			
Massachusetts	36	36			
Michigan	42	42			
Minnesota	26	26			

§ In addition to those of States, the votes of various American territories and possessions are listed.

NATIONAL PARTY CONVENTIONS

DEMOCRATIC: 1948
Roll Call of the States: Selection of a Presidential Nominee
(continued)

States, etc.	Number of Votes	Truman	Russell	Other	
Mississippi	22				
Missouri	34	34			
Montana	12	12			
Nebraska	12	12			
Nevada	10	10			
New Hampshire	12	11			
New Jersey	36	36			
New Mexico	12	12			
New York	98	83		Roe	15
North Carolina	32	13	19		
North Dakota	8	8			
Ohio	50	50			
Oklahoma	24	24			
Oregon	16	16			
Pennsylvania	74	74			
Rhode Island	12	12			
South Carolina	20		20		
South Dakota	8	8			
Tennessee	28		28		
Texas	50		50		
Utah	12	12			
Vermont	6	5-1/2		McNutt	1/2

DEMOCRATIC: 1948
Roll Call of the States: Selection of a Presidential Nominee
(continued)

States, etc.	Number of Votes	Candidates Truman	Russell	Other	
Virginia	26		26		
Washington	20	20			
West Virginia	20	15	4	Barkley	1
Wisconsin	24	24			
Wyoming	6	6			
Alaska	6	6			
Canal Zone	2	2			
District of Columbia	6	6			
Hawaii	6	6			
Puerto Rico	6	6			
Virgin Islands	2	2			
Totals	1,234§	926	266	Roe	15
				McNutt	2-1/2
				Barkley	1
					18-1/2

§Votes not cast: California 1/2; New Hampshire 1; Mississippi 22.

NATIONAL PARTY CONVENTIONS

DEMOCRATIC: 1948
Roll Call of the States

States, etc.	Number of Votes	Moody Resolution on Civil Rights		Biemiller Resolution on Civil Rights	
		Yes	No	Yes	No
Alabama	26	26			26
Arizona	12		12		12
Arkansas	22	22			22
California	54	1-1/2	52-1/2	53	1
Colorado	12	3	9	10	2
Connecticut	20		20	20	
Delaware	10		10		10
Florida	20	20			20
Georgia	28	28			28
Idaho	12		12		12
Illinois	60		60	60	
Indiana	26		26	17	9
Iowa	20		20	18	2
Kansas	16		16	16	
Kentucky	26		26		26
Louisiana	24	24			24
Maine	10		10	3	7
Maryland	20		20		20
Massachusetts	36		36	36	
Michigan	42		42	42	

DEMOCRATIC: 1948
Roll Call of the States
(continued)

States, etc.	Number of Votes	Moody Resolution on Civil Rights		Biemiller Resolution on Civil Rights	
		Yes	No	Yes	No
Minnesota	26		26	26	
Mississippi	22	22			22
Missouri	34		34		34
Montana	12		12	1-1/2	10-1/2
Nebraska	12		12	3	9
Nevada	10		10		10
New Hampshire	12		12	1	11
New Jersey	36		36	36	
New Mexico	12		12		12
New York	98		98	98	
North Carolina	32	32			32
North Dakota	8		8		8
Ohio	50		50	39	11
Oklahoma	24		24		24
Oregon	16	3	13	7	9
Pennsylvania	74		74	74	
Rhode Island	12		12		12
South Carolina	20	20			20
South Dakota	8		8	8	
Tennessee	28	28			28

DEMOCRATIC: 1948
Roll Call of the States
(continued)

States, etc.	Number of Votes	Moody Resolution on Civil Rights		Biemiller Resolution on Civil Rights	
		Yes	No	Yes	No
Texas	50	50			50
Utah	12		12		12
Vermont	6		6	6	
Virginia	26	26			26
Washington	20		20	20	
West Virginia	20		20	7	13
Wisconsin	24		24	24	
Wyoming	6	1-1/2	4-1/2	4	2
Alaska	6	3	3	2	4
Canal Zone	2		2		2
District of Columbia	6		6	6	
Hawaii	6		6	6	
Puerto Rico	6		6	6	
Virgin Islands	2		2	2	
Totals	1,234	310	924	651-1/2	582-1/2

NATIONAL PARTY CONVENTIONS

REPUBLICAN: 1948

Dates: June 21-25, 1948
Site: Philadelphia, Pennsylvania

Presidential Nominee
Thomas E. Dewey of New York
(Nominated on the third ballot.)

Vice Presidential Nominee
Earl Warren of California
(Nominated by acclamation.)

Chairman of the National Committee
Carroll Reese of Tennessee

Secretary of the National Committee and of the Convention
Mrs. Dudley C. Hay of Michigan

Temporary Convention Chairman and Keynoter
Dwight H. Green of Illinois

Permanent Convention Chairman
Joseph W. Martin, Jr. of Massachusetts

Chairman, Committee on Resolutions
Henry Cabot Lodge of Massachusetts

Chairman, Credentials Committee
Alfred Lindley of Minnesota

Chairman, Committee on Rules
E. F. Colladay of the District of Columbia

Chairman, Committee on Permanent Organization
Albert A. Reading of Pennsylvania

NATIONAL PARTY CONVENTIONS

REPUBLICAN: 1948
Roll Call of the States: Selection of a Presidential Nominee
(First Ballot)

States, etc.	Number of Votes	Dewey	Stassen	Taft	Other	
Alabama	14	9		5		
Arizona	8	3	2	3		
Arkansas	14	3	4	7	Warren	53
California	53					
Colorado	15	3	5	7		
Connecticut	19				Baldwin	19
Delaware	9	5	1	2	Martin	1
Florida	16	6	4	6		
Georgia	16	12	1		Martin	2
					Warren	1
Idaho	11	11				
Illinois	56				Green	56
Indiana	29	29				
Iowa	23	3	13	5	MacArthur	2
Kansas	19	12	1	2	Martin	1
					Vandenberg	3
Kentucky	25	10	1	11	MacArthur	1
					Vandenberg	2
Louisiana	13	6		7		
Maine	13		4	1	Vandenberg	1
Maryland	16	8	3	5		
Massachusetts	35	17	1	2	Martin	3
					Vandenberg	12

35

REPUBLICAN: 1948
Roll Call of the States: Selection of a Presidential Nominee
(First Ballot)
(continued)

States, etc.	Number of Votes	Dewey	Candidates Stassen	Taft	Other	
Michigan	41				Vandenberg	41
Minnesota	25		25			
Mississippi	8			8		
Missouri	33	17	6	8	Warren	2
Montana	11	5	3	3		
Nebraska	15	2	13			
Nevada	9	6	1	2		
New Hampshire	8	6	2			
New Jersey	35				Driscoll	35
New Mexico	8	3	2	3		
New York	97	96		1		
North Carolina	26	16	2	5	Martin	3
North Dakota	11		11			
Ohio	53		9	44		
Oklahoma	20	18		1	Martin	1
Oregon	12	12				
Pennsylvania	73	41	1	28	Vandenberg Warren	2 1
Rhode Island	8	1		1	Martin	6
South Carolina	6			6		
South Dakota	11	3		8		

REPUBLICAN: 1948
Roll Call of the States: Selection of a Presidential Nominee
(First Ballot)
(continued)

States, etc.	Number of Votes	Dewey	Candidates Stassen	Taft	Other	
Tennessee	22	6			Reece	15
Texas	33	2	1	30		
Utah	11	5	2	4		
Vermont	9	7	2			
Virginia	21	10		10	Martin	1
Washington	19	14	2	1	Vandenberg Warren	1 1
West Virginia	16	11	5			
Wisconsin	27		19		MacArthur	8
Wyoming	9	4	3	2		
Alaska	3	2		1		
District of Columbia	3	2			Dirksen	1
Hawaii	5	3		1	Warren	1
Puerto Rico	2			2		
Totals	1,094§	434	157	224	Vandenberg Warren Green Driscoll Baldwin Martin Reece MacArthur Dirksen	62 59 56 35 19 18 15 11 1 276

§Votes not cast: Maine 2; Tennessee 1.

NATIONAL PARTY CONVENTIONS

REPUBLICAN: 1948
Roll Call of the States: Selection of a Presidential Nominee
(Second Ballot)

States, etc.	Number of Votes	Dewey	Candidates Stassen	Taft	Other	
Alabama	14	9		5		
Arizona	8	4	2	2		
Arkansas	14	3	4	7		
California	53				Warren	53
Colorado	15	3	8	4		
Connecticut	19				Baldwin	19
Delaware	9	6	1	2		
Florida	16	6	4	6		
Georgia	16	13	1		Martin	1
					Warren	1
Idaho	11	11				
Illinois	56	5		50	Martin	1
Indiana	29	29				
Iowa	23	13	7	2	MacArthur	1
Kansas	19	14	1	2	Martin	1
					Vandenberg	1
Kentucky	25	11	1	11	Vandenberg	2
Louisiana	13	6		7		
Maine	13	5	7		Vandenberg	1
Maryland	16	13		3		
Massachusetts	35	18	1	3	Martin	2
					Vandenberg	11
Michigan	41				Vandenberg	41

REPUBLICAN: 1948
Roll Call of the States: Selection of a Presidential Nominee
(Second Ballot)
(continued)

States, etc.	Number of Votes	Candidates			Other	
		Dewey	Stassen	Taft		
Minnesota	25		25			
Mississippi	8			8		
Missouri	33	18	6	7	Warren	2
Montana	11	6	2	3		
Nebraska	15	6	9			
Nevada	9	6	1	2		
New Hampshire	8	6	2			
New Jersey	35	24	6	2	Vandenberg	3
New Mexico	8	3	2	3		
New York	97	96		1		
North Carolina	26	17	2	4	Martin	3
North Dakota	11		11			
Ohio	53	1	8	44		
Oklahoma	20	19		1		
Oregon	12	12				
Pennsylvania	73	40	1	29	Vandenberg	2
					Warren	1
Rhode Island	8	4		2	Martin	1
					Vandenberg	1
South Carolina	6			6		
South Dakota	11	7	4			
Tennessee	22	8		13	Reece	1

REPUBLICAN: 1948
Roll Call of the States: Selection of a Presidential Nominee
(Second Ballot)§
(continued)

States, etc.	Number of Votes	Candidates			Other	
		Dewey	Stassen	Taft		
Texas	33	2	2	29		
Utah	11	6	2	3		
Vermont	9	7	2			
Virginia	21	13		7	Martin	1
Washington	19	14	2	3		
West Virginia	16	13	3			
Wisconsin	27	2	19		MacArthur	6
Wyoming	9	6	3			
Alaska	3	3				
District of Columbia	3	3				
Hawaii	5	3		2		
Puerto Rico	2	1		1		
Totals	1,094	515	149	274	Vandenberg	62
					Warren	57
					Baldwin	19
					Martin	10
					MacArthur	7
					Reece	1
						156

§After second ballot all candidates withdrew in favor of Governor Dewey who was nominated unanimously on the third ballot.

NATIONAL PARTY CONVENTIONS

DEMOCRATIC: 1952

Dates: July 21-26, 1952
Site: Chicago, Illinois

Presidential Nominee
Adlai E. Stevenson of Illinois
(Nominated on third ballot.)

Vice Presidential Nominee
John J. Sparkman of Alabama
(Nominated by acclamation.)

Chairman of the National Committee
Frank E. McKinney of Indiana

Secretary of the National Committee and of the Convention
Mrs. Dorothy Vredenburgh of Alabama

Temporary Convention Chairman and Keynoter
Paul A. Dever of Massachusetts

Permanent Convention Chairman
Sam Rayburn of Texas

Chairman, Committee on Platform and Resolutions
John W. McCormack of Massachusetts

Chairman, Credentials Committee
Calvin W. Rawlings of Utah

Chairman, Committee on Rules
Blair Moody of Michigan

Chairman, Committee on Permanent Organization
Johnston Murray of Oklahoma

DEMOCRATIC: 1952
Roll Call of the States: Selection of a Presidential Nominee
(First Ballot)

States, etc.	Number of Votes	Harriman	Kefauver	Kerr	Russell	Stevenson	Other
Alabama	22		8		13	1/2	Barkley 1/2
Arizona	12			12			
Arkansas	22						Fulbright 22
California	68		68				
Colorado	16	5	2		8-1/2	1/2	
Connecticut	16					16	
Delaware	6					6	
Florida	24		5		19		
Georgia	28				28		
Idaho	12	3-1/2	3	3	1	1-1/2	
Illinois	60	1	3			53	Douglas 3
Indiana	26		1			25	
Iowa	24	1/2	8	3	2	8	Barkley 2-1/2
Kansas	16					16	
Kentucky	26						Barkley 26
Louisiana	20				20		
Maine	10	1-1/2	1-1/2		2-1/2	3-1/2	Ewing 1
Maryland	18		18				
Massachusetts	36						Dever 36
Michigan	40		40				Humphrey 26
Minnesota	26						

DEMOCRATIC: 1952
Roll Call of the States: Selection of a Presidential Nominee
(First Ballot)
(continued)

States, etc.	Number of Votes	Candidates Harriman	Kefauver	Kerr	Russell	Stevenson	Other
Mississippi	18				18		
Missouri	34	1-1/2	2	4		18	Barkley 7-1/2
Montana	12						Murray 12
Nebraska	12		5	4	1	2	
Nevada	10		1/2	1/2	8	1	
New Hampshire	8		8				
New Jersey	32	1	3			28	
New Mexico	12	1	1-1/2	4-1/2	4	1	
New York	94	83-1/2	1			6-1/2	Ewing 3
North Carolina	32				26	5-1/2	Barkley 1/2
North Dakota	8		2	2	2	2	
Ohio	54	1	29-1/2	1	7	13	Barkley 2-1/2
Oklahoma	24			24			
Oregon	12		12				Douglas 1/2
Pennsylvania	70	4-1/2	22-1/2		1/2	36	Truman 6
Rhode Island	12	1-1/2	3-1/2			5-1/2	Barkley 1/2 Dever 1
South Carolina	16				16		
South Dakota	8		8				
Tennessee	28		28				
Texas	52				52		

DEMOCRATIC: 1952
Roll Call of the States: Selection of a Presidential Nominee
(First Ballot)
(continued)

States, etc.	Number of Votes	Candidates Harriman	Kefauver	Kerr	Russell	Stevenson	Other	
Utah	12	6-1/2	1/2	2-1/2	2	1/2		
Vermont	6		1/2			5	Dever	1/2
Virginia	28				28			
Washington	22	1	12	2-1/2	1/2	6		
West Virginia	20		5-1/2		7	1	Barkley	6-1/2
Wisconsin	28		28					
Wyoming	10	3-1/2	1-1/2	1-1/2	1/2	3		
Alaska	6		6					
Canal Zone	2				2			
District of Columbia	6	6						
Hawaii	6	1	1			2	Barkley	2
Puerto Rico	6					6		
Virgin Islands	2					1		
Totals	1,230§	123-1/2	340	65	268	273	Barkley	48-1/2
							Dever	37-1/2
							Humphrey	26
							Fulbright	22
							Murray	12
							Truman	6
							Ewing	4
							Senator Douglas	3
							Justice Douglas	1/2
								159-1/2

§ Votes not cast: Missouri 1.

NATIONAL PARTY CONVENTIONS

DEMOCRATIC: 1952
Roll Call of the States: Selection of a Presidential Nominee
(Second Ballot)

States, etc.	Number of Votes	Candidates Harriman	Kefauver	Russell	Stevenson	Other	
Alabama	22		7-1/2	14	1/2		
Arizona	12			12			
Arkansas	22	1	1-1/2	18	1-1/2		
California	68		68				
Colorado	16	5	5	2-1/2	3-1/2		
Connecticut	16				16		
Delaware	6				6		
Florida	24		5	19			
Georgia	28			28			
Idaho	12				12		
Illinois	60		3		54	Sen. Douglas	3
Indiana	26		1		25		
Iowa	24	1/2	8-1/2	3	9-1/2	Kerr Barkley	1/2 2
Kansas	16				16		
Kentucky	26					Barkley	26
Louisiana	20			20			
Maine	10	1	1	2-1/2	4-1/2	Ewing	1
Maryland	18		15-1/2	2		Barkley	1/2
Massachusetts	36		2-1/2			Barkley Dever	3 30-1/2
Michigan	40		40				

45

DEMOCRATIC: 1952
Roll Call of the States: Selection of a Presidential Nominee
(Second Ballot)
(continued)

States, etc.	Number of Votes	Candidates Harriman	Kefauver	Russell	Stevenson	Other	
Minnesota	26	1-1/2	17		7-1/2		
Mississippi	18			18			
Missouri	34	1-1/2	2		19-1/2	Barkley	10
Montana	12	3	3	3		Barkley	3
Nebraska	12		5	1	2	Kerr	4
Nevada	10		1/2	7-1/2	2		
New Hampshire	8		8				
New Jersey	32		4		28		
New Mexico	12		1-1/2	6	4-1/2		
New York	94	84-1/2	1		6-1/2	Ewing	2
North Carolina	32			24	7	Barkley	1/2
North Dakota	8					Barkley	8
Ohio	54	1	27-1/2	8	17-1/2		
Oklahoma	24					Barkley	24
Oregon	12		12				
Pennsylvania	70	2-1/2	21-1/2		40	Truman	6
Rhode Island	12		4		8		
South Carolina	16			16			
South Dakota	8		8				
Tennessee	28		28				
Texas	52			52			

DEMOCRATIC: 1952
Roll Call of the States: Selection of a Presidential Nominee
(Second Ballot)
(continued)

States, etc.	Number of Votes	Harriman	Kefauver	Russell	Stevenson	Other	
Utah	12	9	1-1/2		1/2	Kerr	1
Vermont	6		1/2	1/2	5		
Virginia	28			28			
Washington	22	2	12-1/2	1/2	6	Barkley	1
West Virginia	20		7-1/2	6-1/2	5-1/2	Barkley	1/2
Wisconsin	28		28				
Wyoming	10	2-1/2	3		4-1/2		
Alaska	6		6				
Canal Zone	2			2			
District of Columbia	6	6					
Hawaii	6		1		5		
Puerto Rico	6				6		
Virgin Islands	2		1		1		
Totals	1,230§	121	362-1/2	294	324-1/2	Barkley	78-1/2
						Dever	30-1/2
						Truman	6
						Kerr	5-1/2
						Senator Douglas	3
						Ewing	3
							126-1/2

§ Votes not cast: Missouri 1; North Carolina 1/2.

NATIONAL PARTY CONVENTIONS

DEMOCRATIC: 1952
Roll Call of the States: Selection of a Presidential Nominee
(Third Ballot)

States, etc.	Number of Votes	Kefauver	Candidates Russell	Stevenson	Other	
Alabama	22	7-1/2	14	1/2		
Arizona	12		12			
Arkansas	22	1-1/2		20-1/2		
California	68	68				
Colorado	16	4	3-1/2	8-1/2		
Connecticut	16			16		
Delaware	6			6		
Florida	24	5	19			
Georgia	28		28			
Idaho	12			12		
Illinois	60	3		54	Douglas	3
Indiana	26	1		25		
Iowa	24	8	3	10	Barkley	3
Kansas	16			16		
Kentucky	26				Barkley	26
Louisiana	20		20			
Maine	10	1/2	2 1/2	7		
Maryland	18	8-1/2	2-1/2	6	Barkley	1/2
Massachusetts	36	5	1	25	Barkley Dever	4-1/2 1/2
Michigan	40			40		
Minnesota	26	13		13		

DEMOCRATIC: 1952
Roll Call of the States: Selection of a Presidential Nominee
(Third Ballot)
(continued)

States, etc.	Number of Votes	Candidates Kefauver	Russell	Stevenson	Other
Mississippi	18		18		
Missouri	34	2		22	Barkley 9
Montana	12			12	
Nebraska	12	3	1	8	
Nevada	10	1/2	7-1/2	2	
New Hampshire	8	8			
New Jersey	32	4		28	
New Mexico	12	1-1/2	3-1/2	7	
New York	94	4		86-1/2	Ewing 3
North Carolina	32		24	7-1/2	Barkley 1/2
North Dakota	8			8	
Ohio	54	27	1	26	
Oklahoma	24				Barkley 24
Oregon	12	11		1	
Pennsylvania	70			70	
Rhode Island	12			12	
South Carolina	16		16		
South Dakota	8	8			
Tennessee	28	28			
Texas	52		52		
Utah	12	4	1/2	7-1/2	

DEMOCRATIC: 1952
Roll Call of the States: Selection of a Presidential Nominee
(Third Ballot)
(continued)

States, etc.	Number of Votes	Candidates			
		Kefauver	Russell	Stevenson	Other
Vermont	6		1/2	5-1/2	
Virginia	28		28		
Washington	22	11	1/2	10-1/2	
West Virginia	20	7-1/2	3-1/2	9	
Wisconsin	28	28			
Wyoming	10			10	
Alaska	6	6			
Canal Zone	2			2	
District of Columbia	6			6	
Hawaii	6	1		5	
Puerto Rico	6			6	
Virgin Islands	2			2	
Totals§§	1,230§	279-1/2	261-1/2	613	Barkley 67-1/2
					Douglas 3
					Ewing 3
					Dever 1/2
					74

§Votes not cast: Maryland 1/2; Missouri 1; New York 1/2.

§§ This was the vote count when Senator Kefauver withdrew in favor of
Stevenson. The nomination was made unanimous after Utah changed its vote
to 12 for Stevenson.

NATIONAL PARTY CONVENTIONS

DEMOCRATIC: 1952
Roll Call of the States

States, etc.	Number of Votes	Seating of Virginia Delegation		Tabling of Motion to Adjourn	
		Yes	No	Yes	No
Alabama	22	22		13-1/2	8-1/2
Arizona	12	12		12	
Arkansas	22	22		19	3
California	68	4	61		68
Colorado	16	4-1/2	11-1/2	4	12
Connecticut	16		16	16	
Delaware	6	6		6	
Florida	24	24		19	5
Georgia	28	28		28	
Idaho	12	12			12
Illinois	60	52	8	53	7
Indiana	26	14-1/2	6-1/2	25	1
Iowa	24	17	7	8	15
Kansas	16		16	16	
Kentucky	26	26		26	
Louisiana	20	20		20	
Maine	10	2-1/2	7-1/2	4-1/2	5-1/2
Maryland	18	18		18	
Massachusetts	36	16	19	30	4-1/2
Michigan	40		40		40

51

DEMOCRATIC: 1952
Roll Call of the States
(continued)

States, etc.	Number of Votes	Seating of Virginia Delegation		Tabling of Motion to Adjourn	
		Yes	No	Yes	No
Minnesota	26		26		26
Mississippi	18	18		18	
Missouri	34	34		29	5
Montana	12		12	12	
Nebraska	12	8	3		12
Nevada	10	10		9-1/2	1/2
New Hampshire	8	1	7		8
New Jersey	32		32	24	8
New Mexico	12	12		12	
New York	94	7	87	5	89
North Carolina	32	32		32	
North Dakota	8	8		8	
Ohio	54	33-1/2	14-1/2	26	28
Oklahoma	24	24		24	
Oregon	12	4	8	8	12
Pennsylvania	70	57	13	35	35
Rhode Island	12	10	2	10	2
South Carolina	16				
South Dakota	8		8		8
Tennessee	28		28		28

DEMOCRATIC: 1952
Roll Call of the States
(continued)

States, etc.	Number of Votes	Seating of Virginia Delegation§		Tabling of Motion to Adjourn§§	
		Yes	No	Yes	No
Texas	52	52		52	
Utah	12	3	9		12
Vermont	6		6	6	
Virginia	28			28	
Washington	22	12-1/2	9-1/2	3	10
West Virginia	20	13-1/2	5	10	9
Wisconsin	28	1	27		28
Wyoming	10	5-1/2	4-1/2	2-1/2	7-1/2
Alaska	6		6		6
Canal Zone	2	2		2	
District of Columbia	6		6		6
Hawaii	6		6	4	2
Puerto Rico	6	2	4	1	5
Virgin Islands	2		2		2
Totals	1,230	650-1/2	518	671	539-1/2

§ Votes not cast: California 3; Indiana 5; Massachusetts 1; Nebraska 1; Ohio 6; South Carolina 16; Virginia 28; West Virginia 1-1/2.

§§ Votes not cast: Iowa 1; Massachusetts 1-1/2; South Carolina 16; West Virginia 1.

NATIONAL PARTY CONVENTIONS

REPUBLICAN: 1952

Dates: July 7-11, 1952
Site: Chicago, Illinois

Presidential Nominee
Dwight David Eisenhower of Kansas
(Nominated on first ballot.)

Vice Presidential Nominee
Richard M. Nixon of California
(Nominated by acclamation.)

Chairman of the National Committee
Guy G. Gabrielson of New Jersey

Secretary of the National Committee and of the Convention
Mrs. Katherine G. Howard of Massachusetts

Temporary Convention Chairman
Walter S. Hallanan of West Virginia

Keynoter
Douglas MacArthur of New York

Permanent Convention Chairman
Joseph W. Martin, Jr. of Massachusetts

Chairman, Committee on Resolutions
Eugene D. Millikin of Colorado

Chairman, Credentials Committee
Ross Rizley of Oklahoma

Chairman, Committee on Rules
A. Ronald Bulton of California

Chairman, Committee on Permanent Organization
Mrs. Wortz of Colorado

NATIONAL PARTY CONVENTIONS

REPUBLICAN: 1952
Roll Call of the States: Selection of a Presidential Nominee
First Roll Call (Before Changes)

States, etc.	Number of Votes	Candidates Eisenhower	Taft	Other	
Alabama	14	5	9		
Arizona	14	4	10		
Arkansas	11	4	6	MacArthur	1
California	70			Warren	70
Colorado	18	15	2	Stassen	1
Connecticut	22	21	1		
Delaware	12	7	5		
Florida	18	6	12		
Georgia	17	14	2	Warren	1
Idaho	14		14		
Illinois	60	1	59		
Indiana	32	2	30		
Iowa	26	16	10		
Kansas	22	20	2		
Kentucky	20	1	19		
Louisiana	15	13	2		
Maine	16	11	5		
Maryland	24	16	8		
Massachusetts	38	34	4		
Michigan	46	35	11		
Minnesota	28	9		Stassen	19

REPUBLICAN: 1952
Roll Call of the States: Selection of a Presidential Nominee
First Roll Call (Before Changes)
(continued)

States, etc.	Number of Votes	Candidates Eisenhower	Taft	Other	
Mississippi	5		5		
Missouri	26	21	5		
Montana	8	1	7		
Nebraska	18	4	13	Warren	1
Nevada	12	5	7		
New Hampshire	14	14			
New Jersey	38	33	5		
New Mexico	14	6	8		
New York	96	92	4		
North Carolina	26	12	14		
North Dakota	14	4	8	MacArthur	1
				Warren	1
Ohio	56		56		
Oklahoma	16	4	7	MacArthur	5
Oregon	18	18			
Pennsylvania	70	53	15	MacArthur	2
Rhode Island	8	6	1	Warren	1
South Carolina	6	2	4		
South Dakota	14		14		
Tennessee	20		20		
Texas	38	33	5		

REPUBLICAN: 1952
Roll Call of the States: Selection of a Presidential Nominee
First Roll Call (Before Changes)
(continued)

States, etc.	Number of Votes	Candidates Eisenhower	Taft	Other	
Utah	14		14		
Vermont	12	12			
Virginia	23	9	14		
Washington	24	20	4		
West Virginia	16	1	14	MacArthur	1
Wisconsin	30		24	Warren	6
Wyoming	12	6	6		
Alaska	3	1	2		
District of Columbia	6		6		
Hawaii	8	3	4	Warren	1
Puerto Rico	3		3		
Virgin Islands	1	1			
Totals	1,206	595	500	Warren	81
				Stassen	20
				MacArthur	10
					111

NATIONAL PARTY CONVENTIONS

REPUBLICAN: 1952
Roll Call of the States: Selection of a Presidential Nominee
First Roll Call (After Changes)

States, etc.	Number of Votes	Candidates Eisenhower	Taft	Other	
Alabama	14	14			
Arizona	14	4	10		
Arkansas	11	11			
California	70			Warren	70
Colorado	18	17	1		
Connecticut	22	22			
Delaware	12	12			
Florida	18	18			
Georgia	17	16	1		
Idaho	14	14			
Illinois	60	1	59		
Indiana	32	2	30		
Iowa	26	20	6		
Kansas	22	22			
Kentucky	20	13	7		
Louisiana	15	15			
Maine	16	15	1		
Maryland	24	24			
Massachusetts	38	38			
Michigan	46	35	11		
Minnesota	28	28			

NATIONAL PARTY CONVENTIONS

REPUBLICAN: 1952
Roll Call of the States: Selection of a Presidential Nominee
First Roll Call (After Changes)
(continued)

States, etc.	Number of Votes	Candidates Eisenhower	Taft	Other	
Mississippi	5	5			
Missouri	26	26			
Montana	8	1	7		
Nebraska	18	7	11		
Nevada	12	10	2		
New Hampshire	14	14			
New Jersey	38	38			
New Mexico	14	6	8		
New York	96	95	1		
North Carolina	26	26			
North Dakota	14	5	8	Warren	1
Ohio	56		56		
Oklahoma	16	8	4	MacArthur	4
Oregon	18	18			
Pennsylvania	70	70			
Rhode Island	8	8			
South Carolina	6	6			
South Dakota	14	7	7		
Tennessee	20	20			
Texas	38	38			
Utah	14	14			

NATIONAL PARTY CONVENTIONS

REPUBLICAN: 1952
Roll Call of the States: Selection of a Presidential Nominee
First Roll Call (After Changes)
(continued)

States, etc.	Number of Votes	Candidates Eisenhower	Taft	Other
Vermont	12	12		
Virginia	23	19	4	
Washington	24	21	3	
West Virginia	16	3	13	
Wisconsin	30		24	Warren 6
Wyoming	12	12		
District of Columbia	6	6		
Alaska	3	3		
Hawaii	8	4	4	
Puerto Rico	3	1	2	
Virgin Islands	1	1		
Totals	1,206	845	280	MacArthur 4 Warren 77 81

REPUBLICAN: 1952
Roll Call of the States

States, etc.	Number of Votes	Brown Amendment Contested Delegates		Minority Report Georgia Contest		Adoption of Rules Committee Report	
		Yes	No	Yes	No	Yes	No
Alabama	14	9	5	5	9		14
Arizona	14	12	2	3	11		14
Arkansas	11	11		3	8		11
California	70		70	62	8	70	
Colorado	18	1	17	17	1	18	
Connecticut	22	2	20	21	1	22	
Delaware	12	5	7	8	4		12
Florida	18	15	3	5	13		18
Georgia	17	17					16
Idaho	14	14			14	14	
Illinois	60	58	2	1	59		60
Indiana	32	31	1	3	29	32	
Iowa	26	11	15	16	10	24	1
Kansas	22	2	20	20	2	22	
Kentucky	20	18	2	2	18	1	19
Louisiana	15	13	2		2		13
Maine	16	5	11	11	5	16	
Maryland	24	5	19	15	9	24	
Massachusetts	38	5	33	33	5	23	15
Michigan	46	1	45	32	14	44	2
Minnesota	28		28	28		28	

REPUBLICAN: 1952
Roll Call of the States
(continued)

States, etc.	Number of Votes	Brown Amendment Contested Delegates		Minority Report Georgia Contest		Adoption of Rules Committee Report	
		Yes	No	Yes	No	Yes	No
Mississippi	5	5			5		5
Missouri	26	4	22	21	5	18	8
Montana	8	7	1	1	7		8
Nebraska	18	13	5	7	11	15	3
Nevada	12	7	5	2	10	2	10
New Hampshire	14		14	14		8	6
New Jersey	38	5	33	32	6	38	
New Mexico	14	8	6	5	9	14	
New York	96	1	95	92	4	96	
North Carolina	26	14	12	10	16		26
North Dakota	14	11	3	3	11	14	
Ohio	56	56			56	28	28
Oklahoma	16	10	6	4	12		16
Oregon	18		18	18		9	9
Pennsylvania	70	13	57	52	18		70
Rhode Island	8	2	6	6	2	1	1
South Carolina	6	5	1	1	5		6
South Dakota	14	14			14		14
Tennessee	20	20			20		20
Texas	38	22	16				38

REPUBLICAN: 1952
Roll Call of the States
(continued)

States, etc.	Number of Votes	Brown Amendment Contested Delegates		Minority Report Georgia Contest		Adoption of Rules Committee Report	
		Yes	No	Yes	No	Yes	No
Utah	14	14			14	14	
Vermont	12		12	12		12	
Virginia	23	13	10	7	16		23
Washington	24	4	20	19	5	24	
West Virginia	16	15	1	1	15	1	15
Wisconsin	30	24	6	6	24	30	
Wyoming	12	8	4	4	8	12	
Alaska	3	3			3		3
District of Columbia	6	6			6		6
Hawaii	8	7	1	3	5	8	
Puerto Rico	3	2	1	1	2		3
Virgin Islands	1		1	1		1	
Totals	1,206	548	658	607	531§	683	513§§

§ Votes not cast: Georgia 17; Louisiana 13; Texas 38.
§§ Votes not cast: Georgia 1; Iowa 1; Louisiana 2; Rhode Island 6.

NATIONAL PARTY CONVENTIONS

DEMOCRATIC: 1956

Dates: August 13-17, 1956
Site: Chicago, Illinois

Presidential Nominee
Adlai E. Stevenson of Illinois
(Nominated on first ballot.)

Vice Presidential Nominee
Estes Kefauver of Tennessee
(Nominated on second ballot.)

Chairman of the National Committee
Paul M. Butler of Indiana

Secretary of the National Committee and of the Convention
Mrs. Dorothy Vredenburgh of Alabama

Temporary Convention Chairman and Keynoter
Frank Clement of Tennessee

Permanent Convention Chairman
Sam Rayburn of Texas

Chairman, Committee on Platform and Resolutions
John W. McCormack of Massachusetts

Chairman, Credentials Committee
Calvin W. Rawlings of Utah

Chairman, Committee on Rules
John O. Pastore of Rhode Island

Chairman, Committee on Permanent Organization
LeRoy Collins of Florida

DEMOCRATIC: 1956
Roll Call of the States: Selection of a Presidential Nominee

States, etc.	Number of Votes	Stevenson	Candidates Harriman	Other	
Alabama	26	15-1/2		Johnson	1/2
				Davis	1
				Chandler	3
				Battle	1/2
				Timmerman	5-1/2
Arizona	16	16			
Arkansas	26	26			
California	68	68			
Colorado	20	13-1/2	6	Chandler	1/2
Connecticut	20	20			
Delaware	10	10			
Florida	28	25		Symington	3
Georgia	32			Davis	32
Idaho	12	12			
Illinois	64	53-1/2	8-1/2	Chandler	1
				Symington	1
Indiana	26	21-1/2	3	Chandler	1
				Symington	1/2
Iowa	24	16-1/2	7	Chandler	1/2
Kansas	16	16			
Kentucky	30			Chandler	30
Louisiana	24	24			
Maine	14	10-1/2	3-1/2		
Maryland	18	18			
Massachusetts	40	32	7-1/2	Johnson	1/2

DEMOCRATIC: 1956
Roll Call of the States: Selection of a Presidential Nominee
(continued)

States, etc.	Number of Votes	Stevenson	Candidates Harriman	Other	
Michigan	44	39	5		
Minnesota	30	19	11		
Mississippi	22			Johnson	22
Missouri	38			Symington	38
Montana	16	10	6		
Nebraska	12	12			
Nevada	14	5-1/2	7	Johnson Symington	1 1/2
New Hampshire	8	5-1/2	1-1/2	Symington	1
New Jersey	36	36			
New Mexico	16	12	3-1/2	Symington	1/2
New York	98	5-1/2	92-1/2		
North Carolina	36	34-1/2	1	Symington	1/2
North Dakota	8	8			
Ohio	58	52	1/2	Lausche	5-1/2
Oklahoma	28		28		
Oregon	16	16			
Pennsylvania	74	67	7		
Rhode Island	16	16			
South Carolina	20	2		Timmerman	18
South Dakota	8	8			
Tennessee	32	32			

NATIONAL PARTY CONVENTIONS

DEMOCRATIC: 1956
Roll Call of the States: Selection of a Presidential Nominee
(continued)

States, etc.	Number of Votes	Stevenson	Candidates Harriman	Other	
Texas	56			Johnson	56
Utah	12	12			
Vermont	6	5-1/2	1/2		
Virginia	32			Battle	32
Washington	26	19-1/2	6	Symington	1/2
West Virginia	24	24			
Wisconsin	28	22-1/2	5	Chandler	1/2
Wyoming	14	14			
Alaska	6	6			
Canal Zone	3	3			
District of Columbia	6	6			
Hawaii	6	6			
Puerto Rico	6	6			
Virgin Islands	3	3			
Totals	1,372	905-1/2	210	Johnson	80
				Symington	45-1/2
				Chandler	36-1/2
				Davis	33
				Battle	32-1/2
				Timmerman	23-1/2
				Lausche	5-1/2
					256-1/2

DEMOCRATIC: 1956
Roll Call of the States: Selection of a Vice Presidential Nominee
(First Ballot)

States, etc.	Number of Votes	Gore	Kefauver	Kennedy	Humphrey	Wagner	Other	
Alabama	26	12-1/2	3-1/2	1-1/2			Collins Johnson Maurer Clement	1/2 1/2 3 4-1/2
Arizona	16		16					
Arkansas	26	26						
California	68		33	10-1/2	23-1/2		Brown	1
Colorado	20		15	2	3			
Connecticut	20			20				
Delaware	10					10		
Florida	28		17	9-1/2	1/2		Collins	1
Georgia	32			32				
Idaho	12		12					
Illinois	64		12-1/2	46			3-1/2 Symington	1
Indiana	26		22	2-1/2	1-1/2			
Iowa	24		15-1/2	2	6	1/2		
Kansas	16		16					
Kentucky	30						Maner	30
Louisiana	24			24				
Maine	14		6	7-1/2	1/2			
Maryland	18		18					
Massachusetts	40			40				
Michigan	44		40		4			

DEMOCRATIC: 1956
Roll Call of the States: Selection of a Vice Presidential Nominee
(First Ballot)
(continued)

States, etc.	Number of Votes	Candidates					Other
		Gore	Kefauver	Kennedy	Humphrey	Wagner	
Minnesota	30				30		
Mississippi	22	22					
Missouri	38		1	2-1/2	34-1/2		
Montana	16		8	2-1/2	4-1/2	1	
Nebraska	12		12				
Nevada	14		2	11		1	
New Hampshire	8		7-1/2	1/2			
New Jersey	36		4	1/2		31-1/2	
New Mexico	16						Anderson 16
New York	98					98	
North Carolina	36						Hodges 36
North Dakota	8		8				
Ohio	58		50-1/2	5-1/2			
Oklahoma	28	28					
Oregon	16		16				
Pennsylvania	74		54	9-1/2	2	8-1/2	
Rhode Island	16		1/2	15-1/2			
South Carolina	20	1/2		6-1/2			Hodges 4 Clement 9
South Dakota	8		7		1		
Tennessee	32	32					

DEMOCRATIC: 1956
Roll Call of the States: Selection of a Vice Presidential Nominee
(First Ballot)
(continued)

States, etc.	Number of Votes	Gore	Kefauver	Candidates Kennedy	Humphrey	Wagner	Other	
Texas	56	56						
Utah	12		9		2-1/2	1/2		
Vermont	6			6				
Virginia	32			32				
Washington	26		24	1/2	1-1/2			
West Virginia	24		7	5	12			
Wisconsin	28		28					
Wyoming	14		7	5	2			
District of Columbia	6		3		3			
Canal Zone	3			3				
Alaska	6		6					
Puerto Rico	6					6		
Virgin Islands	3		1		1	1		
Totals	1,372§	178	483-1/2	304	134-1/2	162-1/2	Hodges	40
							Maner	30
							Anderson	16
							Clement	13-1/2
							Maurer	3
							Collins	1-1/2
							Symington	1
							Brown	1
							Johnson	1/2
								106-1/2

§Votes not cast: Illinois 1; Ohio 2.

DEMOCRATIC: 1956
Roll Call of the States: Selection of a Vice Presidential Nominee
(Second Ballot)

States, etc.	Number of Votes	Gore	Kefauver	Kennedy	Humphrey	Wagner	Other	
Alabama	26	7	6	12-1/2			Clement	1/2
Arizona	16		16					
Arkansas	26			26				
California	68		37-1/2	25	5		Brown	1/2
Colorado	20		15-1/2	2	2-1/2			
Connecticut	20			20				
Delaware	10			10				
Florida	28		17	10-1/2	1/2			
Georgia	32			32				
Idaho	12		12					
Illinois	64		10-1/2	49-1/2		3-1/2		
Indiana	26		20	3-1/2				
Iowa	24		18-1/2	4	1-1/2			
Kansas	16		16					
Kentucky	30			30				
Louisiana	24			24				
Maine	14		5	9				
Maryland	18		18					
Massachusetts	40			40				
Michigan	44		40		4			
Minnesota	30		13-1/2		16-1/2			

DEMOCRATIC: 1956
Roll Call of the States: Selection of a Vice Presidential Nominee
(Second Ballot)
(continued)

States, etc.	Number of Votes	Candidates Gore	Kefauver	Kennedy	Humphrey	Wagner	Other	
Mississippi	22			22				
Missouri	38	1/2	3	2-1/2	32			
Montana	16		13-1/2	1-1/2	1			
Nebraska	12		12					
Nevada	14		1/2	13-1/2				
New Hampshire	8		8					
New Jersey	36		6	30				
New Mexico	16	2	9-1/2	4-1/2				
New York	98		1-1/2	96-1/2				
North Carolina	36	7-1/2	9-1/2	17-1/2	1/2			
North Dakota	8		8					
Ohio	58		51-1/2	5-1/2				
Oklahoma	28	28						
Oregon	16		16					
Pennsylvania	74		64	8-1/2	1-1/2			
Rhode Island	16		1/2	15-1/2				
South Carolina	20	2-1/2		17			Hodges	1/2
South Dakota	8		8					
Tennessee	32	32						
Texas	56			56				
Utah	12		11		1			

DEMOCRATIC: 1956
Roll Call of the States: Selection of a Vice Presidential Nominee
(Second Ballot^)
(continued)

States, etc.	Number of Votes	Gore	Kefauver	Kennedy	Humphrey	Wagner	Other	
Vermont	6			6				
Virginia	32			32				
Washington	26		25	1				
West Virginia	24		9	9	4			
Wisconsin	28		28					
Wyoming	14		9-1/2	4-1/2				
District of Columbia	6		3		3			
Canal Zone	3			3				
Alaska	6		6					
Puerto Rico	6					6		
Virgin Islands	3		1	2				
Hawaii	6	1	2	2	1			
Totals	1,372§	80-1/2	551-1/2	648	74	9-1/2	Clement	1/2
							Hodges	1/2
							Brown	1/2
								1-1/2

§Votes not cast: Illinois 1/2; Indiana 2-1/2; North Carolina 1; Ohio 1; West Virginia 2.

^Before Senators Gore and Humphrey withdrew in favor of Kefauver.

NATIONAL PARTY CONVENTIONS

DEMOCRATIC: 1956
Roll Call of the States: Selection of a Vice Presidential Nominee
(Second Ballot)

States, etc.	Number of Votes	Gore	Kefauver	Kennedy	Humphrey	Wagner	Other	
Alabama	26	3	6	16-1/2			Clement	1/2
Arizona	16		16					
Arkansas	26			26				
California	68		50	18				
Colorado	20		20					
Connecticut	20			20				
Delaware	10		10					
Florida	28		23-1/2	3-1/2				
Georgia	32			32				
Idaho	12		12					
Illinois	64		9-1/2	54-1/2				
Indiana	26		20	3-1/2				
Iowa	24		24					
Kansas	16		16					
Kentucky	30			30				
Louisiana	24			24				
Maine	14		14					
Maryland	18		18					
Massachusetts	40			40				
Michigan	44		44					
Minnesota	30		30					

NATIONAL PARTY CONVENTIONS

DEMOCRATIC: 1956
Roll Call of the States: Selection of a Vice Presidential Nominee
(Second Ballot)
(continued)

States, etc.	Number of Votes	Gore	Kefauver	Kennedy	Humphrey	Wagner	Other
Mississippi	22			22			
Missouri	38		36	1-1/2	1/2		
Montana	16		15	1			
Nebraska	12		12				
Nevada	14		1/2	13-1/2			
New Hampshire	8		8				
New Jersey	36		6	30			
New Mexico	16	2	9-1/2	4-1/2			
New York	98		1-1/2	96-1/2			
North Carolina	36	7-1/2	9-1/2	17-1/2	1/2		
North Dakota	8		8				
Ohio	58		57				
Oklahoma	28		28				
Oregon	16		16				
Pennsylvania	74		74				
Rhode Island	16		1/2	15-1/2			
South Carolina	20			20			
South Dakota	8		8				
Tennessee	32		32				
Texas	56			56			
Utah	12		12				

DEMOCRATIC: 1956
Roll Call of the States: Selection of a Vice Presidential Nominee
(Second Ballot^)
(continued)

States, etc.	Number of Votes	Gore	Kefauver	Kennedy	Humphrey	Wagner	Other
Vermont	6			6			
Virginia	32			32			
Washington	26		26				
West Virginia	24		24				
Wisconsin	28		28				
Wyoming	14		14				
District of Columbia	6		6				
Canal Zone	3			3			
Alaska	6		6				
Puerto Rico	6					6	
Virgin Islands	3		3				
Hawaii	6	1	2	2	1		
Totals	1,372§	13-1/2	755-1/2	589	2	6	Clement 1/2

§Votes not cast: Florida 1/2; Indiana 2-1/2; North Carolina 1; Ohio 1.

^After Senators Gore and Humphrey withdrew in favor of Kefauver.

NATIONAL PARTY CONVENTIONS

REPUBLICAN: 1956

Dates: August 20-23, 1956
Site: San Francisco, California

Presidential Nominee
Dwight David Eisenhower of Kansas
(Unanimously nominated on first ballot.)

Vice Presidential Nominee
Richard M. Nixon of California
(Unanimously nominated on first ballot.)

Chairman of the National Committee
Leonard W. Hall of New York

Secretary of the National Committee and of the Convention
Mrs. Gladys E. Knowles of Montana

Temporary Convention Chairman
William F. Knowland of California

Keynoter
Arthur B. Langlie of Washington

Permanent Convention Chairman
Joseph W. Martin, Jr. of Massachusetts

Chairman, Committee on Resolutions
Prescott Bush of Connecticut

Chairman, Credentials Committee
C. Wayland Brooks of Illinois

Chairman, Committee on Rules
Theodore R. McKeldin of Maryland

Chairman, Committee on Permanent Organization
Don C. Pierson of Iowa

NATIONAL PARTY CONVENTIONS

REPUBLICAN: 1956
Roll Call of the States: Selection of a Presidential Nominee
(Unanimous Vote for Eisenhower)

States, etc.	Number of Votes	States, etc.	Number of Votes
Alabama	21	Mississippi	15
Arizona	14	Missouri	32
Arkansas	16	Montana	14
California	70	Nebraska	18
Colorado	18	Nevada	12
Connecticut	22	New Hampshire	14
Delaware	12	New Jersey	38
Florida	26	New Mexico	14
Georgia	23	New York	96
Idaho	14	North Carolina	28
Illinois	60	North Dakota	14
Indiana	32	Ohio	56
Iowa	26	Oklahoma	22
Kansas	22	Oregon	18
Kentucky	26	Pennsylvania	70
Louisiana	20	Rhode Island	14
Maine	16	South Carolina	16
Maryland	24	South Dakota	14
Massachusetts	38	Tennessee	28
Michigan	46	Texas	54
Minnesota	28	Utah	14

NATIONAL PARTY CONVENTIONS

REPUBLICAN: 1956
Roll Call of the States: Selection of a Presidential Nominee
(Unanimous Vote for Eisenhower)
(continued)

States, etc.	Number of Votes	States, etc.	Number of Votes
Vermont	12	Alaska	4
Virginia	30	District of Columbia	6
Washington	24	Hawaii	10
West Virginia	16	Puerto Rico	3
Wisconsin	30	Virgin Islands	1
Wyoming	12		
Totals			1,323

NATIONAL PARTY CONVENTIONS

DEMOCRATIC: 1960

Dates: July 11-15, 1960
Site: Los Angeles, California

Presidential Nominee
John F. Kennedy of Massachusetts
(Nominated on first ballot.)

Vice Presidential Nominee
Lyndon Baines Johnson of Texas
(Nominated by acclamation.)

Chairman of the National Committee
John M. Bailey of Connecticut

Secretary of the National Committee and of the Convention
Mrs. Dorothy Vredenburgh of Alabama

Temporary Convention Chairman and Keynoter
Frank Church of Idaho

Permanent Convention Chairman
LeRoy Collins of Florida

Chairman, Committee on Platform and Resolutions
Chester W. Bowles of Connecticut

Chairman, Credentials Committee
Calvin W. Rawlings of Utah

Chairman, Committee on Rules
Herschel C. Loveless of Iowa

Chairman, Committee on Permanent Organization
Margaret Price of Michigan

NATIONAL PARTY CONVENTIONS

DEMOCRATIC: 1960
Roll Call of the States: Selection of a Presidential Nominee

States, etc.	Number of Votes	Kennedy	Johnson	Stevenson	Symington	Other	
Alabama	29	3-1/2	20	1/2	3-1/2	Smathers	1/2
						Meyner	1/2
						Faubus	1/2
Alaska	9	9					
Arizona	17	17					
Arkansas	27		27				
California	81	33-1/2	7-1/2	31-1/2	8	Brown	1/2
Colorado	21	13-1/2		5-1/2	2		
Connecticut	21	21					
Delaware	11		11				
Florida	29					Smathers	29
Georgia	33		33				
Hawaii	9	1-1/2	3	3-1/2	1		
Idaho	13	6	4-1/2	1/2	2		
Illinois	69	61-1/2		2	5-1/2		
Indiana	34	34					
Iowa	26	21-1/2	1/2	2	1/2	Loveless-	1-1/2
Kansas	21	21					
Kentucky	31	3-1/2	25-1/2	1-1/2	1/2		
Louisiana	26	—	26				
Maine	15	15					
Maryland	24	24					

DEMOCRATIC: 1960
Roll Call of the States: Selection of a Presidential Nominee
(continued)

States, etc.	Number of Votes	Kennedy	Johnson	Stevenson	Symington	Other
Massachusetts	41	41				
Michigan	51	42-1/2		2-1/2	6	
Minnesota	31					Humphrey 31
Mississippi	23					Barnett 23
Missouri	39				39	
Montana	17	10	2	2-1/2	2-1/2	
Nebraska	16	11	1/2		4	Humphrey 1/2
Nevada	15	5-1/2	6-1/2	2-1/2	1/2	
New Hampshire	11	11				
New Jersey	41					Meyner 41
New Mexico	17	4	13			
New York	114	104-1/2	3-1/2	3-1/2	2-1/2	
North Carolina	37	6	27-1/2	3		Smathers 1/2
North Dakota	11	11				
Ohio	64	64				
Oklahoma	29		29			
Oregon	17	16-1/2		1/2		
Pennsylvania	81	68	4	7-1/2		Meyner 1-1/2
Rhode Island	17	17				
South Carolina	21		21			
South Dakota	11	4	2	1	2-1/2	Humphrey- 1-1/2

DEMOCRATIC: 1960
Roll Call of the States: Selection of a Presidential Nominee
(continued)

States, etc.	Number of Votes	Candidates				
		Kennedy	Johnson	Stevenson	Symington	Other
Tennessee	33		33			
Texas	61		61			
Utah	13	8	3		1-1/2	
Vermont	9	9				
Virginia	33		33			
Washington	27	14-1/2	2-1/2	6-1/2	3	Rosellini-1/2
West Virginia	25	15	5-1/2	3	1-1/2	
Wisconsin	31	23				Humphrey 8
Wyoming	15	15				
Canal Zone	4		4			
District of Columbia	9	9				
Puerto Rico	7	7				
Virgin Islands	4	4				
Totals	1,521	806	409	79 1/2	86	Meyner 43
						Humphrey 41-1/2
						Smathers 30
						Barnett 23
						Loveless 1-1/2
						Faubus 1/2
						Brown 1/2
						Rosellini 1/2
						140-1/2

NATIONAL PARTY CONVENTIONS

REPUBLICAN: 1960

Dates: July 25-28, 1960
Site: Chicago, Illinois

Presidential Nominee
Richard M. Nixon of California
(Nominated on first ballot.)

Vice Presidential Nominee
Henry Cabot Lodge
(Nominated unanimously on first ballot.)

Chairman of the National Committee
Thruston B. Morton of Kentucky

Secretary of the National Committee and of the Convention
Elizabeth E. Heffelfinger of Minnesota

Temporary Convention Chairman
Cecil H. Underwood of West Virginia

Keynoter
Walter H. Judd of Minnesota

Permanent Convention Chairman
Charles A. Halleck of Indiana

Chairman, Committee on Platform
Charles H. Percy of Illinois

Chairman, Credentials Committee
Robert R. Snodgrass of Georgia

Chairman, Committee on Rules
George F. Etzell of Minnesota

Chairman, Committee on Permanent Organization
Ruth Concilio of Delaware

NATIONAL PARTY CONVENTIONS

REPUBLICAN: 1960
Roll Call of the States: Selection of a Presidential Nominee
(Nearly Unanimous Vote for Nixon)

States, etc.	Number of Votes	States, etc.	Number of Votes
Alabama	22	Michigan	46
Alaska	6	Minnesota	28
Arizona	14	Mississippi	12
Arkansas	16	Missouri	26
California	70	Montana	14
Colorado	18	Nebraska	18
Connecticut	22	Nevada	12
Delaware	12	New Hampshire	14
Florida	26	New Jersey	38
Georgia	24	New Mexico	14
Hawaii	12	New York	96
Idaho	14	North Carolina	28
Illinois	60	North Dakota	14
Indiana	32	Ohio	56
Iowa	26	Oklahoma	22
Kansas	22	Oregon	18
Kentucky	26	Pennsylvania	70
Louisiana	26	Rhode Island	14
Maine	16	South Carolina	13
Maryland	24	South Dakota	14
Massachusetts	38	Tennessee	28

REPUBLICAN: 1960
Roll Call of the States: Selection of a Presidential Nominee
(Nearly Unanimous Vote for Nixon)
(continued)

States, etc.	Number of Votes	States, etc.	Number of Votes
Texas	54	Wisconsin	30
Utah	14	Wyoming	12
Vermont	12	District of Columbia	8
Virginia	30	Puerto Rico	3
Washington	24	Virgin Islands	1
West Virginia	22		
Totals			1,331§

§ Louisiana cast 10 votes for Goldwater.

NATIONAL PARTY CONVENTIONS

DEMOCRATIC: 1964

Dates: August 24-27, 1964
Site: Atlantic City, New Jersey

Presidential Nominee
Lyndon Baines Johnson of Texas
(Nominated by acclamation.)

Vice Presidential Nominee
Hubert H. Humphrey
(Nominated by acclamation.)

Chairman of the National Committee
John M. Bailey of Connecticut

Secretary of the National Committee and of the Convention
Mrs. Dorothy Vredenburgh Bush of Alabama

Temporary Convention Chairman and Keynoter
John O. Pastore of Rhode Island

Permanent Convention Chairman
John W. McCormack of Massachusetts

Chairman, Committee on Platform and Resolutions
Carl Albert of Oklahoma

Chairman, Credentials Committee
David Lawrence of Pennsylvania

Chairman, Committee on Rules
Carl E. Sanders of Georgia

Chairman, Committee on Permanent Organization
Mrs. Geri Joseph of Minnesota

87

NATIONAL PARTY CONVENTIONS

DEMOCRATIC: 1964
Roll Call of the States: Selection of a Presidential Nominee
(Unanimous Vote for Johnson)

States, etc.	Number of Votes	States, etc.	Number of Votes
Alabama	38	Michigan	92
Alaska	12	Minnesota	50
Arizona	19	Mississippi	24
Arkansas	32	Missouri	58
California	154	Montana	17
Colorado	23	Nebraska	19
Connecticut	43	Nevada	22
Delaware	22	New Hampshire	15
Florida	51	New Jersey	77
Georgia	53	New Mexico	26
Hawaii	25	New York	179
Idaho	15	North Carolina	58
Illinois	114	North Dakota	15
Indiana	51	Ohio	99
Iowa	35	Oklahoma	30
Kansas	27	Oregon	24
Kentucky	34	Pennsylvania	125
Louisiana	46	Rhode Island	27
Maine	16	South Carolina	38
Maryland	48	South Dakota	15
Massachusetts	69	Tennessee	40

DEMOCRATIC: 1964
Roll Call of the States: Selection of a Presidential Nominee
(Unanimous Vote for Johnson)
(continued)

States, etc.	Number of Votes	States, etc.	Number of Votes
Texas	99	Wyoming	15
Utah	16	District of Columbia	16
Vermont	12	Canal Zone	5
Virginia	42	Guam	3
Washington	35	Puerto Rico	8
West Virginia	37	Virgin Islands	5
Wisconsin	46	Mississippi Freedom Dems	2
Totals			2,318

NATIONAL PARTY CONVENTIONS

REPUBLICAN: 1964

Dates: July 13-16, 1964
Site: San Francisco, California

Presidential Nominee
Barry Goldwater of Arizona
(Nominated on first ballot.)

Vice Presidential Nominee
William E. Miller of New York
(Nominated by acclamation.)

Chairman of the National Committee
William E. Miller of New York

Secretary of the National Committee and of the Convention
Mrs. C. Douglass Buck of Delaware

Temporary Convention Chairman and Keynoter
Mark O. Hatfield of Oregon

Permanent Convention Chairman
Thruston B. Morton of Kentucky

Chairman, Committee on Resolutions
Melvin R. Laird of Wisconsin

Chairman, Credentials Committee
Charles E. Wittenmeyer of Iowa

Chairman, Committee on Rules
George F. Etzell of Minnesota

Chairman, Committee on Permanent Organization
Jack Crichton of Texas

NATIONAL PARTY CONVENTIONS

REPUBLICAN: 1964
Roll Call of the States: Selection of a Presidential Nominee

States, etc.	Number of Votes	Goldwater	Candidates Rockefeller	Scranton	Other	
Alabama	20	20				
Alaska	12			8	Fong	1
					Judd	1
					Smith	2
Arizona	16	16				
Arkansas	12	9	1	2		
California	86	86				
Colorado	18	15		3		
Connecticut	16	4		12		
Delaware	12	7		5		
Florida	34	32		2		
Georgia	24	22		2		
Hawaii	8	4			Fong	4
Idaho	14	14				
Illinois	58	56	2			
Indiana	32	32				
Iowa	24	14		10		
Kansas	20	18		1	Romney	1
Kentucky	24	21		3		
Louisiana	20	20				
Maine	14				Smith	14
Maryland	20	6	1	13		

NATIONAL PARTY CONVENTIONS

REPUBLICAN: 1964
Roll Call of the States: Selection of a Presidential Nominee
(continued)

States, etc.	Number of Votes	Goldwater	Candidates Rockefeller	Scranton	Other	
Massachusetts	34	5		26	Lodge	2
Michigan	48	8			Romney	40
Minnesota	26	8			Judd	18
Mississippi	13	13				
Missouri	24	23		1		
Montana	14	14				
Nebraska	16	16				
Nevada	6	6				
New Hampshire	14			14		
New Jersey	40	20		20		
New Mexico	14	14				
New York	92	5	87			
North Carolina	26	26				
North Dakota	14	7	1		Judd Smith	3 3
Ohio	58	57			Smith	1
Oklahoma	22	22				
Oregon	18		18			
Pennsylvania	64	4		60		
Rhode Island	14	3		11		
South Carolina	16	16				
South Dakota	14	12		2		

REPUBLICAN: 1964
Roll Call of the States: Selection of a Presidential Nominee
(continued)

States, etc.	Number of Votes	Goldwater	Candidates Rockefeller	Scranton	Other	
Tennessee	28	28				
Texas	56	56				
Utah	14	14				
Vermont	12	3	2	2	Smith	5
Virginia	30	29		1		
Washington	24	22		1	Smith	1
West Virginia	14	10	2	2		
Wisconsin	30	30				
Wyoming	12	12				
District of Columbia	9	4		5		
Puerto Rico	5			5		
Virgin Islands	3			3		
Totals	1,308	883	114	214	Romney	41
					Smith	27
					Judd	22
					Fong	5
					Lodge	2
						97

NATIONAL PARTY CONVENTIONS

REPUBLICAN: 1964
Roll Call of the States: Scott Amendment on Civil Rights

States, etc.	Number of Votes	Yes	No	States, etc.	Number of Votes	Yes	No
Alabama	20		20	Michigan	48	37	9
Alaska	12	12		Minnesota	26	17	9
Arizona	16		16	Mississippi	13		13
Arkansas	12		12	Missouri	24	1	23
California	86		86	Montana	14		14
Colorado	18		18	Nebraska	16		16
Connecticut	16	11	5	Nevada	6		6
Delaware	12	11	1	New Hampshire	14	14	
Florida	34		34	New Jersey	40	40	
Georgia	24		24	New Mexico	14		14
Hawaii	8	4	4	New York	92	86	6
Idaho	14		14	North Carolina	26		26
Illinois	58	4	54	North Dakota	14	1	13
Indiana	32		32	Ohio	58		58
Iowa	24	2	22	Oklahoma	22		22
Kansas	20	2	18	Oregon	18	10	8
Kentucky	24	1	23	Pennsylvania	64	62	2
Louisiana	20		20	Rhode Island	14	11	3
Maine	14	11	3	South Carolina	16		16
Maryland	20	17	3	South Dakota	14		14
Massachusetts	34	27	7	Tennessee	28		28

REPUBLICAN: 1964
Roll Call of the States: Scott Amendment on Civil Rights
(continued)

States, etc.	Number of Votes	Yes	No	States, etc.	Number of Votes	Yes	No
Texas	56		56	Wisconsin	30		30
Utah	14		14	Wyoming	12		12
Vermont	12	8	4	District of Columbia	9	7	2
Virginia	30		30				
Washington	24	1	23	Puerto Rico	5	5	
West Virginia	14	4	10	Virgin Islands	3	3	
Totals					1,308§	409	897

§ Votes not cast: Michigan 2.

NATIONAL PARTY CONVENTIONS

DEMOCRATIC: 1968

Dates: August 26-29, 1968
Site: Chicago, Illinois

Presidential Nominee
Hubert H. Humphrey of Minnesota
(Nominated on first ballot.)

Vice Presidential Nominee
Edmund S. Muskie of Maine
(Nominated on first ballot.)

Chairman of the National Committee
John M. Bailey of Connecticut

Secretary of the National Committee and of the Convention
Mrs. Dorothy Vredenburgh Bush of Alabama

Temporary Convention Chairman and Keynoter
Daniel K. Inouye of Hawaii

Permanent Convention Chairman
Carl Albert of Oklahoma

Chairman, Committee on Platform and Resolutions
Hale Boggs of Louisiana

Chairman, Credentials Committee
Richard J. Hughes of New Jersey

Chairman, Committee on Rules
Samuel H. Shapiro of Illinois

Chairman, Committee on Permanent Organization
Fay Broderick of Maine

NATIONAL PARTY CONVENTIONS

DEMOCRATIC: 1968
Roll Call of the States: Selection of a Presidential Nominee
(First Ballot)

States, etc.	Number of Votes	Humphrey	McCarthy	McGovern	Phillips	Other	
Alabama	32	23				Moore	1/2
						Kennedy	3-1/2
						Bryant	1-1/2
						Wallace	1/2
Alaska	22	17	2	3			
Arizona	19	14-1/2	2-1/2	2			
Arkansas	33	30	2				
California	174	14	91	51	17		
Colorado	35	16-1/2	10	5-1/2	3		
Connecticut	44	35	8		1		
Delaware	22	21					
Florida	63	58	5				
Georgia Regular	22-1/2	17				Moore	2
						Gray	1/2
Georgia Loyal	20-1/2	2-1/2	13-1/2	1	3	Kennedy	1/2
Hawaii	26	26					
Idaho	25	21	3-1/2	1/2			
Illinois	118	112	3	3			
Indiana	63	49	11	2	1		
Iowa	46	18-1/2	19-1/2	5		Kennedy	3
Kansas	38	34	1	3			
Kentucky	46	41	5				
Louisiana	36	35					

NATIONAL PARTY CONVENTIONS

DEMOCRATIC: 1968
Roll Call of the States: Selection of a Presidential Nominee
(First Ballot)
(continued)

States, etc.	Number of Votes	Humphrey	McCarthy	McGovern	Phillips	Other
Maine	27	23	4			
Maryland	49	45	2	2		
Massachusetts	72	2	70			
Michigan	96	72-1/2	9-1/2	7-1/2	6-1/2	
Minnesota	52	38	11-1/2		2-1/2	
Mississippi	24	9-1/2	6-1/2	4	2	
Missouri	60	56	3-1/2		1/2	
Montana	26	23-1/2	2-1/2			
Nebraska	30	15	6	9		
Nevada	22	18-1/2	2-1/2	1		
New Hampshire	26	6	20			
New Jersey	82	62	19		1	
New Mexico	26	15	11			
New York	190	96-1/2	87	1-1/2	2	Kennedy 3
North Carolina	59	44-1/2	2	1/2		Moore 12
North Dakota	25	18	7			
Ohio	115	94	18	2		Kennedy 1
Oklahoma	41	37-1/2	2-1/2	1/2	1/2	
Oregon	35		35			
Pennsylvania	130	103-3/4	21-1/2	2-1/2	1-1/2	Kennedy 3/4

DEMOCRATIC: 1968
Roll Call of the States: Selection of a Presidential Nominee
(First Ballot)
(continued)

States, etc.	Number of Votes	Candidates Humphrey	McCarthy	McGovern	Phillips	Other	
Rhode Island	27	23-1/2	2-1/2				
South Carolina	28	28					
South Dakota	26	2		24			
Tennessee	51	49-1/2	1/2	1			
Texas	104	100-1/2	2-1/2		1		
Utah	26	23	2		1		
Vermont	22	9	6	7			
Virginia	54	42-1/2	5-1/2		2	Moore	3
Washington	47	32-1/2	8-1/2	6			
West Virginia	38	34	3			Kennedy	1
Wisconsin	59	8	49	1	1		
Wyoming	22	18-1/2	3-1/2				
Canal Zone	5	4		1			
District of Columbia	23	2			21		
Guam	5	5					
Puerto Rico	8	8					
Virgin Islands	5	5					
Totals§	2,622	1,760-1/4	601	146-1/2	67-1/2	Moore 17-1/2 Kennedy 12-3/4 Bryant 1-1/2 Wallace 1/2 Gray 1/2 ——— 32-3/4	

§ Votes not cast: Alabama 3; Arkansas 1; California 1;
Delaware 1; Georgia Regular 3; Louisiana 1; Mississippi 2;
Rhode Island 1; Virginia 1.

NATIONAL PARTY CONVENTIONS

DEMOCRATIC: 1968
Roll Call of the States: Selection of a Vice Presidential Nominee

States, etc.	Number of Votes	Muskie	Bond	Other			Not Voting
Alabama	32			Daley	1-1/2		30-1/2
Alaska	22					Passed	22
Arizona	19	17-1/2	1				1/2
Arkansas	33	32					1
California	174					Passed	174
Colorado	35					Passed	35
Connecticut	44					Passed	44
Delaware	22	21					1
Florida	63	58	5				
Georgia Regular	22-1/2	22	1/2				
Georgia Loyal	20-1/2					Passed	20-1/2
Hawaii	26	25		McCarthy	1		
Idaho	25	25					
Illinois	118	116					2
Indiana	63	63					
Iowa	46	46					
Kansas	38	38					
Kentucky	46	46					
Louisiana	36	36					
Maine	27	27					
Maryland	49	49					
Massachusetts	72	72					

100

DEMOCRATIC: 1968
Roll Call of the States: Selection of a Vice Presidential Nominee
(continued)

States, etc.	Number of Votes	Muskie	Bond	Other		Not Voting
Michigan	96	96				
Minnesota	52	39-1/2	12-1/2			
Mississippi	24				Passed	24
Missouri	60	60				
Montana	26	26				
Nebraska	30	24		McCarthy	2	
				Edwards	2	2
Nevada	22	19-1/2		Shriver	1	
				Kennedy	1-1/2	
New Hampshire	26				Passed	26
New Jersey	82	65	1			16
New Mexico	26	23-1/2				2-1/2
New York	190	100				90
North Carolina	59	58		Sanford	1	
North Dakota	25	21	3	McGovern	1	
Ohio	115	115				
Oklahoma	41	41				
Oregon	35				Passed	35
Pennsylvania	130	118		Tate	1-1/2	
				Ryan	3/4	9-3/4
Rhode Island	27	27				
South Carolina	28	26-1/2		McNair	1-1/2	

DEMOCRATIC: 1968
Roll Call of the States: Selection of a Vice Presidential Nominee
(continued)

States, etc.	Number of Votes	Muskie	Bond	Other		Not Voting	
South Dakota	26	26					
Tennessee	51	51					
Texas	104	104					
Utah	26	25	1				
Vermont	22					Passed	22
Virginia	54	50	3-1/2				1/2
Washington	47	42		Hoeh	3	2	
West Virginia	38	38					
Wisconsin	59	8		Lowenstein	1	42	
				McGovern	1		
				Reuss	1		
				Kennedy	2		
				O'Dwyer	1		
				Hoeh	1		
				Ribicoff	2		
Wyoming	22	22					
Canal Zone	5	5					
District of Columbia	23	2	21				
Guam	5	5					
Puerto Rico	8	8					
Virgin Islands	5	5					
Totals	2,622	1,944-1/2	48-1/2		26-3/4	602-1/4	

NATIONAL PARTY CONVENTIONS

DEMOCRATIC: 1968
Roll Call of the States

States, etc.	Number of Votes	Adoption of Minority Report Vietnam Plank Yes	No	States, etc.	Number of Votes	Adoption of Minority Report Vietnam Plank Yes	No
Alabama	32	1-1/2	30-1/2	Maryland	49	12	37
Alaska	22	10	12	Massachusetts	72	56	16
Arizona	19	6-1/2	12-1/2	Michigan	96	52	44
Arkansas	33	7	25	Minnesota	52	16-1/2	34-1/2
California	174	166	6	Mississippi	24	19-1/2	2-1/2
Colorado	35	21	14	Missouri	60	10	50
Connecticut	44	13	30	Montana	26	6	20
Delaware	22		21	Nebraska	30	19	11
Florida	63	7	56	Nevada	22	3-1/2	18-1/2
Georgia Regulars			22-1/2	New Hampshire	26	23	3
Georgia Loyal		19-1/2	1	New Jersey	82	24	57
Hawaii	26		26	New Mexico	26	11-1/2	14-1/2
Idaho	25	10	15	New York	190	148	42
Illinois	118	13	105	North Carolina	59	7	51
Indiana	63	15	47-1/2	North Dakota	25	6	19
Iowa	46	36	10	Ohio	115	48	67
Kansas	38	4-1/2	33-1/2	Oklahoma	41	4	37
Kentucky	46	7	39	Oregon	35	29	6
Louisiana	36	2-1/2	33-1/2	Pennsylvania	130	35-1/4	92-1/4
Maine	27	4-1/2	22-1/2	Rhode Island	27	5	22

DEMOCRATIC: 1968
Roll Call of the States
(continued)

States, etc.	Number of Votes	Adoption of Minority Report Vietnam Plank		States, etc.	Number of Votes	Adoption of Minority Report Vietnam Plank	
		Yes	No			Yes	No
South Carolina	28	1	27	West Virginia	38	8	30
South Dakota	26	26		Wisconsin	59	52	7
Tennessee	51	2	49	Wyoming	22	3-1/2	18-1/2
Texas	104		104	Canal Zone	5	1-1/2	3-1/2
Utah	26	6	20	District of Columbia	22	21	2
Vermont	22	17	5				
				Guam	5	1/2	4-1/2
Virginia	54	8	46				
				Puerto Rico	8		8
Washington	47	15-1/2	31-1/2				
				Virgin Islands	5		5
Totals					2,622	1,041-1/4	1,567-3/4

DEMOCRATIC: 1968
Roll Call of the States

States, etc.	Number of Votes	Motion to Delay Credentials Dispute To August 27		Motion to Seat Regular Texas Delegation		Motion to Seat Georgia Loyal National Democrats	
		Yes	No	Yes	No	Yes	No
Alabama	32	1/2	31-1/2	32		10	22
Alaska	22		22	17	5	5	17
Arizona	19	4-1/2	14	1-1/2	17	17	2
Arkansas	33		33	33		3	29
California	174	173	1	1	173	173	1
Colorado	35	31	4		35	30	5
Connecticut	44		44	30	12	13	27
Delaware	22		21	21		3	18
Florida	63	5	58	58	4	9	54
Georgia	43		43				
Hawaii	26		26	26		4	22
Idaho	25	2	23	22-1/2	2-1/2	4-1/2	20-1/2
Illinois	118		118	114	4	12	83
Indiana	63	13	48	34	10	25	38
Iowa	46	33-1/2	12-1/2	37-1/2	8-1/2	32	12
Kansas	38		38	38		3-1/2	34-1/2
Kentucky	46	3	43	40-1/2	5-1/2	6	40
Louisiana	36		36	32	4	7	29
Maine	27	2	24	25	1	5	22
Maryland	49	5	44	46	3	3	46

DEMOCRATIC: 1968
Roll Call of the States
(continued)

States, etc.	Number of Votes	Motion to Delay Credentials Dispute To August 27		Motion to Seat Regular Texas Delegation		Motion to Seat Georgia Loyal National Democrats	
		Yes	No	Yes	No	Yes	No
Massachusetts	72	19	53	16	47	39	24
Michigan	96	20	69	70	23	35	58
Minnesota	52	16	32	34-1/2	14-1/2	16	33
Mississippi	24	24		2	18-1/2	18	2
Missouri	60	3	57	48	12	12	48
Montana	26	3	23	20	4	2-1/2	21-1/2
Nebraska	30	16	14	12	16	11	18
Nevada	22	1	21	13	7	14	6
New Hampshire	26	21	4	6	20	23	2
New Jersey	82	20	62	43	25	22	51
New Mexico	26	11	15	13	13	11	15
New York	190	190			190	190	
North Carolina	59	3-1/2	55-1/2	54-1/2	4-1/2	3-1/2	55-1/2
North Dakota	25	6	17	17	5	5	17
Ohio	115	30	85	37-1/2	27	21	80
Oklahoma	41	5	36	40	1	1	40
Oregon	35	21	13	10	23	32	
Pennsylvania	130	24	102	81	42	31-1/2	90-1/4
Rhode Island	27	1-1/2	25-1/2	24-1/2	2-1/2	12	11

DEMOCRATIC: 1968
Roll Call of the States
(continued)

States, etc.	Number of Votes	Motion to Delay Credentials Dispute To August 27		Motion to Seat Regular Texas Delegation		Motion to Seat Georgia Loyal National Democrats	
		Yes	No	Yes	No	Yes	No
South Carolina	28		28	28		4	22
South Dakota	26	26		1	25	26	
Tennessee	51	1/2	50-1/2	48-1/2	1		51
Texas	104		104			2-1/2	101-1/2
Utah	26	10	16	18	8	7	19
Vermont	22	14	7	5	13	17	4
Virginia	54	9	36	21-1/2	22-1/2	6-1/2	35-1/2
Washington	47	13-1/2	29-1/2	31-1/2	15-1/2	18	29
West Virginia	38	15	17	19	12	8	22
Wisconsin	59	54	5	5	54	52	7
Wyoming	22	3-1/2	18-1/2	18-1/2	3-1/2	2	20
Canal Zone	5	1	3	4		2	3
District of Columbia	22	21	1		22	22	
Guam	5		5	4-1/2	1/2		5
Puerto Rico	8		8	8		7-1/2	
Virgin Islands	5		5	5		2-1/2	
Totals	2,622	875	1,691-1/2§	1,368	955	1,041-1/2	1,413

§ Georgia vote cast before credentials decision and later disallowed.

DEMOCRATIC: 1968
Roll Call of the States

States, etc.	Number of Votes	Motion to Seat Insurgent Alabama Delegation		Motion to Eliminate Unit Rule		Motion Adding State Party Chairmen and Young Democratic Presidents to National Committee	
		Yes	No	Yes	No	Yes	No
Alabama	32			5-1/2	24-1/2	20-1/2	9
Alaska	22	14	8	22		22	
Arizona	19	7-1/2	11-1/2		19	16-1/2	2-1/2
Arkansas	33	8	23		33	18	14
California	174	173	1	173	1	15	122
Colorado	35	34	1	35		19	16
Connecticut	44	21	21	9	30		44
Delaware	22	2	19		21	20	1
Florida	63	6	57	11	52	23	20
Georgia	43	25	17-1/2	39	4	8-1/2	34-1/2
Hawaii	26		26	3	23		26
Idaho	25	2	23	1	24	11	11
Illinois	118	18	100	3	115	1	117
Indiana	63	13	41-1/2	63		61	2
Iowa	46	24-1/2	21-1/2	46		43	3
Kansas	38	5-1/2	31-1/2	6	20	16	19
Kentucky	46	6-1/2	39-1/2	6-1/2	39-1/2	43-1/2	2-1/2
Louisiana	36		36		36	4	32

DEMOCRATIC: 1968
Roll Call of the States
(continued)

States, etc.	Number of Votes	Motion to Seat Insurgent Alabama Delegation		Motion to Eliminate Unit Rule		Motion Adding State Party Chairmen and Young Democratic Presidents to National Committee	
		Yes	No	Yes	No	Yes	No
Maine	27		26	27		19	8
Maryland	49	2	47	49		48	1
Massachusetts	72	29	29	37	31	24	47
Michigan	96	26	67	43-1/2	44-1/2	19	61
Minnesota	52	23-1/2	28-1/2	16	33-1/2	11-1/2	38
Mississippi	24	12-1/2	8-1/2	21-1/2	1/2	22	
Missouri	60	8	52	60		4-1/2	53-1/2
Montana	26	3-1/2	22-1/2	12-1/2	12	17-1/2	8
Nebraska	30	13	15	26	2	30	
Nevada	22	12-1/2	9-1/2	22		19	3
New Hampshire	26	25		23	3	16	10
New Jersey	82	21	61	21	61	4	78
New Mexico	26	11	15	11	15	5-1/2	20-1/2
New York	190	80	82	190		17	173
North Carolina	59	1	58	2	57	59	
North Dakota	25	7	18	17	5	3	19
Ohio	115	30-1/2	65	23	92	113	2
Oklahoma	41	6-1/2	34-1/2	6	35		41

DEMOCRATIC: 1968
Roll Call of the States
(continued)

States, etc.	Number of Votes	Motion to Seat Insurgent Alabama Delegation		Motion to Eliminate Unit Rule		Motion Adding State Party Chairmen and Young Democratic Presidents to National Committee	
		Yes	No	Yes	No	Yes	No
Oregon	35	31	3	31		14	20
Pennsylvania	130	22-1/4	100-1/2	39-3/4	79-1/2	89-3/4	9-3/4
Rhode Island	27	2-1/2	24-1/2	3-1/2	23-1/2		27
South Carolina	28		28	4-1/2	23-1/2	18	10
South Dakota	26	24	2	26		2	23
Tennessee	51	1/2	49-1/2	2-1/2	46-1/2	47	
Texas	104		104	5	99	7-1/2	84-1/2
Utah	26	5	21	26		21	3
Vermont	22	14	7	22		10	12
Virginia	54	1	53	9-1/2	43-1/2	15	38
Washington	47	16	28	21-1/2	25-1/2	5	42
West Virginia	38	9	29	38		38	
Wisconsin	59	54	4	58	1	40-1/2	17-1/2
Wyoming	22	6-1/2	15-1/2	3	19	2-1/2	19-1/2
Canal Zone	5		4	1	4	5	
District of Columbia	22	23		23		23	
Guam	5		5	1/2	4-1/2	1/2	4-1/2

NATIONAL PARTY CONVENTIONS

DEMOCRATIC: 1968
Roll Call of the States
(continued)

States, etc.	Number of Votes	Motion to Seat Insurgent Alabama Delegation		Motion to Eliminate Unit Rule		Motion Adding State Party Chairmen and Young Democratic Presidents to National Committee	
		Yes	No	Yes	No	Yes	No
Puerto Rico	8		8	1	7	8	
Virgin Islands	5		5	5		5	
Totals	2,622	883-1/2	1,605	1,350	1,206	1,125-3/4	1,349-1/4

111

NATIONAL PARTY CONVENTIONS

REPUBLICAN: 1968

Dates: August 5-8, 1968
Site: Miami Beach, Florida

Presidential Nominee
Richard M. Nixon of California
(Nominated on first ballot.)

Vice Presidential Nominee
Spiro T. Agnew of Maryland
(Nominated on first ballot.)

Chairman of the National Committee
Ray C. Bliss of Ohio

Secretary of the National Committee and of the Convention
Mrs. Consuelo Northrop Bailey of Vermont

Temporary Convention Chairman and Keynoter
Edward W. Brooke of Massachusetts

Permanent Convention Chairman
Gerald R. Ford of Michigan

Chairman, Committee on Platform and Resolutions
Everett Dirksen of Illinois

Chairman, Credentials Committee
Orvas Beers of Indiana

Chairman, Committee on Rules
Charles E. Wittenmeyer of Iowa

Chairman, Committee on Permanent Organization
Mrs. Estelle Stacy of Wyoming

NATIONAL PARTY CONVENTIONS

REPUBLICAN: 1968
Roll Call of the States: Selection of a Presidential Nominee
(First Ballot)

States, etc.	Number of Votes	Nixon	Rockefeller	Reagan	Other	
Alabama	26	14		12		
Alaska	12	11	1			
Arizona	16	16				
Arkansas	18				W. Rockefeller	18
California	86			86		
Colorado	18	14	3	1		
Connecticut	16	4	12			
Delaware	12	9	3			
Florida	34	32	1	1		
Georgia	30	21	2	7		
Hawaii	14				Fong	14
Idaho	14	9		5		
Illinois	58	50	5	3		
Indiana	26	26				
Iowa	24	13	8	3		
Kansas	20				Carlson	20
Kentucky	24	22	2			
Louisiana	26	19		7		
Maine	14	7	7			
Maryland	26	18	8			
Massachusetts	34		34			

REPUBLICAN: 1968
Roll Call of the States: Selection of a Presidential Nominee
(First Ballot)
(continued)

States, etc.	Number of Votes	Nixon	Candidates Rockefeller	Reagan	Other	
Michigan	48	4			Romney	44
Minnesota	26	9	15		Stassen	1
					Lindsay	1
Mississippi	20	20				
Missouri	24	16	5	3		
Montana	14	11		3		
Nebraska	16	16				
Nevada	12	9	3			
New Hampshire	8	8				
New Jersey	40	18			Case	22
New Mexico	14	8	1	5		
New York	92	4	88			
North Carolina	26	9	1	16		
North Dakota	8	5	2	1		
Ohio	58	2			Rhodes	55
					Stassen	1
Oklahoma	22	14	1	7		
Oregon	18	18				
Pennsylvania	64	22	41	1		
Rhode Island	14		14			
South Carolina	22	22				
South Dakota	14	14				

REPUBLICAN: 1968
Roll Call of the States: Selection of a Presidential Nominee
(First Ballot)
(continued)

States, etc.	Number of Votes	Nixon	Candidates Rockefeller	Reagan	Other	
Tennessee	28	28				
Texas	56	41		15		
Utah	8	2			Romney	6
Vermont	12	9	3			
Virginia	24	22	2			
Washington	24	15	3	6		
West Virginia	14	11	3			
Wisconsin	30	30				
Wyoming	12	12				
District of Columbia	9	6	3			
Puerto Rico	5		5			
Virgin Islands	3	2	1			
Totals	1,333	692	277	182	Rhodes	55
					Romney	50
					Case	22
					Carlson	20
					W. Rockefeller	18
					Fong	14
					Stassen	2
					Lindsay	1
						182

REPUBLICAN: 1968
Roll Call of the States: Selection of a Vice Presidential Nominee
(First Ballot)

States, etc.	Number of Votes	Candidates		Other
		Agnew	Romney	
Alabama	26	25		
Alaska	12	11	1	
Arizona	16	16		
Arkansas	18	9	9	
California	86	86		
Colorado	18	14	4	
Connecticut	16	16		
Delaware	12	3	9	
Florida	34	34		
Georgia	30	29	1	
Hawaii	14	14		
Idaho	14	14		
Illinois	58	56		
Indiana	26	26		
Iowa	24	18	6	
Kansas	20	19		
Kentucky	24	24		
Louisiana	26	26		
Maine	14	13	1	
Maryland	26	26		
Massachusetts	34	26	8	

NATIONAL PARTY CONVENTIONS

REPUBLICAN: 1968
Roll Call of the States: Selection of a Vice Presidential Nominee
(First Ballot)
(continued)

States, etc.	Number of Votes	Candidates Agnew	Romney	Other	
Michigan	48	5	43		
Minnesota	26	4	22		
Mississippi	20	20			
Missouri	24	24			
Montana	14	14			
Nebraska	16	16			
Nevada	12	11	1		
New Hampshire	8	8			
New Jersey	40	36	4		
New Mexico	14	14			
New York	92	84	8		
North Carolina	26	22			
North Dakota	8	8			
Ohio	58	56		Brooke Rhodes	1 1
Oklahoma	22	22			
Oregon	18	3	15		
Pennsylvania	64	30	24	Lindsay	10
Rhode Island	14	1	13		
South Carolina	22	22			
South Dakota	14	14			

REPUBLICAN: 1968
Roll Call of the States: Selection of a Vice Presidential Nominee
(First Ballot)
(continued)

States, etc.	Number of Votes	Candidates Agnew	Romney	Other	
Tennessee	28	27	1		
Texas	56	48			
Utah	8	6	2		
Vermont	12	12			
Virginia	24	24			
Washington	24	19	5		
West Virginia	14	14			
Wisconsin	30	25	5		
Wyoming	12	12			
District of Columbia	9	5	4		
Puerto Rico	5	5			
Virgin Islands	3	3			
Totals	1,333§	1,119	186	Lindsay	10
				Brooke	1
				Rhodes	1
					12

§ Votes not cast: Alabama 1; Illinois 2; Kansas 1; North Carolina 4; Texas 8.

PART III

Presidential Campaign Staff

NOTE

The inclusions in Part III are the major advisors and aides of the Presidential candidates.

SOURCES

1948–1964 Presidential Campaign Staffs

Reprinted by permission of Congressional Quarterly, Inc. CONGRESS AND THE NATION: 1945–1964, pp. 7, 8, 15, 16, 25, 26, 38, 39, 55, and 58.

1968 Presidential Campaign Staffs

Reprinted by permission of Congressional Quarterly, Inc. CONGRESS AND THE NATION: 1965–1968, pp. 16 and 19.

THE CAMPAIGN

Perhaps above all, I always believed that a national campaign—
far from being a kind of superfluous carnival to celebrate a secretly
accomplished fact—reached the stage of decision only in its last
three or four weeks. To that point, the time was essentially spent
in two exercises: the slow striving to catch the ear of the people, and
the gradual staking of claims to positions and policies on which
to speak loudly, once the people's attention was truly engaged.[1]

The statistics describing the modern, or post-World War II, presidential campaign underscore the changes in technique, though not in the purpose or the substance, of the campaign process. Today's candidate seeking "the ear of the people" has television and radio at his disposal, and his "slow striving" has been enhanced by the jet age. He has expert pollsters to discern the issues on "which to speak loudly," and he has the awesome responsibility of paying for these new techniques. In 1968, over sixty-two million dollars was spent on presidential campaigns. This figure is almost double the costs of the 1964 presidential campaign and over six times greater than the total expenditures for all campaigns—*i.e.*, presidential and congressional campaigns—in the 1948 election year. The costs of media exposure, in particular television time, has been the major cause of spiralling campaign expenses. The Republican party has gained a distinct advantage in this media revolution due to the fact that it has more money at its disposal, if one defines more media exposure as an advantage.

The costliness of media exposure is partly due to the Equal Time ruling of the Federal Communications Commission. As a result of this 1934 statute, television broadcasters are bound to give all candidates equal access to the media; *i.e.*, if a Democrat appears on the air for a half-hour, all of his opponents, third and fourth party candidates included, are entitled to equal broadcast time. The television industry circumscribes this problem by charging standard rates for broadcast time so that all candidates have an equal opportunity to *pay* for broadcast time.

The staff of a presidential candidate has become increasingly specialized due to the changes in campaign techniques. Aside from the broad and traditional concerns of fund raising, strategy construction, research and coordination, the modern staff must also be equipped to handle

---

[1] Emmet John Hughes, *The Ordeal of Power* (New York: Dell Publishing Co., 1962), pp. 27–28.

121

the technical and artistic problems relating to television and radio advertising. In 1968 Richard Nixon had a manager of communications and an
aide in charge of television production, as well as campaign trip specialists. Aside from the staff, presidential candidates have numerous professional campaign management agencies at their disposal, a situation
unheard of in 1948.[2] There are professional campaign managers, like
Joseph Napolitan and F. Clifton White, who provide general campaign
direction, as well as polling, advertising, research, and publicity services.
Napolitan was hired by candidates Kennedy, Johnson, and Humphrey,
while White has worked for both Nixon and Goldwater. There are television specialists like the Rudner Agency that worked for the 1952
Eisenhower-Nixon campaign and the Doyle Dane Bernbach Agency that
handled the television advertising for the 1964 Johnson-Humphrey ticket.
There are also professional campaign researchers like Kevin Phillips, who
did a potential voter study for Richard Nixon in 1968. The rise in campaign costs is in part due to the employment of these professionals, for,
unlike the regular staff, these services must be paid for and they are costly.

There are different types of campaign organization, a topology that is
not immediately evident in the data as presented. Organization is largely
dependent upon the personality of the candidate, for the only national
party machinery at his disposal is the national committee. A candidate
may choose to staff the national committee with his own key advisors and
utilize it as the core of his organization, as Kennedy and Goldwater did.
A candidate may also choose to erect his own organization essentially
by-passing the national committee, as Nixon did in 1960. Only an incumbent President has a "built-in" staff to organize around, such as the White
House staff and the Executive Department, and he is likely to utilize the
national committee as well, since ostensibly he has staffed and worked
with it for four years. Organization is also contingent upon candidate
personality insofar as the candidate chooses to use it once it is constructed.
In 1960 Nixon personally made most of the major campaign decisions
while his predecessor, Eisenhower, delegated this power to his staff.

One of the major campaign decisions to be made by the candidate
and/or his staff is determining where he is going to campaign; i.e., the
itinerary. It is remarkable that, despite the modernization of campaign
techniques, in general the strategy of where to campaign has been fairly
consistent. The campaign itineraries of 1968 are remarkably similar in
content to the itineraries of 1948. In fact, no jet-age candidate has cam-
paigned in as many places as Harry Truman did in 1948. Air transportation and television have had the effect of cutting down travel and
increased scheduling flexibility so that a candidate could conceivably
appear in New York in the morning, be in Cleveland in the afternoon, and

---

[2] See Dan Nimmo, *The Political Persuaders* (New Jersey: Prentice-Hall, 1970).

in Los Angeles that same evening. In terms of strategy, the itinerary is crucial in that the candidate should be appearing before and turning out those who will most likely vote for him and those voters who are undecided. That has meant, for example, that Democratic candidates concentrate on large urban centers. Kennedy did this with remarkable effectiveness in 1960. Nixon, on the other hand, made a serious strategic mistake by publicly pledging to campaign in all fifty states. As a result he was campaigning in Anchorage, Alaska, one day before the election, essentially fulfilling a campaign promise but accomplishing little else. As a rule the campaign itinerary is less significant to the incumbent President, though President Truman was an obvious exception to this rule. The incumbent President, however, usually assumes a "statesmanlike" role, remaining close to Washington, fulfilling his presidential responsibilities, and utilizing the news media to reach the voters. The President is always at an advantage in terms of the media simply because what he does is "news." Thus the question of exposure and the expense of exposure is less significant for him.

Public opinion polls have grown in significance since the 1948 error, when all the major pollsters predicted a Dewey victory. Polls have perhaps a disproportionate amount of influence, especially as a vehicle for creating a "winner" image—*i.e.*, as a demonstration of popularity—but they have become increasingly significant in determining campaign strategy. They are helpful in gauging candidate strengths, weaknesses, and issues on "which to speak loudly." In 1960 John Kennedy employed his own personal pollster, Louis Harris, for this purpose. Harris's expertise was particularly effective in the West Virginia primary. Based on his survey of the situation, he advised Kennedy to handle the religion issue head-on in an attempt to assure an already favorable electorate that the man preferred was indeed all right despite the fact that he was Catholic.

The drastic change in technique and the ensuing rise in campaign expenses has been analyzed with alarm and dismay by both journalists and political scientists. The criticism varies as to the degree the new campaign has meant a degeneration of democratic politics. Journalists are more alarmed over the media explosion, while academics dismiss their apocalyptic cry in the absence of concrete, objective data proving that the media does change votes. This difference in opinion can be partially explained in terms of the bias of the analyzer; journalists, being part and parcel of the media industry, will no doubt attach more importance to it. But the question remains: What does the media explosion mean for the future of democratic politics?

While it is extremely difficult to ascertain the influence of political commercials and while, thus far, no academic study has demonstrated changed voter attitudes as a result of media exposure, those who make the strongest case against the media base their opinion on their assess-

123

ment of the impact of television in general. In this area, there is evidence that while television may not change minds, it does not have to, for the vast majority of the audience viewing television news programs receive all of their information from only that source.[3] Only a small percentage of the audience reads either magazines or newspapers regularly.

If television is the only source of news information for most people, then the issue must be raised as to the kind of information communicated in political broadcasts. It is evident from the data on media exposure that most political broadcasts are not effective vehicles for informing the people but rather, like soap commercials, are one minute of selling the people. A one-minute or thirty-second spot is hardly enough time for an intelligent discussion of the issues. The more serious question of media usefulness must be raised in light of this fact and particularly in view of the costliness of this media exposure. If the trend continues, it will mean that only the rich or those who have access to large amounts of money will be able to run for the Presidency. It will also mean that the gap between the Republican and Democratic parties will widen, with Republican candidates having the edge of money and media over their opponents. This is hardly an advance for democratic politics.

---

[3] *See* Robert MacNeil, *The People Machine* (New York: Harper and Row, 1968), pp. 3–18.

PRESIDENTIAL CAMPAIGN STAFF

Major Advisers and Staff: Truman, 1948

Clark Clifford of Missouri - Special Counsel, chief speechwriter.

Charles Ross of Missouri - Press Secretary.

Matthew J. Connelly of Massachusetts - Appointments Secretary, campaign train adviser.

William M. Boyle Jr. of Missouri - Advance campaign train planning, contact with state Democratic leaders.

Donald S. Dawson of Missouri - Personnel Manager, advance worker for campaign train.

J. Howard McGrath of Rhode Island - Chairman, Democratic National Committee.

Mrs. India Edwards of the District of Columbia - Executive Director, Women's Division, Democratic National Committee.

Charles J. Murphy of North Carolina - Assistant White House General Counsel, in charge of speech preparation.

Samuel I. Rosenman of New York - Speechwriter, adviser.

George Elsey of Pennsylvania - "Whistle stop" speechwriter.

Oscar Chapman of Colorado - Advance man for campaign train, on leave from Secretary of Interior post.

Leslie Biffle of Arkansas - Secretary of Senate, personal friend of President; made tour (disguised as chicken farmer) of West Virginia, Kentucky, and Ohio to sound out chances for Truman's re-election.

Jonathan Daniels of North Carolina - Adviser.

Representative Michael J. Kirwan of Ohio - Chairman, Democratic Congressional Campaign Committee, traveled on campaign train, considered a key adviser.

Major General Harry S. Vaughan - Military aide to President.

John Blythe of North Carolina - Treasurer, Democratic National Committee, administrator of campaign funds.

Louis Johnson of West Virginia - A key fund raiser.

Jack Redding of the District of Columbia - Director of Publicity, Democratic National Committee

John Nangle of Missouri - Adviser to President Truman.

PRESIDENTIAL CAMPAIGN STAFF

Major Advisers and Staff: **Dewey, 1948**

Herbert Brownell Jr. of New York - Campaign manager.

Elliott V. Bell of New York - Headed policy section of campaign organization; chief adviser on fiscal matters.

Edwin Jaeckle of New York - Buffalo Republican leader and aide to Brownell.

J. Russell Sprague of New York - Nassau County Republican leader and National Committeeman; Brownell aide.

Paul Lockwood of New York - Personal secretary to Dewey; head of operations for campaign including transportation.

James C. Hagerty of New York - Press secretary and public relations.

Thomas E. Stephens of New York - Executive secretary to Brownell.

Harold E. Talbott of New York - Chief fund raiser.

The Reverend **Stanley** High of Connecticut - Speechwriter.

Representative Hugh Scott of Pennsylvania - Republican National Chairman.

Mrs. Jane Hamilton Macauley of the District of Columbia - Assistant Chairman, Republican National Committee.

House Speaker Joseph W. Martin Jr. of Massachusetts - General consultant on Congressional matters.

Senator Henry Cabot Lodge of Massachusetts - Consultant on Senate elections; foreign policy adviser.

John Foster Dulles and Allen W. Dulles of New York - Foreign policy advisers.

Harry Darby of Kansas - Adviser on Middle West.

Representative Everett McKinley Dirksen of Illinois - Farm policy.

Val Washington of Illinois - Adviser on Negro affairs.

Mrs. Jessica McC. Weis of New York - Women's affairs.

John E. Burton of New York - Policy adviser.

Charles D. Breitel of New York - Policy adviser.

PRESIDENTIAL CAMPAIGN STAFF

Major Advisers and Staff: Stevenson, 1952

Wilson W. Wyatt of Kentucky - Campaign manager.

Carl McGowen of Illinois - Administrative assistant, consultant on policy
    matters.

William McCormick Blair Jr. of Illinois - Administrative assistant, in charge
    of daily schedule, appointments.

Stephen A. Mitchell of Illinois - Democratic National Chairman.

Clayton Fritchey of the District of Columbia - Public relations adviser.

William Neale Roach of the District of Columbia - Director of operations from
    Springfield, aide to Wyatt on campaign trains.

James S. Lanigan of New York - Worked with local organizations, briefed
    advance men.

Richard J. Nelson of Illinois - President of Young Democratic Clubs; worked
    with party politicians and organizations.

Arthur Schlesinger Jr. of Massachusetts - Research, gathering of basic
    materials for speeches.

David E. Bell of the District of Columbia - Head of research staff.

William I. Flanagan of Illinois - Press Secretary.

Newton Minow of Illinois - General assistant to McGowen.

Oscar Chapman of Colorado - Advance man on campaign trips, kept in touch
    with state and local party leaders.

James H. Rowe of the District of Columbia - Campaign advance man.

W. Willard Wirtz of Illinois - Research in the labor field.

Jacob M. Arvey of Illinois - Democratic National Committeeman and Cook
    County Democratic Chairman; moving force in Stevenson nomination.

Representative Michael J. Kirwan of Ohio - Chairman, Democratic Congressional
    Campaign Committee, campaign adviser.

PRESIDENTIAL CAMPAIGN STAFF

Major Advisers and Staff: Eisenhower, 1952

Governor Sherman Adams of New Hampshire - Chief of staff of personal campaign.

Senator Henry Cabot Lodge of Massachusetts - Pre-convention campaign manager, chairman of advisory committee.

Arthur E. Summerfield of Michigan - Post-convention campaign manager; Republican National Chairman.

Arthur H. Vandenberg Jr. of Michigan - Executive assistant, speechwriter; head of personal campaign staff.

James C. Hagerty of New York - Press Secretary.

Representative Leonard W. Hall of New York - Manager, campaign train; political operations.

Representative Hugh Scott of Pennsylvania - Pre-conventions strategist; headed national post-convention headquarters in New York.

Governor Thomas E. Dewey of New York - Adviser on campaign strategy.

Governor James H. Duff of Pennsylvania - Adviser on campaign strategy.

Fred A. Seaton of Nebraska - Adviser, assisted Adams.

Senator Frank Carlson of Kansas - Adviser, assisted Adams.

Senator William F. Knowland of California - Adviser, assisted Adams.

Sinclair Weeks of Massachusetts - Adviser, assisted Adams.

Thomas E. Stephens of New York - Secretary; aide to Adams.

Harold E. Talbott of New York - Republican National Finance Chairman.

C. D. Jackson of New York - Vice president of Time; adviser.

Albert B. Hermann of North Dakota - Executive director, Republican National Committee.

Kevin McCann of Ohio - President of Defiance College of Ohio; major speechwriter.

Gabriel Hauge of New York - Speechwriter; research director.

Emmet J. Hughes of New York - Speechwriter.

Milton Eisenhower of Pennsylvania - President, Pennsylvania State College and brother of the candidate.

PRESIDENTIAL CAMPAIGN STAFF

Major Advisers and Staff: Eisenhower, 1952
(continued)

Bertha Adkins of Maryland - Assistant to Republican National Chairman.

Fred C. Scribner Jr. of Maine - General Counsel, Republican National
Committee.

PRESIDENTIAL CAMPAIGN STAFF

Major Advisers and Staff: Stevenson, 1956

James A. Finnegan of Pennsylvania - Campaign manager.

Paul M. Butler of Indiana - Democratic National Chairman.

Roger Tubby of New York - In charge of public relations.

Harry S. Ashmore of Arkansas - Adviser on news media.

John Brademas of Indiana - Set up research division.

Ken Hechler of West Virginia - Executive assistant for research.

Rogers Stevens of Illinois - Solicitation of large individual campaign
    contributions.

Thomas K. Finletter of New York - Co-director of New York campaign head-
    quarters.

Mrs. Anna Rosenberg of New York - Co-director of New York campaign head-
    quarters.

Archibald S. Alexander of New Jersey - Director of activities, National
    Stevenson for President Committee.

Mrs. Edison Dick of Illinois - A director of the National Stevenson for
    President Committee.

Barry Bingham of Kentucky - A director of the National Stevenson for
    President Committee.

Hyman B. Raskin of Illinois - Advance man for the campaign.

James H. Rowe of the District of Columbia - Coordinated campaign trips from
    Washington.

William McCormick Blair Jr. of Illinois - Adviser on political and legal
    affairs.

George F. Kennan of New Jersey - Foreign policy adviser.

Dr. Karl Meyer of Illinois - Adviser on matters relating to public health.

Wilson W. Wyatt of Kentucky - Personal manager.

Clayton Fritchey of the District of Columbia - Press Secretary.

Stephen A. Mitchell of Illinois - Adviser.

PRESIDENTIAL CAMPAIGN STAFF

Major Advisers and Staff: Eisenhower, 1956

Sherman Adams of New Hampshire - Assistant to the President; chief of staff of personal campaign.

Wilton B. Persons of Alabama - Deputy Assistant to the President.

Leonard W. Hall of New York - Republican National Chairman and key campaign adviser.

Postmaster General Arthur E. Summerfield of Michigan - Political adviser.

Gerald Morgan of the District of Columbia - Counsel to the President.

Bernard M. Shanley of New Jersey. - Secretary to the President.

James C. Hagerty of New York - Press Secretary.

Secretary of the Interior Fred A. Seaton of Nebraska - Campaign adviser.

Maxwell Rabb of Massachusetts - Secretary to the Cabinet; campaign adviser on ethnic groups.

Fred C. Scribner, Jr. of Maine - Assistant to Hall.

Representative Hugh Scott of Pennsylvania - General Counsel, Republican National Committee.

Gabriel Hauge of New York - Special Presidential Assistant on economic affairs; campaign speechwriter.

Kevin McCann - President, Defiance College of Ohio; speechwriter.

Bryce Harlow of Virginia - Special Presidential Assistant; speechwriter.

Emmet J. Hughes of New York - Speechwriter.

C.D. Jackson of New York - Vice president, Time, Inc.; campaign adviser.

Milton Eisenhower of Maryland - President, Johns Hopkins University; brother of President; adviser.

Secretary of State John Foster Dulles of New York - Chief foreign policy adviser.

Harold E. Stassen of Pennsylvania - Adviser on peace and disarmament problems.

Edward A. McCabe of the District of Columbia - Assistant to Adams.

PRESIDENTIAL CAMPAIGN STAFF

Major Advisers and Staff: Kennedy, 1960

Robert F. Kennedy of Massachusetts - National Campaign Manager.

Lawrence F. O'Brien of Massachusetts - National director of organization.

Theodore C. Sorenson of Nebraska - Chief Kennedy speechwriter.

P. Kenneth O'Donnell of Massachusetts - Director, campaign scheduling.

Neil Staebler of Michigan - Democratic state chairman, Director of special projects.

Stephen E. Smith of New York - Director of fund raising and financing, brother-in-law of the candidate.

Edward M. (Ted) Kennedy of Massachusetts - Coordinator of the campaign in the Western states.

R. Sargent Shriver of Illinois - Active in formation of civil rights, farm, and businessmen's activities in the campaign; brother-in-law of the candidate.

John M. Bailey of Connecticut - Democratic state chairman; "personal liaison" with state and local party leaders.

Representative Chester Bowles of Connecticut - Foreign policy adviser.

Adlai E. Stevenson of Illinois - Foreign policy adviser.

W. Averell Harriman of New York - Foreign policy adviser.

Governor Abraham A. Ribicoff of Connecticut - Adviser and frequent speech-maker for the campaign.

Paul H. Nitze of Massachusetts - Adviser on national security matters.

Myer Feldman of Pennsylvania - Chief of research.

Archibald Cox of Massachusetts - Director of Kennedy "brain trust."

Pierre Salinger of California - Press secretary.

Louis Harris of New York - Public opinion pollster.

Byron R. White of Colorado - Director, Citizens for Kennedy-Johnson.

Senator J. W. Fulbright of Arkansas - Foreign policy adviser.

PRESIDENTIAL CAMPAIGN STAFF

Major Advisers and Staff: Kennedy, 1960
(continued)

Senator Albert Gore of Tennessee - Economic policy adviser.

George Ball of Washington, D.C. - Coordinator of advisory panels.

Clark Clifford of Washington, D.C. - Policy adviser.

Senator George A. Smathers of Florida - Southern states coordinator.

Senator Henry M. Jackson of Washington - Democratic National Chairman.

Matthew H. McCloskey of Pennsylvania - Treasurer, Democratic National
    Finance Committee.

Representative Frank Thompson Jr. of New Jersey - Chief of Kennedy organized
    National Voters Registration Committee.

PRESIDENTIAL CAMPAIGN STAFF

Major Advisers and Staff: Nixon, 1960

Leonard W. Hall of New York - General Campaign Chairman for Nixon-Lodge; member of strategy board.

Robert H. Finch of California - Campaign director; member of strategy board.

Senator Thruston B. Morton of Kentucky - Chairman of National Committee; member of strategy board.

Meade Alcorn of Connecticut - Member of strategy board.

Senator Hugh Scott of Pennsylvania - Member of strategy board.

Secretary of Interior Fred A. Seaton of Nebraska - Member of strategy board.

Under Secretary of Treasury Fred C. Scribner Jr. of Maine - Member of strategy board.

J. Clifford Folger of Washington, D.C. - Chief campaign fund raiser; member of strategy board.

Charles K. McWhorter of New York - Liaison between activites appealing to independent voters and the regular party machinery.

James Bassett of California - Director of scheduling and itineraries.

Representative Bob Wilson of California - In charge of Nixon's itinerary.

Robert Haldeman of California - Chief of advance-man team.

James Shepley of New York - Chief assistant on policy formulation.

George L. Grassmuck of Michigan - Director of research.

Attorney General William P. Rogers of New York - Close friend and policy adviser to Nixon.

Secretary of Labor James P. Mitchell of New Jersey - Adviser on labor and economic problems.

Herbert G. Klein of California - Press secretary.

Charles S. Rhyne of Washington, D.C. - Chairman, Volunteers for Nixon-Lodge.

Peter M. Flanigan of New York - National Director, Volunteers for Nixon-Lodge.

PRESIDENTIAL CAMPAIGN STAFF

Major Advisers and Staff: Johnson, 1964

Lawrence F. O'Brien of Massachusetts - Director of campaign organization, National Committee; member of strategy board. Regular Presidential assistant for Congressional relations.

P. Kenneth O'Donnell of Massachusetts - Executive director, National Committee; member of strategy board. Regular White House aide.

Walter W. Jenkins of Texas (prior to resignation October 14) - Administrative assistant to the President.

Bill Don Moyers of Texas - Media and speech coordinator prior to Jenkins' resignation; took over Jenkins' duties thereafter.

Jack Joseph Valenti of Texas - In charge of scheduling Johnson campaign appearances; regular White House aide.

George E. Reedy of Texas - Presidential Press Secretary.

Lady Bird (Mrs. Claudia T.) Johnson of Texas - President's wife; campaign adviser.

Clifton Carter of Texas - Untitled White House representative at the National Committee with general campaign coordination role; member of strategy board.

Wayne Phillips of Washington, D.C. - Director of news and information, National Committee; member of strategy board.

Frederick G. Dutton of California - Director of research, National Committee; member of strategy board.

John M. Bailey of Connecticut - Chairman of National Committee; member of strategy board.

Mrs. Margaret Price of Michigan - Vice chairman, National Committee; member of strategy board.

Charles D. Roche of Massachusetts - Deputy chairman, National Committee (Senate, House campaigns); member of strategy board.

Louis Martin of Illinois - Deputy chairman, National Committee (minorities and nationalities); member of strategy board.

Robert Short of Minnesota - Humphrey staff man; member of strategy board.

Myer Feldman of Massachusetts - White House research coordinator; member of strategy board.

PRESIDENTIAL CAMPAIGN STAFF

Major Advisers and Staff: Johnson, 1964
(continued)

Secretary of Labor W. Willard Wirtz of Illinois - Speechwriter and co-
    ordinator.

Douglass Cater of Washington, D.C. - Speechwriter and coordinator.

Richard Goodwin of Massachusetts - Speechwriter.

Horace Busby of Texas - Speechwriter.

Samuel C. Brightman of Washington, D.C. - Deputy chairman for public affairs,
    National Committee; member of strategy board.

Richard Maguire of Massachusetts - Treasurer, National Committee.

Arthur Krim of New York - Head of New York City "President's Club" (fund
    raising group).

James H. Rowe Jr. of Washington D.C. - Director of all non-party-oriented
    volunteer activities.

Mrs. Elizabeth Carpenter of Washington, D.C. - Mrs. Johnson's press secretary
    and staff director.

136

PRESIDENTIAL CAMPAIGN STAFF

Major Advisers and Staff: Goldwater, 1964

Denison Kitchel of Arizona - Campaign director; chief Goldwater strategy and
    policy adviser; member of steering committee.

Dean Burch of Arizona - Chairman of National Committee; member of steering
    committee.

John E. Grenier of Alabama- Executive director of National Committee; member
    of steering committee.

F. Clifton White of New York - Director, Citizens for Goldwater-Miller;
    member of steering committee.

Wayne J. Hood of Wisconsin - Director of National Committee campaign organi-
    zation division; member of steering committee.

Edward A. McCabe of Washington, D.C. - Director of research, National Com-
    mittee; member of steering committee.

Ray C. Bliss of Ohio - Member of steering committee.

Leonard W. Hall of New York - Member of steering committee.

L. Richard Guylay of New York - Director of public relations for National
    Committee; member of steering committee.

Ralph Cordiner of New York - Chairman, Republican National Finance Committee;
    member of steering committee.

William F. Knowland of California - Member of steering committee.

Karl Hess of Washington, D.C. - Chief speechwriter.

Paul F. Wagner of Washington, D.C. - Press secretary.

Raymond V. Humphreys of West Virginia - Director of political education and
    training, National Committee.

Douglas Whitlock of Washington, D.C. - Tour director.

Mrs. Laddie F. (Pat) Hutar of Illinois - Assistant chairman, Republican
    National Committee.

Mrs. Emery (Ann-Eve) Johnson of Arizona - Special campaign assistant for Mrs.
    Goldwater.

William S. Warner of Indiana - Miller campaign director; member of steering
    committee.

137

Major Advisers and Staff: Goldwater, 1964
(continued)

Charles Lichenstein of Washington, D.C. - Deputy director of research, National Committee.

William J. Baroody of Washington, D.C. - Policy adviser.

W. Lee Edwards of Washington, D.C. - Deputy director of public relations, National Committee.

PRESIDENTIAL CAMPAIGN STAFF

Major Advisers and Staff: Humphrey, 1968

Lawrence F. O'Brien of Massachusetts - Campaign manager for Humphrey and Democratic National Chairman.

Senators Fred R. Harris of Oklahoma and Walter F. Mondale of Minnesota - Key advisers; were co-chairmen of Humphrey's pre-nomination campaign.

James H. Rowe, Jr. of Washington, D.C. - Adviser.

Orville L. Freeman of Minnesota - Secretary of Agriculture, during campaign in charge of issues and scheduling division of Democratic National Committee.

W. Willard Wirtz of Illinois - Secretary of Labor; adviser.

Max Kampelman of Washington, D.C. - Washington attorney; adviser.

John A. Gronouski of Wisconsin - Executive secretary of preconvention United Democrats for Humphrey.

George W. Ball of Washington, D.C. - Foreign affairs adviser; former U.S. Ambassador to United Nations.

Mrs. Geri Joseph of Minnesota - Vice chairman, Democratic National Committee.

William Connell of Maryland - Humphrey's executive assistant.

William B. Welsh of Virginia - Humphrey's administrative assistant.

John Reilly and John G. Stewart - "Idea" men on foreign and domestic affairs respectively.

Ted VanDyke - Humphrey aide, "executive officer" of campaign tour.

Terry Sanford of North Carolina - Chairman of Citizens for Humphrey-Muskie; former Governor of North Carolina.

Robert E. Short of Minnesota - Treasurer, Democratic National Committee.

PRESIDENTIAL CAMPAIGN STAFF

Major Advisers and Staff: Nixon, 1968

John N. Mitchell of New York - National campaign manager.

H.R. (Bob) Haldeman of California - Chief of staff for Nixon campaign.

Herbert G. Klein of California - Manager of communications (including press).

Leonard Garment of New York - Chief talent scout and organization "trouble shooter".

Peter M. Flanigan of New York - Deputy campaign manager.

Robert F. Ellsworth of Kansas - National political director.

Maurice H. Stans of New York - Chairman, Republican National Finance Committee.

Frank Shakespeare of New York - In charge of television productions.

Charles S. Rhyne of Washington, D.C. - National chairman of United Citizens for Nixon-Agnew.

Ray C. Bliss of Ohio - Chairman, Republican National Committee.

Mrs. Patricia R. Hitt of California - National co-chairman of Nixon-Agnew campaign committee.

Richard G. Kleindienst of Arizona - Liaison between Nixon campaign organization and Republican National Committee.

Robert H. Finch of California - Key adviser; the Lieutenant Governor of California.

Raymond K. Price, Patrick J. Buchanan, William Safire, William F. Gavin - Principal speechwriters.

Charles K. McWhorter of New York and Dwight Chapin of New York - Campaign trip political specialists.

John Ehrlichman of New York - Tour manager.

Campaign Itineraries

NOTE

Except for 1960 and the campaigns of incumbent Presidents, no official records were kept of Presidential Campaign Itineraries. The other itineraries in Part IV were reconstructed from the sources indicated below. In all cases the itineraries begin on September 1 and continue through election day.

SOURCES

1960 Campaign Itineraries

U.S. Senate. Committee on Commerce. THE SPEECHES, RE-MARKS, PRESS CONFERENCES, AND STUDY PAPERS OF VICE PRESIDENT RICHARD M. NIXON, AUGUST 25 THROUGH NOVEMBER 7, 1960. Report 994, Part 2, 87th Congress, 1st Session, 1961.
————. THE SPEECHES, REMARKS, PRESS CONFERENCES, AND STATEMENTS OF JOHN F. KENNEDY AUGUST 17 THROUGH NOVEMBER 7, 1960. Report 994, Part 1, 87th Congress, 1st Session, 1961.

1948, 1956, and 1964 Campaign Itineraries

U.S. President. Public Papers of the Presidents of the United States. Washington, D.C.: Office of the Federal Register, National Archives and Records Service, 1948: Harry S. Truman.
————. Public Papers of the Presidents of the United States. Washington, D.C.: Office of the Federal Register, National Archives and Records Service, 1956: Dwight D. Eisenhower.
————. Public Papers of the Presidents of the United States. Washington, D.C.: Office of the Federal Register, National Archives and Records Service, 1964: Lyndon B. Johnson.

Other 1948, 1952, 1956, 1964, and 1968 Campaign Itineraries

Compiled on the basis of Campaign Press Releases, *The New York Times*, and information supplied by the Republican National Committee.

CAMPAIGN ITINERARIES: PRESIDENTIAL CANDIDATES

September 1 - November 2, 1948§

Date	Truman	Dewey	Wallace
9/ 1/48	Washington, D.C.	Albany, N.Y.	Birmingham, Ala.
9/ 2/48	Washington, D.C.	Albany, N.Y.	Shreveport, La. Monroe, La. Jackson, Miss.
9/ 3/48	Washington, D.C.	Albany, N.Y.	Little Rock, Ark.
9/ 4/48	Washington, D.C.	Albany, N.Y.	Nashville, Tenn. Knoxville, Tenn.
9/ 5/48	Washington, D.C.	Albany, N.Y.	South Salem, N.Y.
9/ 6/48	Grand Rapids, Mich. Lansing, Mich. Detroit, Mich. Hamtramck, Mich. Pontiac, Mich. Flint, Mich. Toledo, Ohio	Albany, N.Y.	New York City, N.Y.
9/ 7/48	Washington, D.C.	Albany, N.Y.	New York City, N.Y.
9/ 8/48	Washington, D.C.	Albany, N.Y.	New York City, N.Y.
9/ 9/48	Washington, D.C.	Albany, N.Y.	New York City, N.Y.
9/10/48	Washington, D.C.	New York City, N.Y.	New York City, N.Y.
9/11/48	Washington, D.C.	Pawling, N.Y.	Philadelphia, Pa.
9/12/48	Washington, D.C.	New York City, N.Y.	Baltimore, Md.
9/13/48	Washington, D.C.	Albany, N.Y.	New York City, N.Y.
9/14/48	Washington, D.C.	Albany, N.Y.	Chicago, Ill.
9/15/48	Washington, D.C.	Albany, N.Y.	Chicago, Ill.
9/16/48	Washington, D.C.	Albany, N.Y.	Buffalo, N.Y.
9/17/48	Pittsburg, Pa. Crestline, Ohio	Albany, N.Y.	Rochester, N.Y.
9/18/48	Rock Island, Ill. Davenport, Iowa Iowa City, Iowa Oxford, Iowa Grinnell, Iowa Des Moines, Iowa Dexter, Iowa Melcher, Iowa Chariton, Iowa Trenton, Mo. Polo, Mo.	Albany, N.Y.	Boston, Mass.
9/19/48	Junction City, Kan.	Albany, N.Y.	Westchester, N.Y.
9/20/48	Denver, Colo. Colorado Springs, Colo. Pueblo, Colo. Canon City, Colo.	Des Moines, Iowa	New York City, N.Y.

§ Comparable data was not available for the inclusion of Strom Thurmond's itinerary.

CAMPAIGN ITINERARIES: PRESIDENTIAL CANDIDATES

September 1 - November 2, 1948
(continued)

Date	Truman	Dewey	Wallace
9/21/48	Salita, Colo. Grand Junction, Colo. Price, Utah Helper, Utah Springville, Utah Provo, Utah American Fork, Utah Salt Lake City, Utah Ogden, Utah	Denver, Colo.	New York City, N.Y.
9/22/48	Sparks, Nev. Reno, Nev. Truckee, Calif. Roseville, Calif. San Francisco, Calif. Oakland, Calif. Sacramento, Calif.	Albuquerque, N.M.	New York City, N.Y.
9/23/48	Merced, Calif. Fresno, Calif. Tulare, Calif. Bakersfield, Calif. Tehachapi, Calif. Mojave, Calif. Burbank, Calif. Los Angeles, Calif.	Phoenix, Ariz.	Toledo, Ohio
9/24/48	San Diego, Calif. Oceanside, Calif. Colton, Calif. Yuma, Ariz. Phoenix, Ariz.	Los Angeles, Calif.	Youngstown, Ohio
9/25/48	Lordsburg, N.M. Deming, N.M. El Paso, Tex. Sierra Blanca, Tex. Valentine, Tex. Marfa, Tex. Alpine, Tex. Sanderson, Tex.	SanFrancisco, Calif.	St. Louis, Mo.
9/26/48	San Antonio, Tex.		Chicago, Ill. South Bend, Ind.
9/27/48	San Marcos, Tex. Austin, Tex. Georgetown, Tex. Temple, Tex. Waco, Tex.	Portland, Ore. Tacoma, Wash.	Dallas, Tex.

CAMPAIGN ITINERARIES: PRESIDENTIAL CANDIDATES

September 1 - November 2, 1948
(continued)

Date	Truman	Dewey	Wallace
9/27/48	Hillsboro, Tex. Fort Worth, Tex. Grand Prairie, Tex. Dallas, Tex. Greenville, Tex. Bells, Tex. Bonham, Tex.		
9/28/48	Sherman, Tex. Whitesboro, Tex. Gainesville, Tex. Marietta, Okla. Ardmore, Okla. Davis, Okla. Pauls Valley, Okla. Purcell, Okla. Norman, Okla. Oklahoma City, Okla.	Spokane, Wash. Missouia, Mont.	Dallas, Tex.
9/29/48	Shawnee, Okla. Seminole, Okla. Wewoka, Okla. Holdenville, Okla. McAlester, Okla. Eufaula, Okla. Muskogee, Okla. Tulsa, Okla. Claremore, Okla. Chelsea, Okla. Vinita, Okla. Afton, Okla. Neosho, Mo. Monett, Mo. Springfield, Mo. Marshfield, Mo.	Helena, Mont. Great Falls, Mont.	Houston, Tex.
9/30/48	Mount Vernon, Ill. West Frankfort, Ill. Herrin, Ill. Carbondale, Ill. Marion, Ill. Eldorado, Ill. Carmi, Ill. Mount Vernon, Ind. Evansville, Ind. Henderson, Ky. Owensboro, Ky.	Pocatello, Idaho Falls, Idaho Salt Lake City, Utah	ElPaso, Tex.

CAMPAIGN ITINERARIES: PRESIDENTIAL CANDIDATES

September 1 - November 2, 1948
(continued)

Date	Truman	Dewey	Wallace
9/30/48	Hawesville, Ky. Irvington, Ky. Louisville, Ky.		
10/ 1/48	Shelbyville, Ky. Frankfort, Ky. Lexington, Ky. Winchester, Ky. Mt. Sterling, Ky. Morehead, Ky. Obric Hill, Ky. Ashland, Ky. Huntington, W.Va. Montgomery, W.Va. Charleston, W.Va.	Cheyenne, Wyo.	LosAngeles, Calif.
10/ 2/48	Washington, D.C.	St. Louis, Mo.	Los Angeles, Calif.
10/ 3/48	Washington, D.C.	Albany, N.Y.	Bakersfield, Calif.
10/ 4/48	Washington, D.C.	Albany, N.Y.	Fresno, Calif.
10/ 5/48	Washington, D.C.	Albany, N.Y.	Sacramento, Calif.
10/ 6/48	Wilmington, Del. Philadelphia, Pa. Camden, N.J.	Albany, N.Y.	San Francisco, Cal.
10/ 7/48	Bridgeport, Pa. Reading, Pa. Allentown, Pa. Bethlehem, Pa. Easton, Pa. Elizabeth, N.J. Newark, N.J. Jersey City, N.J.	Albany, N.Y.	Portland, Ore.
10/ 8/48	Albany, N.Y. Schenectady, N.Y. Amsterdam, N.Y. Little Falls, N.Y. Utica, N.Y. Rome, N.Y. Oneida, N.Y. Syracuse, N.Y. Auburn, N.Y. Seneca Falls, N.Y. Geneva, N.Y. Rochester, N.Y. Batavia, N.Y. Buffalo, N.Y.	New York City, N.Y.	Seattle, Wash.

CAMPAIGN ITINERARIES: PRESIDENTIAL CANDIDATES

September 1 - November 2, 1948
(continued)

Date	Truman	Dewey	Wallace
10/ 9/48	Washington, D.C.	Albany, N.Y.	Tacoma, Wash.
10/10/48	Washington, D.C.	Albany, N.Y.	
10/11/48	Cincinnati, Ohio Hamilton, Ohio Dayton, Ohio Sidney, Ohio Lima, Ohio Ottawa, Ohio Deshler, Ohio Fostoria, Ohio Willard, Ohio Rittman, Ohio Akron, Ohio	Erie, Pa. Sharon, Pa. New Castle, Pa. Rochester, Pa. Pittsburgh, Pa.	Benson, Minn. Chicago, Ill.
10/12/48	Richmond, Ind. Greenfield, Ind. Crawfordsville, Ind. Danville, Ill. Tolono, Ill. Decatur, Ill. Springfield, Ill.	Beaucoup, Ill. Louisville, Ky. Mt. Vernon, Ill.	Chicago, Ill.
10/13/48	Adams, Wis. Altoona, Wis. Spooner, Wis. Superior, Wis. Duluth, Minn. St. Paul, Minn.	Oklahoma City, Okla.	Chicago, Ill.
10/14/48	Mankato, Minn. Waseca, Minn. Rochester, Minn. Winona, Minn. Sparta, Wis. Elroy, Wis. Madison, Wis. Waukesha, Wis. Milwaukee, Wis.	Kansas City, Mo.	Milwaukee, Wis.
10/15/48	Hammond, Ind. North Judson, Ind. Logansport, Ind. Kokomo, Ind. Tyston, Ind. Noblesville, Ind. Indianapolis, Ind.	St. Paul, Minn.	Chicago, Ill.

CAMPAIGN ITINERARIES: PRESIDENTIAL CANDIDATES

September 1 - November 2, 1948
(continued)

Date	Truman	Dewey	Wallace
10/16/48	Clarkesburg, W.Va. Grafton, W.Va. Keyser, W.Va.	Rensselair, Ind. Hammond, Ind. Owasso, Mich.	Dalton, Ga.
10/17/48	Washington, D.C.	Owasso, Mich.	Detroit, Mich.
10/18/48	Miami, Fla.	Buffalo, N.Y. Rochester, N.Y. Syracuse, N.Y. Schenectady, N.Y. Albany, N.Y.	Pittsburgh, Pa.
10/19/48	Raleigh, N.C.	Albany, N.Y.	Reading, Pa. Philadelphia, Pa.
10/20/48	Washington, D.C.	New York City, N.Y.	Wilkes-Barre, Pa.
10/21/48	Washington, D.C.	New York City, N.Y.	New York City, N.Y.
10/22/48	Washington, D.C.	New York City, N.Y.	New York City, N.Y.
10/23/48	Scranton, Pa. Wilkes-Barre, Pa. Lock Haven, Pa. Johnston, Pa. Pittsburgh, Pa.	Albany, N.Y.	South Salem, N.Y.
10/24/48		Albany, N.Y.	Newark, N.J.
10/25/48	Garrett, Ind. Gary, Ind. Chicago, Ill.	Albany, N.Y.	Jersey City, N.J. Elizabeth, N.J.
10/26/48	South Bend, Ind. Elkhart, Ind. Toledo, Ohio Sandusky, Ohio Elyria, Ohio Cleveland, Ohio	Chicago, Ill.	New York City, N.Y.
10/27/48	Pittsfield, Mass. Thompsonville, Conn. Hartford, Conn. Springfield, Mass. Worcester, Mass. Framingham, Mass. Boston, Mass.	Cleveland, Ohio	New Haven, Conn.
10/28/48	Quincy, Mass. Brockton, Mass. Taunton, Mass. Fall River, Mass. Providence, R.I. New London, Conn. New Haven, Conn. Bridgeport, Conn.	Boston, Mass.	New York City, N.Y.

CAMPAIGN ITINERARIES: PRESIDENTIAL CANDIDATES

September 1 - November 2, 1948
(continued)

Date	Truman	Dewey	Wallace
10/28/48	South Norwalk, Conn. New York City, N.Y.		
10/29/48	Bronx, N.Y. Yonkers, N.Y. Queens, N.Y. Brooklyn, N.Y. New York City, N.Y.	New London, Conn. New Haven, Conn. Bridgeport, Conn.	New York City, N.Y.
10/30/48	Bellefontaine, Ohio Terre Haute, Ind. Mattoon, Ill. St. Louis, Mo.	New York City, N.Y.	Philadelphia, Pa.
10/31/48	Independence, Mo.	Pawling, N.Y.	Brooklyn, N.Y.
11/ 1/48	Independence, Mo.	New York City, N.Y.	Bronx, N.Y.
11/ 2/48	Independence, Mo.	New York City, N.Y.	South Salem, N.Y.

CAMPAIGN ITINERARIES: PRESIDENTIAL CANDIDATES

September 1 - November 4, 1952

Date	Stevenson	Eisenhower
9/ 1/52	Detroit, Michigan Hamtramck, Michigan Grand Rapids, Michigan Flint, Michigan Pontiac, Michigan	New York City, New York
9/ 2/52	Springfield, Illinois	Atlanta, Georgia Jacksonville, Florida Miami, Florida
9/ 3/52	Springfield, Illinois	Tampa, Florida Birmingham, Alabama Little Rock, Arkansas
9/ 4/52	Springfield, Illinois	Philadelphia, Pennsylvania
9/ 5/52	Denver, Colorado	Chicago, Illinois
9/ 6/52	Rochester, Minnesota Kassen, Minnesota	Kassen, Minnesota
9/ 7/52	Cheyenne, Wyoming Billings, Montana Lewistown, Iowa	Minneapolis, Minnesota
9/ 8/52	Portland, Oregon Seattle, Washington	Cleveland, Ohio
9/ 9/52	San Francisco, California San Jose, California Fresno, California Bakersfield, California	Indianapolis, Indiana
9/10/52	Los Angeles, California	Washington, D.C.
9/11/52	Los Angeles, California	New York City, New York
9/12/52	Phoenix, Arizona Albuquerque, New Mexico	New York City, New York
9/13/52	Albuquerque, New Mexico	New York City, New York
9/14/52	Springfield, Illinois	New York City, New York
9/15/52	Springfield, Illinois	Fort Wayne, Indiana Warsaw, Indiana Plymouth, Indiana South Bend, Indiana Gary, Indiana Chicago, Illinois Ottawa, Illinois
9/16/52	Springfield, Illinois	St. Paul, Minnesota
9/17/52	Springfield, Illinois	New York City, New York
9/18/52	Bridgeport, Connecticut New Haven, Connecticut Hartford, Connecticut	Iowa City, Iowa Des Moines, Iowa Omaha, Nebraska
9/19/52	Springfield, Massachusetts	Nebraska City, Nebraska Falls City, Nebraska Kansas City, Missouri

CAMPAIGN ITINERARIES: PRESIDENTIAL CANDIDATES

September 1 - November 4, 1952
(continued)

Date	Stevenson	Eisenhower
9/20/52	Quantico, Virginia	Jefferson City, Missouri
	Richmond, Virginia	St. Louis, Missouri
9/21/52	New York City, New York	St. Louis, Missouri
9/22/52	New York City, New York	Evansville, Indiana
		Louisville, Kentucky
		Cincinnati, Ohio
9/23/52	Baltimore, Maryland	Dayton, Ohio
		Springfield, Ohio
		Columbus, Ohio
		Cleveland, Ohio
9/24/52	Springfield, Illinois	Columbus, Ohio
		Chillicothe, Ohio
		Portsmith, Ohio
		Kenova, West Virginia
		Huntington, West Virginia
9/25/52	Springfield, Illinois	Silver Spring, Maryland
		Baltimore, Maryland
		Washington, D.C.
9/26/52	Indianapolis, Indiana	Charlotte, North Carolina
		Winston-Salem, N. Carolina
		Richmond, Virginia
9/27/52	Paducah, Kentucky	New York City, New York
	Louisville, Kentucky	
9/28/52	Louisville, Kentucky	New York City, New York
9/29/52	Chicago, Illinois	New York City, New York
9/30/52	Springfield, Illinois	Columbia, South Carolina
10/ 1/52	Springfield, Illinois	Cleveland, Ohio
		Flint, Michigan
		Lansing, Michigan
		Grand Rapids, Michigan
10/ 2/52	Springfield, Illinois	Bradley, Illinois
		Champaign, Illinois
		Peoria, Illinois
		Springfield, Illinois
10/ 3/52	Columbus, Ohio	Green Bay, Wisconsin
		Milwaukee, Wisconsin
10/ 4/52	Minneapolis, Minnesota	Fargo, North Dakota
	St. Paul, Minnesota	Duluth, Minnesota
	St. Cloud, Minnesota	
	Fort Dodge, Iowa	
10/ 5/52	Springfield, Illinois	Livingston, Montana
		Billings, Montana
		Missoula, Montana

CAMPAIGN ITINERARIES: PRESIDENTIAL CANDIDATES

September 1 – November 4, 1952
(continued)

Date	Stevenson	Eisenhower
10/ 6/52	Springfield, Illinois	Spokane, Washington
		Seattle, Washington
10/ 7/52	Sajenew, Michigan	Tacoma, Washington
	Detroit, Michigan	Eugene, Oregon
		Portland, Oregon
10/ 8/52	Madison, Wisconsin	San Francisco, California
10/ 9/52	St. Louis, Missouri	Fresno, California
		San Diego, California
		Long Beach, California
		Los Angeles, California
10/10/52	New Orleans, Louisiana	Phoenix, Arizona
		Albuquerque, New Mexico
		Salt Lake City, Utah
10/11/52	Miami, Florida	Denver, Colorado
	Tampa, Florida	
	Nashville, Tennessee	
10/12/52	Springfield, Illinois	Denver, Colorado
10/13/52	Springfield, Illinois	Casper, Wyoming
		Cheyenne, Wyoming
10/14/52	Casper, Wyoming	Houston, Texas
		San Antonio, Texas
10/15/52	San Francisco, California	Fort Worth, Texas
		Shreveport, Louisiana
		Memphis, Tennessee
		Knoxville, Tennessee
10/16/52	San Francisco, California	New York City, New York
	Los Angeles, California	
10/17/52	San Diego, California	Wilmington, Delaware
	Forth Worth, Texas	Newark, New Jersey
	Dallas, Texas	
10/18/52	San Antonio, Texas	New York City, New York
	Houston, Texas	
	Springfield, Illinois	
10/19/52	Springfield, Illinois	New York City, New York
10/20/52	Springfield, Illinois	New Haven, Connecticut
		Bridgeport, Connecticut
		Attleboro, Massachusetts
		Worcester, Massachusetts
		Providence, Rhode Island
10/21/52	Chicago, Illinois	Boston, Massachusetts
10/22/52	Buffalo, New York	Albany, New York
	Dunkirk, New York	
10/23/52	Cleveland, Ohio	Buffalo, New York

CAMPAIGN ITINERARIES: PRESIDENTIAL CANDIDATES

September 1 - November 4, 1952
(continued)

Date	Stevenson	Eisenhower
10/24/52	Niagara Falls, New York Albany, New York	New York City, New York Detroit, Michigan
10/25/52	Hyde Park, New York Poughkeepsie, New York Boston, Massachusetts	New York City, New York
10/26/52	Boston, Massachusetts	New York City, New York
10/27/52	Quincy, Massachusetts Brockton, Massachusetts Providence, Rhode Island New London, Connecticut Bridgeport, Connecticut New York City, New York	Harrisburg, Pennsylvania Pittsburgh, Pennsylvania
10/28/52	New York City, New York	New York City, New York
10/29/52	Scranton, Pennsylvania Wilkes-Barre, Pennsylvania Bethlehem, Pennsylvania Philadelphia, Pennsylvania	New York City, New York
10/30/52	York, Pennsylvania Harrisburg, Pennsylvania Reading, Pennsylvania	New York City, New York
10/31/52	Brooklyn, New York	Chicago, Illinois
11/ 1/52	Fort Wayne, Indiana Gary, Indiana Chicago, Illinois	New York City, New York
11/ 2/52	Bloomington, Indiana Springfield, Illinois	New York City, New York
11/ 3/52	Chicago, Illinois	Boston, Massachusetts
11/ 4/52	Libertyville, Illinois	New York City, New York

152

CAMPAIGN ITINERARIES: PRESIDENTIAL CANDIDATES

September 1 - November 5, 1956

Date	Stevenson	Eisenhower
9/ 1/56	Chicago, Illinois	Washington, D.C.
	Libertyville, Illinois	
9/ 2/56	Libertyville, Illinois	Washington, D.C.
9/ 3/56	Detroit, Michigan	Washington, D.C.
9/ 4/56	Los Angeles, California	Washington, D.C.
9/ 5/56	Los Angeles, California	Washington, D.C.
9/ 6/56	Chicago, Illinois	Washington, D.C.
9/ 7/56	Chicago, Illinois	Washington, D.C.
9/ 8/56	Columbus, Ohio	Washington, D.C.
	Springfield, Illinois	
	New York City, New York	
9/ 9/56	Palisades Park, New Jersey	Washington, D.C.
9/10/56	Hartford, Connecticut	Washington, D.C.
	Albany, New York	
9/11/56	New York City, New York	Washington, D.C.
9/12/56	Philadelphia, Pennsylvania	Gettysburg, Pennsylvania
9/13/56	Harrisburg, Pennsylvania	Washington, D.C.
9/14/56	Washington, D.C.	Washington, D.C.
9/15/56	Washington, D.C.	Washington, D.C.
9/16/56	Delaplane, Virginia	Gettysburg, Pennsylvania
9/17/56	Washington, D.C.	Washington, D.C.
9/18/56	Washington, D.C.	Washington, D.C.
9/19/56	Washington, D.C.	Washington, D.C.
9/20/56	Silver Spring, Maryland	Iowa
	Kansas City, Missouri	
9/21/56	Washington, D.C.	Newton, Iowa
		Des Moines, Iowa
9/22/56	Des Moines, Iowa	Washington, D.C.
	Denver, Colorado	
9/23/56	Denver, Colorado	Washington, D.C.
9/24/56	Oklahoma City, Oklahoma	Salt Lake City, Utah
	Tulsa, Oklahoma	Phoenix, Arizona
9/25/56	Little Rock, Arkansas	Peoria, Illinois
	New Orleans, Louisiana	
	Miami, Florida	
9/26/56	Kansas City, Missouri	Washington, D.C.
	Kansas City, Kansas	
9/27/56	St. Louis, Missouri	Washington, D.C.
9/28/56	Indianapolis, Indiana	Washington, D.C.
	Milwaukee, Wisconsin	
9/29/56	Minneapolis, Minnesota	Washington, D.C.
	St. Paul, Minnesota	
9/30/56	Washington, D.C.	Cleveland, Ohio

CAMPAIGN ITINERARIES: PRESIDENTIAL CANDIDATES

September 1 - November 5, 1956
(continued)

Date	Stevenson	Eisenhower
10/ 1/56	Washington, D.C.	Cleveland, Ohio
		Lexington, Kentucky
10/ 2/56	Morristown, New Jersey	Washington, D.C.
	Jersey City, New Jersey	
	Teaneck, New Jersey	
	Paterson, New Jersey	
10/ 3/56	Pittsburgh, Pennsylvania	New York City, New York
10/ 4/56	Pennsylvania	Washington, D.C.
	Elkins, West Virginia	
	New York City, New York	
10/ 5/56	Brooklyn, New York	Washington, D.C.
	New Haven, Connecticut	
10/ 6/56	New York City, New York	Washington, D.C.
	Providence, Rhode Island	
10/ 7/56	New York City, New York	Washington, D.C.
	Chicago, Illinois	
10/ 8/56	Libertyville, Illinois	Washington, D.C.
		Pittsburgh, Pennsylvania
10/ 9/56	Montana	Pittsburgh, Pennsylvania
	Boise, Idaho	
	Seattle, Washington	
10/10/56	Portland, Oregon	Washington, D.C.
10/11/56	Oakland, California	Washington, D.C.
	San Francisco, California	
10/12/56	San Diego, California	Washington, D.C.
10/13/56	Chicago, Illinois	Washington, D.C.
10/14/56	Libertyville, Illinois	Washington, D.C.
10/15/56	Chicago, Illinois	Washington, D.C.
10/16/56	Chicago, Illinois	Minneapolis, Minnesota
		St. Paul, Missouri
		Seattle, Washington
10/17/56	Flint, Michigan	Seattle, Washington
10/18/56	Ohio	Portland, Oregon
10/19/56	Cincinnati, Ohio	Los Angeles, California
	Louisville, Kentucky	Burbank, California
	Lexington, Kentucky	
10/20/56	South Bend, Indiana	Denver, Colorado
	Chicago, Illinois	Washington, D.C.
10/21/56	Chicago, Illinois	Washington, D.C.
10/22/56		Washington, D.C.
10/23/56	New York City, New York	Washington, D.C.
10/24/56	New York City, New York	Washington, D.C.
10/25/56	Springfield, Illinois	New York City, New York

CAMPAIGN ITINERARIES: PRESIDENTIAL CANDIDATES

September 1 - November 5, 1956
(continued)

Date	Stevenson	Eisenhower
10/26/56	Rock Island, Illinois Albuquerque, New Mexico	Washington, D.C.
10/27/56	Los Angeles, California San Francisco, California	Washington, D.C.
10/28/56	Boston, Massachusetts	Washington, D.C.
10/29/56	Boston, Massachusetts	Miami, Florida Jacksonville, Florida Richmond, Florida
10/30/56	Philadelphia, Pennsylvania Baltimore, Maryland	Washington, D.C.
10/31/56	New York City, New York Pittsburgh, Pennsylvania	Washington, D.C.
11/ 1/56	Buffalo, New York	Philadelphia, Pennsylvania
11/ 2/56	Detroit, Michigan Cleveland, Ohio	Washington, D.C.
11/ 3/56	Chicago, Illinois	Washington, D.C.
11/ 4/56	Chicago, Illinois	Washington, D.C.
11/ 5/56	Minneapolis, Minnesota Boston, Massachusetts	Washington, D.C.

CAMPAIGN ITINERARIES: PRESIDENTIAL CANDIDATES

September 1 - November 7, 1960

Date	Kennedy	Nixon
9/ 1/60	Washington, D.C.	Washington, D.C.
9/ 2/60	Manchester, New Hampshire	(Walter Reed Hospital)
	Presque Isle, Maine	Washington, D.C.
	Bangor, Maine	(Walter Reed Hospital)
	Portland, Maine	
9/ 3/60	San Francisco, California	Washington, D.C.
	Anchorage, Alaska	(Walter Reed Hospital)
	Palmer, Alaska	
9/ 4/60	Anchorage, Alaska	Washington, D.C.
	Detroit, Michigan	(Walter Reed Hospital)
9/ 5/60	Detroit, Michigan	Washington, D.C.
	Pontiac, Michigan	(Walter Reed Hospital)
	Flint, Michigan	
	Muskegon, Michigan	
9/ 6/60	Pocatello, Idaho	Washington, D.C.
	Spokane, Washington	(Walter Reed Hospital)
	Seattle, Washington	
9/ 7/60	Seattle, Washington	Washington, D.C.
	Eugene, Oregon	(Walter Reed Hospital)
	Salem, Oregon	
	Portland, Oregon	
9/ 8/60	Dunsmuir, California	Washington, D.C.
	Redding, California	(Walter Reed Hospital)
	Red Bluff, California	
	Chico, California	
	Marysville, California	Washington, D.C.
	Sacramento, California	(Walter Reed Hospital)
	Martinez, California	
	Richmond, California	
	Oakland, California	
9/ 9/60	Stockton, California	Washington, D.C.
	Modesto, California	(Walter Reed Hospital)
	Merced, California	
	Madera, California	
	Fresno, California	
	Tulare, California	
	Turlock, California	
	Burbank, California	
	Bakersfield, California	
	Los Angeles, California	
9/10/60	Los Angeles, California	Washington, D.C.
9/11/60	San Diego, California	Washington, D.C.
	Los Angeles, California	

CAMPAIGN ITINERARIES: PRESIDENTIAL CANDIDATES

September 1 - November 7, 1960
(continued)

Date	Kennedy	Nixon
9/12/60	El Paso, Texas	Baltimore, Maryland
	Lubbock, Texas	Indianapolis, Indiana
	San Antonio, Texas	Dallas, Texas
	Houston, Texas	San Francisco, California
9/13/60	Austin, Texas	San Francisco, California
	Fort Worth, Texas	Portland, Oregon
	Grand Prairie, Texas	Vancouver, Washington
	Dallas, Texas	Boise, Idaho
	Texarkana, Arkansas-Texas	
9/14/60	St. Louis, Missouri	Grand Forks, North Dakota
	New York City, New York	Peoria, Illinois
9/15/60	Jersey City, New Jersey	St. Louis, Missouri
	Paramus, New Jersey	Atlantic City, New Jersey
	Paterson, New Jersey	Roanoke, Virginia
	Clifton, New Jersey	
	Newark, New Jersey	
	New Brunswick, New Jersey	
	Trenton, New Jersey	
	Harrisburg, Pennsylvania	
9/16/60	Lebanon, Pennsylvania	Omaha, Nebraska
	Reading, Pennsylvania	Council Bluffs, Iowa
	Columbus Park, Pennsylvania	Red Oak, Iowa
	York, Pennsylvania	Atlantic, Iowa
	Towson, Maryland	Guthrie Center, Iowa
	Pikesville, Maryland	Des Moines, Iowa
9/17/60	Greenville, North Carolina	Sioux City, Iowa
	Greensboro, North Carolina	Minneapolis, Minnesota
	Charlotte, North Carolina	St. Paul, Minnesota
	Raleigh, North Carolina	
9/18/60	Washington, D.C.	Washington, D.C.
9/19/60	Atlantic City, New Jersey	Washington, D.C.
	Charleston, West Virginia	Wilkes-Barre, Pennsylvania
		Scranton, Pennsylvania
9/20/60	Washington, D.C.	Scranton, Pennsylvania
		Mount Clemens, Michigan
		Flint, Michigan
		Saginaw, Michigan
		Bay City, Michigan
9/21/60	Bristol, Virginia-Tennessee	Fort Wayne, Indiana
	Knoxville, Tennessee	Louisville, Kentucky
	Nashville, Tennessee	Springfield, Missouri
	Memphis, Tennessee	
	Sioux City, Iowa	

CAMPAIGN ITINERARIES: PRESIDENTIAL CANDIDATES

September 1 - November 7, 1960
(continued)

Date	Kennedy	Nixon
9/22/60	Sioux City, Iowa Fort Dodge, Iowa Sioux Falls, South Dakota Mitchell, South Dakota Fargo, North Dakota Billings, Montana	St. Joseph, Missouri Sullivan, Illinois Rockford, Illinois
9/23/60	Cheyenne, Wyoming Denver, Colorado Salt Lake City, Utah	Beloit, Wisconsin Rock County, Wisconsin Sioux Falls, South Dakota Kansas City, Kansas
9/24/60	Washington, D.C.	Kansas City, Kansas Lafayette, Louisiana Jackson, Mississippi
9/25/60	Cleveland, Ohio	Washington, D.C.
9/26/60	Chicago, Illinois	Chicago, Illinois
9/27/60	Painesville, Ohio Lorain, Ohio Mansfield, Ohio Akron, Ohio Canton, Ohio Erie, Pennsylvania	Memphis, Tennessee West Memphis, Arkansas Charleston, West Virginia
9/28/60	Erie, Pennsylvania Niagara Falls, New York Lockport, New York North Tonawanda, New York Rochester, New York Buffalo, New York	New York City, New York Forest Hills, New York Hicksville, New York Mineola, New York Commack, New York
9/29/60	Albany, New York Troy, New York Schenectady, New York Amsterdam, New York Syracuse, New York	Burlington, Vermont Manchester, New Hampshire Boston, Massachusetts
9/30/60	Hyannis Port, Massachusetts	Bangor, Maine Binghamton, New York Schenectady, New York Troy, New York
10/ 1/60	Chicago, Illinois Minneapolis, Minnesota	Akron, Ohio Canton, Ohio Mansfield, Ohio
10/ 2/60	St. Paul, Minnesota Duluth, Minnesota Hibbing, Minnesota St. Louis, Missouri	New York City, New York

CAMPAIGN ITINERARIES: PRESIDENTIAL CANDIDATES

September 1 - November 7, 1960
(continued)

Date	Kennedy	Nixon
10/ 3/60	Alton, Illinois Grante City, Illinois East St. Louis, Illinois Belleville, Illinois Carbondale, Illinois Marion, Illinois Harrisburg, Illinois Venice, Illinois Springfield, Illinois	Washington, D.C. Richmond, Virginia Charlotte, North Carolina
10/ 4/60	Evansville, Illinois Indianapolis, Indiana	Paterson, New Jersey Hackensack, New Jersey Elizabeth, New Jersey Plainfield, New Jersey Newark, New Jersey West Orange, New Jersey
10/ 5/60	Pendleton, Indiana Muncie, Indiana Anderson, Indiana Terre Haute, Indiana Louisville, Kentucky	Bronx, New York New York City, New York Philadelphia, Pennsylvania
10/ 6/60	Cincinnati, Ohio	Nashville, Tennessee Cleveland, Ohio
10/ 7/60	Washington, D.C.	Washington, D.C.
10/ 8/60	Lexington, Kentucky Bowling Green, Kentucky Paducah, Kentucky	La Crosse, Wisconsin Rochester, Minnesota Milwaukee, Wisconsin
19/ 9/60	Youngstown, Ohio Gerard, Ohio Warren, Ohio Salem, Ohio Louisville, Kentucky	Billings, Montana
10/10/60	Columbus, Georgia Warm Springs, Georgia La Grange, Georgia Columbia, South Carolina Pittsburgh, Pennsylvania	Billings, Montana Denver, Colorado Salt Lake City, Utah
10/11/60	New York City, New York	Albuquerque, New Mexico San Diego, California Burbank, California
10/12/60	New York City, New York Mineola, New York	Los Angeles, California Long Beach, California
10/13/60	New York City, New York	Los Angeles, California

CAMPAIGN ITINERARIES: PRESIDENTIAL CANDIDATES

September 1 - November 7, 1960
(continued)

Date	Kennedy	Nixon
10/14/60	Ann Arbor, Michigan Jackson, Michigan Albion, Michigan Marshall, Michigan Battle Creek, Michigan Kalamazoo, Michigan Grand Rapids, Michigan Lansing, Michigan Owasso, Michigan Saginaw, Michigan	Los Angeles, California West Covina, California Beverly Hills, California
10/15/60	Sharon, Pennsylvania New Castle, Pennsylvania Beaver Falls, Pennsylvania Butler, Pennsylvania Kitlanning, Pennsylvania Johnstown, Pennsylvania	Phoenix, Arizona Tulsa, Oklahoma Springfield, Illinois
10/16/60	Levittown, New Jersey Wilmington, Delaware Silver Spring, Maryland	Hartford, Connecticut
10/17/60	Middletown, Ohio Dayton, Ohio Fairburn, Ohio Springfield, Ohio London, Ohio Columbus, Ohio	Hartford, Connecticut New Haven, Connecticut Bridgeport, Connecticut Buffalo, New York
10/18/60	Miami Beach, Florida Tampa, Florida Jacksonville, Florida	Jacksonville, Florida Miami, Florida St. Petersburg, Florida
10/19/60	New York City, New York	Wilmington, Delaware New York City, New York
10/20/60	Brooklyn, New York	New York City, New York
10/21/60	New York City, New York	New York City, New York
10/22/60	Crestwood, Missouri Jennings, Missouri St. Louis, Missouri Joplin, Missouri Wichita, Kansas Kansas City, Kansas Grand View, Missouri Kansas City, Missouri	Chester, Pennsylvania West Chester, Pennsylvania Narrestown, Pennsylvania
10/23/60	Green Bay, Wisconsin Madison, Wisconsin La Crosse, Wisconsin Milwaukee, Wisconsin	Washington, D.C.

CAMPAIGN ITINERARIES: PRESIDENTIAL CANDIDATES

September 1 - November 7, 1960
(continued)

Date	Kennedy	Nixon
10/24/60	Rockford, Illinois Champaign-Urbana, Illinois Peoria, Illinois East Peoria, Illinois Moline, Illinois Rock Island, Illinois	Harrisburg, Pennsylvania Lewistown, Pennsylvania Huntington, Pennsylvania Altoona, Pennsylvania Johnstown, Pennsylvania Greensburg, Pennsylvania Pittsburgh, Pennsylvania
10/25/60	Des Plaines, Illinois Libertyville, Illinois Barrington, Illinois Carpentersville, Illinois Elgin, Illinois St. Charles, Illinois Geneva, Illinois Batavia, Illinois Aurora, Illinois Elmhurst, Illinois	Marietta, Ohio Parkersburg, West Virginia Athens, Ohio Chillicothe, Ohio Cincinnati, Ohio
10/26/60	Mount Clemens, Michigan Warren, Michigan Roseville, Michigan Hamtramck, Michigan Detroit, Michigan New York City, New York	Middletown, Ohio Dayton, Ohio Springfield, Ohio Columbus, Ohio Marion, Ohio Lima, Ohio Deschler, Ohio London, Ohio Toledo, Ohio
10/27/60	New York City, New York Brooklyn, New York Queens, New York	Monroe, Michigan Ann Arbor, Michigan Jackson, Michigan Battle Creek, Michigan Kalamazoo, Michigan Grand Rapids, Michigan Muskegon, Michigan
10/28/60	Bethlehem, Pennsylvania Allentown, Pennsylvania Pottsville, Pennsylvania Hazleton, Pennsylvania Wilkes-Barre, Pennsylvania Hazleton, Pennsylvania Scranton, Pennsylvania	Danville, Illinois Tolono, Illinois Tuscola, Illinois Mattoon, Illinois Centralia, Illinois Carbondale, Illinois Quincy, Illinois Davenport, Iowa

CAMPAIGN ITINERARIES: PRESIDENTIAL CANDIDATES

September 1 - November 7, 1960
(continued)

Date	Kennedy	Nixon
10/29/60	Philadelphia, Pennsylvania Chester, Pennsylvania Upper Darby, Pennsylvania Philadelphia, Pennsylvania Norristown, Pennsylvania Willow Grove, Pennsylvania Valley Forge, Pennsylvania	Moline, Illinois Chicago, Illinois Wheaton, Illinois Park Forest, Illinois
10/30/60	Levittown, Pennsylvania Philadelphia, Pennsylvania	Washington, D.C.
10/31/60	Philadelphia, Pennsylvania	Ridgewood, New Jersey Newark, New Jersey
11/ 1/60	Los Angeles, California Redondo Beach, California Long Beach, California	Philadelphia, Pennsylvania Lancaster, Pennsylvania Erie, Pennsylvania Syracuse, New York Rochester, New York
11/ 2/60	Los Angeles, California San Diego, California Oakland, California San Francisco, California	Brooklyn, New York Garden City, New York Bronx, New York New York City, New York
11/ 3/60	Phoenix, Arizona Albuquerque, New Mexico Amarillo, Texas Wichita Falls, Texas Oklahoma City, Oklahoma	New York City, New York Columbia, South Carolina San Antonio, Texas Houston, Texas
11/ 4/60	Norfolk, Virginia Roanoke, Virginia Toledo, Ohio Chicago, Illinois	Fort Worth, Texas Casper, Wyoming Spokane, Washington Fresno, California
11/ 5/60	Bronx, New York Queens, New York Nassau County, New York Flushing, New York New York City, New York	San Jose, California Hayward, California Oakland, California Los Angeles, California
11/ 6/60	Waterbury, Connecticut New Haven, Connecticut Bridgeport, Connecticut Commack, New York Newark, New Jersey Teterboro, New Jersey Jersey City, New Jersey Lewiston, Maine	Los Angeles, California Anchorage, Alaska

CAMPAIGN ITINERARIES: PRESIDENTIAL CANDIDATES

September 1 - November 7, 1960
(continued)

Date	Kennedy	Nixon
11/ 7/60	Providence, Rhode Island Springfield, Massachusetts Hartford, Connecticut Manchester, New Hampshire Boston, Massachusetts	Madison, Wisconsin Detroit, Michigan Southfield, Michigan Chicago, Illinois

CAMPAIGN ITINERARIES: PRESIDENTIAL CANDIDATES

September 1 - November 2, 1964

Date	Johnson	Goldwater
9/ 1/64	Washington, D.C.	Washington, D.C.
		Los Angeles, California
		Phoenix, Arizona
9/ 2/64	Washington, D.C.	Phoenix, Arizona
9/ 3/64	Washington, D.C.	Phoenix, Arizona
		Prescott, Arizona
9/ 4/64	Washington, D.C.	Washington, D.C.
9/ 5/64	Washington, D.C.	Washington, D.C.
		Niagara Falls, New York
		Lockport, New York
9/ 6/64	Washington, D.C.	Phoenix, Arizona
9/ 7/64	Detroit, Michigan	Phoenix, Arizona
9/ 8/64	Washington, D.C.	San Diego, California
		Chavey Ravine, California
		Los Angeles, California
9/ 9/64	Washington, D.C.	Sacramento, California
		Klamath Falls, Oregon
		Eugene, Oregon
		Seattle, Washington
9/10/64	Harrisburg, Pennsylvania	Boise, Idaho
		Great Falls, Montana
		Minneapolis, Minnesota
9/11/64	Washington, D.C.	Chicago, Illinois
		Rockford, Illinois
		Oregon, Illinois
		Washington, D.C.
9/12/64	Washington, D.C.	Washington, D.C.
9/13/64	Washington, D.C.	Washington, D.C.
9/14/64	Washington, D.C.	Washington, D.C.
9/15/64	Miami Beach, Florida	Winston-Salem, N. Carolina
	Cape Kennedy, Florida	Atlanta, Georgia
		Orlando, Florida
		Tampa-St. Petersburg, Fla.
9/16/64	Great Falls, Montana	Knoxville, Tennessee
	Vancouver, British Columbia	Memphis, Tennessee
	Seattle, Washington	Macon, Georgia
		Montgomery, Alabama
9/17/64	Sacramento, California	Raleigh, North Carolina
		Greenville, South Carolina
		Shreveport, Louisiana
		New Orleans, Louisiana
9/18/64	Washington, D.C.	Longview, Texas
		Springfield, Missouri
		Evansville, Indiana
		Charleston, West Virginia

CAMPAIGN ITINERARIES: PRESIDENTIAL CANDIDATES

September 1 - November 2, 1964
(continued)

Date	Johnson	Goldwater
9/19/64	Washington, D.C.	Washington, D.C. Fargo, North Dakota St. Louis, Missouri
9/20/64	Morgantown, West Virginia	Washington, D.C.
9/21/64	Washington, D.C.	Charlotte, North Carolina
9/22/64	Atlantic City, New Jersey	Tulsa, Oklahoma Amarillo, Texas Albuquerque, New Mexico Midland-Odessa, Texas
9/23/64		Forth Worth, Texas Dallas, Texas
9/24/64	Washington, D.C.	Wichita, Texas Mason City, Iowa Madison, Wisconsin Boston, Massachusetts
9/25/64	El Paso, Texas Eufaula Dam, Texas Oklahoma City, Oklahoma Texarkana, Arkansas-Texas	Portland, Maine Concord, New Hampshire Burlington, Vermont Albany, New York Louisville, Kentucky
9/26/64	Washington, D.C.	South Bend, Indiana Niles, Michigan Midland, Michigan Detroit, Michigan
9/27/64	Washington, D.C.	Washington, D.C.
9/28/64	Hartford, Connecticut Burlington, Vermont Portland, Maine Manchester, New Hampshire	Washington, D.C.
9/29/64	Omaha, Nebraska	Marietta, Ohio Athens, Ohio Chillicothe, Ohio Blanchester, Ohio Cincinnati, Ohio
9/30/64	Washington, D.C.	Middletown, Ohio Dayton, Ohio Springfield, Ohio Columbus, Ohio Marion, Ohio Lima, Ohio Deshler, Ohio Toledo, Ohio

CAMPAIGN ITINERARIES: PRESIDENTIAL CANDIDATES

September 1 - November 2, 1964
(continued)

Date	Johnson	Goldwater
10/ 1/64	Baltimore, Maryland	Jeffersonville, Indiana
		Seymour, Indiana
		Columbus, Indiana
		Indianapolis, Indiana
		Frankfort, Indiana
		Logansport, Indiana
		Lake County, Indiana
10/ 2/64	Washington, D.C.	Cairo, Illinois
		Carbondale, Illinois
		Centralia, Illinois
		Effingham, Illinois
		Mattoon, Illinois
		Champaign, Illinois
		Decatur, Illinois
		Pekin-Peoria, Illinois
10/ 3/64	Washington, D.C.	Galesburg, Illinois
		Rock Island, Illinois
		La Salle-Perce, Illinois
		Joliet, Illinois
		Chicago, Illinois
10/ 4/64	Washington, D.C.	Washington, D.C.
10/ 5/64	Washington, D.C.	Washington, D.C.
10/ 6/64	Alexandria, Virginia	Horsham Twp., Pennsylvania
	Raleigh, North Carolina	Warminster, Pennsylvania
		Glenside, Pennsylvania
		Ardmore, Pennsylvania
		Washington, D.C.
10/ 7/64	Des Moines, Iowa	Atlantic City, New Jersey
	Springfield, Illinois	Asbury Park, New Jersey
	Peoria, Illinois	Newark, New Jersey
		Teaneck, New Jersey
10/ 8/64	Lake County, Indiana	Lubbock, Texas
	Indianapolis, Indiana	El Paso, Texas
	Cleveland, Ohio	Phoenix, Arizona
10/ 9/64	Louisville, Kentucky	Los Angeles, California
	Nashville, Tennessee	San Francisco, California
	New Orleans, Louisiana	
10/10/64	Austin, Texas	Spokane, Washington
		Portland, Oregon
		Salt Lake City, Utah
		Phoenix, Arizona
10/11/64	Phoenix, Arizona	Phoenix, Arizona
	South Gate, California	
	San Francisco, California	

CAMPAIGN ITINERARIES: PRESIDENTIAL CANDIDATES

September 1 - November 2, 1964
(continued)

Date	Johnson	Goldwater
10/11/64	Las Vegas, Nevada	
10/12/64	Reno, Nevada	Phoenix, Arizona
	Butte, Wyoming	
	Casper, Wyoming	
	Denver, Colorado	
	Boise, Idaho	
10/13/64	Washington, D.C.	Topeka, Kansas
		Des Moines, Iowa
		Milwaukee, Wisconsin
10/14/64	Paramus, New Jersey	Kansas City, Missouri
	Wilkes-Barre, Pennsylvania	Omaha, Nebraska
	Scranton, Pennsylvania	Denver, Colorado
	New York City, New York	
10/15/64	Rochester, New York	Harlingen, Texas
	Buffalo, New York	Beaumont, Texas
	Brooklyn, New York	Houston, Texas
	New York City, New York	
10/16/64	Washington, D.C.	Sioux City, Iowa
	Cincinnati, Ohio	Sioux Falls, South Dakota
	Dayton, Ohio	Chicago, Illinois
10/17/64	Washington, D.C.	Mansfield, Ohio
		Akron-Canton, Ohio
		Youngstown, Ohio
		Washington, D.C.
10/18/64	Washington, D.C.	Washington, D.C.
10/19/64	Washington, D.C.	Washington, D.C.
10/20/64	Washington, D.C.	Salisbury, Maryland
		Baltimore, Maryland
		Pikesville, Maryland
		Washington, D.C.
10/21/64	Akron, Ohio	Philadelphia, Pennsylvania
	Belleville, Illinois	West Chester, Pennsylvania
	St. Louis, Missouri	Upper Darby, Pennsylvania
		Washington, D.C.
10/22/64	Washington, D.C.	Cheyenne, Wyoming
		Las Vegas, Nevada
		San Francisco, California
10/23/64	Washington, D.C.	Los Angeles, California
		Pico Revera, California
		Fullerton, California
		Santa Ana, California
		San Clemente, California
		Oceanside, California
		San Diego, California

CAMPAIGN ITINERARIES: PRESIDENTIAL CANDIDATES

September 1 – November 2, 1964
(continued)

Date	Johnson	Goldwater
10/23/64		Westgate Park, California Phoenix, Arizona
10/24/64	Memphis, Tennessee Chattanooga, Tennessee Baltimore, Maryland	Austin, Texas Corpus Christi, Texas Wichita Falls, Texas Washington, D.C.
10/25/64	Boca Raton, Florida Miami, Florida	Washington, D.C.
10/26/64	Orlando, Florida Jacksonville, Florida Macon, Georgia Augusta, Georgia Columbia, South Carolina	Dover, Delaware New York City, New York
10/27/64	Boston, Massachusetts Pittsburgh, Pennsylvania Evansville, Indiana	Cleveland, Ohio Lakewood, Ohio
10/28/64	Albuquerque, New Mexico Los Angeles, California Riverside, California San Bernardino, California San Diego, California	Oshkosh, Wisconsin Cedar Rapids, Iowa Belleville, Illinois
10/29/64	Salt Lake City, Utah Wichita, Kansas Philadelphia, Pennsylvania	Pittsburgh, Pennsylvania Lewistown, Pennsylvania Huntington, Pennsylvania Altoona, Pennsylvania Johnstown, Pennsylvania Greensburg, Pennsylvania
10/30/64	Detroit, Michigan Milwaukee, Wisconsin Rockford, Illinois Chicago, Illinois	Cheyenne, Wyoming Las Vegas, Nevada Tucson, Arizona Los Angeles, California
10/31/64	Dover, Delaware Wilmington, Delaware New York City, New York	Phoenix, Arizona Columbia, South Carolina
11/ 1/64	Washington, D.C.	Phoenix, Arizona
11/ 2/64	Houston, Texas Pasadena, Texas Austin, Texas Johnson City, Texas	San Francisco, California Fredonia, Arizona Phoenix, Arizona

CAMPAIGN ITINERARIES: PRESIDENTIAL CANDIDATES

September 1 - November 4, 1968

Date	Nixon	Humphrey	Wallace
9/ 1/68	New York City, N.Y.	Waverly, Minn.	Knoxville, Tenn.
9/ 2/68	New York City, N.Y.	New York City, N.Y.	Darlington, S.C.
9/ 3/68	New York City, N.Y.	Waverly, Minn.	Long Beach, Calif.
9/ 4/68	Chicago, Ill.	Washington, D.C.	Miami, Fla.
9/ 5/68	San Francisco, Calif.	Washington, D.C.	Miami, Fla.
	Santa Clara, Calif.		
9/ 6/68	Houston, Texas	Minneapolis, Minn.	Miami, Fla.
		Waverly, Minn.	
9/ 7/68	Oklahoma City, Okla.	Waverly, Minn.	Miami, Fla.
	Pittsburgh, Penna.		
9/ 8/68	Washington, D.C.	Washington, D.C.	Montgomery, Ala.
9/ 9/68	New York City, N.Y.	Philadelphia, Penna.	Montgomery, Ala.
		Denver, Colo.	
		Los Angeles, Calif.	
9/10/68	Westchester Co., N.Y.	Los Angeles, Calif.	Mongtomery, Ala.
	White Plains, N.Y.	Houston, Texas	
9/11/68	New York City, N.Y.	New Orleans, La.	New Orleans, La.
	Charlotte, N.C.	Houston, Texas	Little Rock, Ark.
		Flint, Mich.	
9/12/68	Charlotte, N.C.	Wilmington, Del.	Springfield, Mo.
	New Orleans, La.	Sea Girt, N.J.	Springfield, Ill.
	Indianapolis, Ind.		Milwaukee, Wis.
9/13/68	Cleveland, Ohio	Island Beach Pk,N.J.	Cincinnati, Ohio
		Pittsburgh, Penna.	Wheeling, W.Va.
			Charlottesville,S.C.
9/14/68	Cleveland, Ohio	Pittsburgh, Penna.	Lexington, Ky.
	Des Moines, Iowa		Columbia, S.C.
	Santa Barbara, Calif.		Albany, Ga.
9/15/68	Santa Barbara, Calif.	Washington, D.C.	Montgomery, Ala.
9/16/68	Yorba Linda, Calif.	Washington, D.C.	Dallas, Texas
	Annaheim, Calif.		
	Los Angeles, Calif.		
9/17/68	Annaheim, Calif.	Rochester, N.Y.	Dallas, Texas
		Buffalo, N.Y.	Wichita Falls, Texas
		Syracuse, N.Y.	Tulsa, Okla.
9/18/68	Anaheim, Calif.	Washington, D.C.	Cape Girardeau, Mo.
	Los Angeles, Calif.		Kansas City, Mo.
	Fresno, Calif.		
	Salt Lake City, Utah		
9/19/68	Springfield, Mo.	Boston, Mass.	Montgomery, Ala.
	Peoria, Ill.	Sioux Falls, S.D.	
	New York City, N.Y.		
9/20/68	Philadelphia, Penna.	Springfield, Ill.	Tallahassee, Fla.
		Louisville, Ky.	Orlando, Fla.
9/21/68	Philadelphia, Penna.	Independence, Mo.	Orlando, Fla.
		Huron, S.D.	

CAMPAIGN ITINERARIES: PRESIDENTIAL CANDIDATES

September 1 - November 4, 1968
(continued)

Date	Nixon	Humphrey	Wallace
9/22/68	New York City, N.Y.	Columbus, Ohio Cleveland, Ohio Toledo, Ohio	Atlanta, Ga.
9/23/68	Milwaukee, Wis.	Toledo, Ohio Waverly, Minn.	Atlanta, Ga.
9/24/68	Sioux Falls, S.D. Bismarck, N.D. Boise, Idaho Seattle, Wash.	Waverly, Minn. Los Angeles, Calif.	Montgomery, Ala.
9/25/68	Seattle, Wash. Denver, Colo.	Long Beach, Calif. Los Angeles, Calif. Sacramento, Calif.	Montgomery, Ala.
9/26/68	St. Louis, Mo. Louisville, Ky.	San Francisco, Calif.	Montgomery, Ala.
9/27/68	Louisville, Ky. Chattanooga, Tenn. Orlando, Fla. Tampa, Fla. Miami, Fla. Key Biscayne, Fla.	Portland, Ore.	Montgomery, Ala.
9/28/68	Key Biscayne, Fla.	Takoma, Wash. Seattle, Wash.	Montgomery, Ala.
9/29/68	Key Biscayne, Fla.	Seattle, Wash.	Montgomery, Ala.
9/30/68	Detroit, Mich.	Salt Lake City, Utah	Chicago, Ill.
10/ 1/68	Erie, Penna. Wilkes-Barre, Penna. Scranton, Penna.	Nashville, Tenn. Knoxville, Tenn.	Grand Rapids, Mich. Kalamazoo, Mich. Lansing, Mich.
10/ 2/68	Williamsburg, Va. Norfolk, Va.	Knoxville, Tenn. Jacksonville, Fla. Charlotte, N.C.	Canton, Ohio Pittsburgh, Penna.
10/ 3/68	Norfolk, Va. Atlanta, Ga.	Washington, D.C.	Pittsburgh, Penna. Indianapolis, Ind. Toledo, Ohio
10/ 4/68	Greenville, S.C. Spartansburg, S.C. Hartford, Conn. New York City, N.Y.	Washington, D.C.	Buffalo, N.Y.
10/ 5/68	New York City, N.Y. Nassau Co., N.Y. Suffolk Co., N.Y.	Washington, D.C.	Jersey City, N.J. Newark, N.J. Cleveland, Ohio
10/ 6/68	New York City, N.Y.	Detroit, Mich.	Montgomery, Ala.
10/ 7/68	Washington, D.C. Buffalo, N.Y.	Erie, Penna. Scranton, Penna. Wilkes-Barre, Penna.	Washington, D.C.

CAMPAIGN ITINERARIES: PRESIDENTIAL CANDIDATES

September 1 - November 4, 1968
(continued)

Date	Nixon	Humphrey	Wallace
10/ 8/68	Flint, Mich. Minneapolis, Minn. Los Angeles, Calif.	Washington, D.C. Utica, N.Y.	Baltimore, Md. Boston, Mass. Bridgeport, Conn.
10/ 9/68	Santa Monica, Calif. Moline, Ill.	Boston, Mass. New York City, N.Y.	Albany, N.Y. Albany, N.Y. Evansville, Ind.
10/10/68	Moline, Ill. Akron, Ohio	New York City, N.Y.	Peoria, Ill. Duluth, Minn.
10/11/68	Dallas, Texas	New York City, N.Y.	Fargo, N.D. Casper, Wyo. Denver, Colo.
10/12/68	Key Biscayne, Fla.	Washington, D.C.	Salt Lake City, Utah Boise, Idaho Seattle, Wash.
10/13/68	Key Biscayne, Fla.	Washington, D.C.	San Francisco, Calif. Fresno, Calif.
10/14/68	Key Biscayne, Fla.	Washington, D.C.	Fresno, Calif. San Diego, Calif.
10/15/68	Miami, Fla. Greensboro, N.C. Knoxville, Tenn.	St. Louis, Mo.	Los Angeles, Calif. San Diego, Calif.
10/16/68	Kansas City, Mo. New York City, N.Y.	New York City, N.Y.	Alamogordo, N.M. El Paso, Texas
10/17/68	Johnstown, Penna. Rochester, N.Y.	Detroit, Mich. Hartford, Conn.	Fort Worth, Texas Longview, Texas
10/18/68	Boston, Mass. Chicago, Ill.	Hartford, Conn. Stratford, Conn. Waterbury, Conn. Bridgeport, Conn. New York City, N.Y.	Montgomery, Ala.
10/19/68	Chicago, Ill. Eatonwood, N.J. New York City, N.Y.	Washington, D.C. Suitland, Md.	Montgomery, Ala.
10/20/68	New York City, N.Y.	Washington, D.C.	Washington, D.C.
10/21/68	New York City, N.Y. Cincinnati, Ohio	New York City, N.Y. Fort Worth, Texas	Bristol, Ill. Davenport, Iowa Rock Island, Ill. Moline, Ill.
10/22/68	Columbus, Ohio Middletown, Ohio Marion, Ohio Lima, Ohio Dayton, Ohio London, Ohio Springfield, Ohio	Forth Worth, Texas Dallas Texas Waco, Texas Austin, Texas San Antonio, Texas	Oshkosh, Wis. Racine, Wis.

171

CAMPAIGN ITINERARIES: PRESIDENTIAL CANDIDATES

September 1 - November 4, 1968
(continued)

Date	Nixon	Humphrey	Wallace
10/22/68	Toledo, Ohio		
10/23/68	Saginaw, Mich.	San Antonio, Texas	Youngstown, Ohio
	Battle Creek, Mich.	Harlingen, Texas	Roanoke, Va.
	Grand Rapids, Mich.	El Paso, Texas	Salem, Va.
		Los Angeles, Calif.	
10/24/68	Grand Rapids, Mich.	Los Angeles, Calif.	Durham, N.C.
	Allentown, Penna.	San Diego, Calif.	New York City, N.Y.
	Reading, Penna.		
	Pottsville, Penna.		
	Haselton, Penna.		
	Wilkes-Barre, Penna.		
	New York City, N.Y.		
10/25/68	New York City, N.Y.	San Jose, Calif.	Erie, Penna.
		Compton, Calif.	Hershey, Penna.
		Los Angeles, Calif.	Harrisburg, Penna.
			Trenton, N.J.
10/26/68	Ft. Lee, N.J.	Washington, D.C.	Terre Haute, Ind.
	Bloomfield, N.J.		Cincinnati, Ohio
	Jersey City, N.J.		
10/27/68	New York City, N.Y.	Washington, D.C.	Montgomery, Ala.
10/28/68	Albany, N.Y.	Canton, Ohio	Hannibal, Mo.
	Pittsburgh, Penna.	Akron, Ohio	Beaumont, Texas
		Lorain, Ohio	
		Brooklyn, Ohio	
		Cleveland, Ohio	
10/29/68	Syracuse, N.Y.	Pittsburgh, Penna.	Enid, Okla.
	Detroit, Mich.	McKeesport, Penna.	Detroit, Mich.
		Bethlehem, Penna.	
10/30/68	Rochester, Minn.	New York City, N.Y.	Philadelphia, Penna.
	Marion, Ill.	Baltimore, Md.	Wheeling, W.Va.
	Cleveland, Ill.		
10/31/68	New York City, N.Y.	Teaneck, N.J.	Norfolk, Va.
		Harrison, N.J.	Hagerstown, Md.
		Elizabeth, N.J.	
		Battle Creek, Mich.	
11/ 1/68	San Antonio, Texas	South Gate, Mich.	Ashville, N.C.
	Fort Worth, Texas	Peoria, Ill.	Chicago, Ill.
	Lubbock, Texas	Rockville, Ill.	
		Chicago, Ill.	
11/ 2/68	El Paso, Texas	New York City, N.Y.	St. Louis, Mo.
	Austin, Texas	Youngstown, Ohio	Atlanta, Ga.
11/ 3/68	Los Angeles, Calif.	Houston, Texas	Atlanta, Ga.
		Los Angeles, Calif.	

CAMPAIGN ITINERARIES: PRESIDENTIAL CANDIDATES

September 1 - November 4, 1968
(continued)

Date	Nixon	Humphrey	Wallace
11/ 4/68	Los Angeles, Calif.	Los Angeles, Calif. Waverly, Minn.	Atlanta, Ga. Montgomery, Ala.

PART V

The Cost of Presidential Campaigns

NOTE

For additional information see:

Alexander, Herbert E. FINANCING THE 1960 ELECTION. Princeton: Citizens Research Foundation, 1961.
————. FINANCING THE 1964 ELECTION. Princeton: Citizens Research Foundation, 1966.
Heard, Alexander. THE COSTS OF DEMOCRACY. Chapel Hill: University of North Carolina Press, 1960.
————. CONGRESSIONAL QUARTERLY ALMANACS, Volumes IV–XXV. Washington, D.C.: Congressional Quarterly Service, 1948–1969.
U.S. Senate Subcommittee on Privileges and Elections Report. 1956 GENERAL ELECTION CAMPAIGNS (GORE COMMITTEE REPORT). 85th Congress, 1st Session, 1957.

SOURCES

Reprinted by permission of Congressional Quarterly, Inc.
  Congressional Quarterly Almanac, 1949. pp. 82 and 83.
  Congressional Quarterly Almanac, 1965. p. 1550.
  Congressional Quarterly Weekly Report, December 5, 1969. p. 2435.

THE COST OF PRESIDENTIAL CAMPAIGNS

Expenditures: 1948-1968

National Committees	1948	1952	1956
Republican	3,686,779	12,229,239	13,220,144
Democratic	2,266,261	5,121,698	6,492,634
Progressive	1,365,399		
States Rights	162,081		
Labor	1,291,733	2,070,350	1,805,482
Miscellaneous	542,078	1,003,124	732,783
Total National Committees	9,314,331	20,424,411	22,251,043
Congressional Expenditure	1,978,695	2,639,955	6,169,616
Grand Total	11,293,026	23,064,366	28,420,659

National Committees	1960	1964	1968
Republican	12,950,232	19,314,796	29,563,337
Democratic	11,800,979	13,348,791	13,577,715
American Independent			7,242,896
Labor	2,450,944	3,816,242	7,631,868
Miscellaneous	872,588	2,121,172	4,869,400
Total National Committees	28,074,743	38,601,001	62,885,216
Congressional Expenditure	4,821,578	9,161,889	8,482,857
Grand Total	32,896,321	47,762,890	71,368,073

THE COST OF PRESIDENTIAL CAMPAIGNS

Receipts and Expenditures: 1948

Republican Committees (Number)	6
Receipts	$ 3,509,421
Expenditures	3,686,779
National Committee Debt	Unknown
Total Spending	$ 3,686,779
Republican Percentage of	
National Spending	39.6%
Democratic Committees (Number)	8
Receipts	$ 2,451,006
Expenditures	2,266,261
National Committee Debt	Unknown
Total Spending	$ 2,266,261
Democratic Percentage of	
National Spending	24.3%
Labor Committees (Number)	13
Receipts	$ 889,937
Expenditures	$ 1,291,733
Labor Percentage of	
National Spending	13.9%
Progressive Committees (Number)	3
Receipts	$ 1,133,108
Expenditures	1,365,399
Total Spending	$ 1,365,399
Progressive Percentage of	
National Spending	14.7%
States Rights Committees (Number)	1
Receipts	$ 163,442
Expenditures	$ 162,081
States Rights Percentage of	
National Spending	1.7%
Miscellaneous Committees (Number)	13
Receipts	$ 630,328
Expenditures	$ 542,078
Miscellaneous Committee Per-	
centage of National Spending	5.8%
Total National Committee Expenditures	$ 9,314,331

THE COST OF PRESIDENTIAL CAMPAIGNS

Receipts and Expenditures: 1952

Republican Committees (Number)	42
Receipts	$13,260,758
Expenditures	12,229,239
National Committee Debt	Unknown
Total Spending	$12,229,239
Republican Percentage of	
National Spending	59.9%
Democratic Committees (Number)	22
Receipts	$ 5,267,481
Expenditures	5,121,698
National Committee Debt	Unknown
Total Spending	$ 5,121,698
Democratic Percentage of	
National Spending	25.1%
Labor Committees (Number)	35
Receipts	$ 2,099,535
Expenditures	$ 2,070,350
Labor Percentage of	
National Spending	10.1%
Miscellaneous Committees (Number)	34
Receipts	$ 956,270
Expenditures	$ 1,003,124
Miscellaneous Committee Per-	
centage of National Spending	4.9%
Total National Committee Expenditures	$20,424,411

178

THE COST OF PRESIDENTIAL CAMPAIGNS

Receipts and Expenditures: 1956

Republican Committees (Number)	31
Receipts	$13,583,511
Expenditures	13,091,561
National Committee Debt	128,583
Total Spending	$13,220,144
Republican Percentage of	
National Spending	59.4%
Democratic Committees (Number)	22
Receipts	$ 5,705,722
Expenditures	5,795,827
National Committee Debt	696,807
Total Spending	$ 6,492,634
Democratic Percentage of	
National Spending	29.2%
Labor Committees (Number)	43
Receipts	$ 1,727,521
Expenditures	$ 1,805,482
Labor Percentage of	
National Spending	8.1%
Miscellaneous Committees (Number)	16
Receipts	$ 762,352
Expenditures	718,764
Plus Unpaid Bills	14,019
Total Spending	$ 732,783
Miscellaneous Committee Per-	
centage of National Spending	3.3%
Total National Committee Expenditures	$22,251,043

THE COST OF PRESIDENTIAL CAMPAIGNS

Receipts and Expenditures: 1960

Republican Committees (Number)	43
Receipts	$13,040,263
Expenditures	12,200,232
National Committee Debt	750,000
Total Spending	$12,950,232
Republican Percentage of National Spending	46.1%
Democratic Committees (Number)	29
Receipts	$ 8,074,311
Expenditures	7,980,979
National Committee Debt	3,820,000
Total Spending	$11,800,979
Democratic Percentage of National Spending	42.0%
Labor Committees (Number)	60
Receipts	$ 2,154,244
Expenditures	$ 2,450,944
Labor Percentage of National Spending	8.7%
Miscellaneous Committees (Number)	22
Receipts	$ 904,039
Expenditures	$ 872,588
Miscellaneous Committee Percentage of National Spending	3.1%
Total National Committee Expenditures	$28,074,743

THE COST OF PRESIDENTIAL CAMPAIGNS

Receipts and Expenditures: 1964

Republican Committees (Number)	41
Receipts	$19,828,673
Expenditures	19,314,796
National Committee Debt	None
Total Spending	$19,314,796
Republican Percentage of	
National Spending	50.0%
Democratic Committees (Number)	49
Receipts	$11,062,957
Expenditures	12,148,791
National Committee Debt	1,200,000
Total Spending	$13,348,791
Democratic Percentage of	
National Spending	34.6%
Labor Committees (Number)	40
Receipts	$ 3,163,945
Expenditures	$ 3,816,242
Labor Percentage of	
National Spending	9.9%
Miscellaneous Committees (Number)	34
Receipts	$ 1,951,981
Expenditures	$ 2,121,172
Miscellaneous Committee Per-	
centage of National Spending	5.5%
Total National Committee Expenditures	$38,601,001

THE COST OF PRESIDENTIAL CAMPAIGNS

Receipts and Expenditures: 1968

Republican Committees (Number)	46
Receipts	$29,563,337
Expenditures	29,442,832
National Committee Debt	None
Total Spending	$29,563,337
Republican Percentage of	
National Spending	47.0%
Democratic Committees (Number)	97
Receipts	$14,145,677
Expenditures	12,577,715
National Committee Debt	1,000,000
Total Spending	$13,577,715
Democratic Percentage of	
National Spending	21.6%
Wallace Campaign	
Receipts	$ 6,973,745
Expenditures	7,242,896
Total Spending	$ 7,242,896
Wallace Percentage of	
National Spending	11.5%
Labor Committees (Number)	46
Receipts	$ 5,645,700
Expenditures	7,631,868
Labor Percentage of	
National Spending	12.2%
Miscellaneous Committees (Number)	66
Receipts	$ 4,405,551
Expenditures	4,869,400
Miscellaneous Committee Per-	
centage of National Spending	7.7%
Total National Committee Expenditures	$62,885,236

Presidential Campaign Media Exposure

Section A | Time and Cost of Media Exposure 1956-1968

NOTE

Very little information is available on Media Exposure prior to 1956. Future research will hopefully fill the gap between 1948 and 1956. Section B of Part VI does include the Television Network Exposure of the candidates' campaign and it begins with the 1952 election.

SOURCES

1956 Campaign Media Exposure

U.S. Senate Subcommittee on Privileges and Election Report. 1956 GENERAL ELECTION CAMPAIGNS (GORE COMMITTEE REPORT). 85th Congress, 1st Session, 1957.

1960, 1964, and 1968 Campaign Media Exposure

Federal Communications Commission. SURVEYS OF POLITICAL BROADCASTING: 1960, 1964, 1968. Washington: FCC, April 1961, July 1965, and August 1969.

PRESIDENTIAL CAMPAIGN MEDIA EXPOSURE

TOTAL CHARGES FOR POLITICAL BROADCASTS
General Elections 1968, 1964, 1960, and 1956

	1968	1964	1960	1956
Total Charges	$40,403,498	$24,603,989	$14,195,278	$9,818,342
Republican	22,504,858	13,032,575	7,558,809	5,381,891
Democratic	15,447,989	11,012,626	6,204,986	4,120,712
Other	2,450,651	558,788	431,483	315,739
Television - Total	27,087,027	17,496,405	10,052,322	6,635,946
Network - Total	7,362,240	3,807,011	2,927,235	2,930,514
Republican	4,189,298	1,911,616	1,820,360	1,733,073
Democratic	2,500,517	1,895,395	1,106,875	1,197,441
Other	672,425			
Stations - Total	19,724,787	13,689,394	7,125,087	3,705,432
Republican	10,993,574	7,519,494	3,610,933	2,004,090
Democratic	7,923,423	5,819,699	3,307,987	1,159,347
Other	807,790	350,201	206,167	151,995
Radio - Total	13,316,471	7,107,584	4,142,956	3,182,396
Network - Total	662,674	119,365	78,867	320,940
Republican	468,871	88,863	44,546	144,645
Democratic	177,803	30,502	34,321	176,295
Other	16,000			
Stations - Total	12,653,797	6,988,219	4,064,089	2,861,456
Republican	6,853,115	3,512,602	2,082,970	1,500,083
Democratic	4,846,246	3,267,030	1,755,803	1,197,629
Other	954,436	208,587	225,316	163,744

PRESIDENTIAL CAMPAIGN MEDIA EXPOSURE

NETWORKS: SUSTAINING (FREE) TIME PROVIDED TO CANDIDATES AND THEIR SUPPORTERS
General Elections 1968, 1964, 1960, and 1956
(In Hours and Minutes)

	Total	Republican	Democratic	Other
3 Television Networks				
1968	3:01	1:05	0:39	1:17
1964	4:28	2:47	1:41	0:00
1960	39:22	18:21	19:26	1:35
1956	29:38	10:43	8:25	10:30
Radio Networks[§]				
1968	24:17	6:41	10:56	6:40
1964	21:14	12:26	8:18	0:30
1960	43:14	21:18	21:05	0:51
1956	32:23	11:23	9:15	11:45

§ Seven networks in 1968, four in all other years.

PRESIDENTIAL CAMPAIGN MEDIA EXPOSURE: 1956-1968

Total Broadcasting Expenditures for Presidential
and Vice Presidential Candidates in General Election Campaigns

	1956		1960	
	Republican	Democratic	Republican	Democratic
Network TV	$1,698,882	$1,166,751	$1,820,360	$1,106,875
Local TV	481,869	305,809	§	§
Network Radio	142,408	175,853	44,546	34,321
Local Radio	415,944	301,452	§	§
Supplemental	67,118	22,485		
Totals	2,806,221	1,972,350		

Grand Total 1956:
$4,778,571

	1964		1968	
Network TV	$1,911,616	$1,895,395	$4,189,298	$2,500,917
Local TV	3,204,686	1,870,112	4,817,814	1,973,560
Network Radio	88,863	30,502	468,871	177,803
Local Radio	1,163,599	877,859	3,121,970	1,490,997
Totals	6,368,764	4,673,868	12,597,953	6,143,277

Grand Total 1964:   Grand Total 1968:
$11,042,632 $18,741,230

§ Information not available.

PRESIDENTIAL CAMPAIGN MEDIA EXPOSURE: 1956

Total Expenditures: Political Broadcasts for
Presidential and Vice Presidential Candidates

	Democratic	Republican
Network Radio		
ABC	$38,432	$19,070
NBC	26,647	49,694
CBS	93,818	66,110
MBS	16,956	7,534
Sub total	175,853	142,408
Local Radio	301,452	415,944
Total Radio	477,305	558,352
Network Television		
ABC	275,330	163,002
NBC	409,943	639,676
CBS	481,478	896,204
Sub total	1,166,751	1,698,882
Local Television	305,809	481,869
Total Television	1,472,560	2,180,751
Supplemental	22,485	67,118
Grand Total	1,972,350	2,806,221

PRESIDENTIAL CAMPAIGN MEDIA EXPOSURE: 1956

Total Expenditures: Network Political Broadcasts for
Presidential and Vice Presidential Candidates

Television and Radio	Democratic	Republican
ABC		
Spots	$250,029	$136,022
Programs	62,459	45,584
Production, Preemptions, etc.	1,274	466
Sub total ABC	313,762	182,072
NBC		
Spots		14,700
Programs	406,724	576,179
Production, Preemptions, etc.	29,866	98,491
Sub total NBC	436,590	689,370
CBS		
Spots		
Programs	529,637	771,937
Production, Preemptions, etc.	45,659	190,377
Sub total CBS	575,296	962,314
MBS		
Spots		
Programs	16,956	7,534
Production, Preemptions, etc.		
Sub total MBS	16,956	7,534
Total ABC, NBC, CBS, MBS	1,342,604	1,841,290

PRESIDENTIAL CAMPAIGN MEDIA EXPOSURE: 1956

Total Expenditures: Network Television Political Broadcasts for
Presidential and Vice Presidential Candidates

	Democratic	Republican
ABC		
Spots	$250,029	$136,022
Programs	25,301	26,980
Production, Preemptions, etc.		
Sub total ABC	275,330	163,002
NBC		
Spots		
Programs	380,077	541,185
Production, Preemptions, etc.	29,866	98,491
Sub total NBC	409,943	639,676
CBS		
Spots		
Programs	437,962	712,501
Production, Preemptions, etc.	43,516	183,703
Sub total CBS	481,478	896,204
Total ABC, NBC, CBS	1,166,751	1,698,882

PRESIDENTIAL CAMPAIGN MEDIA EXPOSURE: 1956

Total Expenditures: Network Radio Political Broadcasts for
Presidential and Vice Presidential Candidates

	Democratic	Republican
ABC		
Spots		
Programs	$37,158	18,604
Production, Preemptions, etc.	1,274	466
Sub total ABC	38,432	19,070
NBC		
Spots		14,700
Programs	26,647	34,994
Production, Preemptions, etc.		
Sub total NBC	26,647	49,694
CBS		
Spots		
Programs	91,675	59,436
Production, Preemptions, etc.	2,143	6,674
Sub total CBS	93,818	66,110
MBS		
Spots		
Programs	16,956	7,534
Production, Preemptions, etc.		
Sub total MBS	16,956	7,534
Total ABC, NBC, CBS, MBS	175,853	142,408

PRESIDENTIAL CAMPAIGN MEDIA EXPOSURE: 1956

Total Expenditures: Local Stations Political Broadcasts for Presidential and Vice Presidential Candidates

	Democratic	Republican	Other
Radio			
Spots	$215,694	$324,841	$ 7,255
Programs	76,849	84,456	9,274
Production, Preemptions, etc.	8,909	6,647	1,064
Sub total	301,452	415,944	17,593
Television			
Spots	118,532	240,274	1,460
Programs	144,953	177,871	11,759
Production, Preemptions, etc.	42,324	63,724	3,367
Sub total	305,809	481,869	16,586
Total Radio and Television	607,261	897,813	34,179
Supplemental	22,485^	67,118	793
Grand Total	629,746	964,931	34,972

^ Data not divided as above.

PRESIDENTIAL CAMPAIGN MEDIA EXPOSURE: 1956

Network and Local Station Free Time[§] for
Presidential and Vice Presidential Candidates

	Democratic	Republican	Other
Network			
ABC			
Radio	15	15	230
Television	15	15	225
	30	30	455
CBS			
Radio	248	235	265
Television	228	180	210
	476	415	475
NBC			
Radio	408	278	195
Television	400	310	195
	808	588	390
MBS			
Radio		15	15
		15	15
Local			
Radio	3,891	4,236	1,275
Television	678	835	466
	4,569	5,071	1,741

§ Time in minutes

192

PRESIDENTIAL CAMPAIGN MEDIA EXPOSURE: 1960

Total Charges for Political Broadcasts[§]

	Republican	Democratic	Other	Total All Parties
3 TV Networks	$ 1,820,360	$ 1,106,875	$	$ 2,927,235
TV Stations	3,610,933	3,307,987	206,167	7,125,087
4 Radio Networks	44,546	34,321		78,867
Radio Stations	2,082,970	1,755,803	225,316	4,064,089
Total	$ 7,558,809	$ 6,204,986	$431,483	$14,195,278

§ Before commissions and after discounts.

PRESIDENTIAL CAMPAIGN MEDIA EXPOSURE: 1960

Networks: Amount of Program Time and Number of
Appearances of Presidential and Vice Presidential Candidates

		Television	
	Republican	Democratic	Other
Sustaining Time:			
Programs on which candidate's appearance was 5 minutes or longer:			
President	6 hrs. 36 mins.	7 hrs. 6 mins.	1 hr. 20 mins.
Vice President	1 hr. 30 mins.	1 hr.	None
Total	8 hrs. 6 mins.	8 hrs. 6 mins.	1 hr. 20 mins.
Non-Sustaining Time:			
Programs on which candidate's appearance was 5 minutes or longer:			
President	9 hrs. 17 mins.	9 hrs. 51 mins.	None
Vice President	4 hrs. 17 mins.	1 hr. 24 mins.	None
Total	13 hrs. 34 mins.	11 hrs. 15 mins.	None
Programs on which the candidate's appearance was less than 5 minutes			
President	162 appearances	173 appearances	None
Vice President	36 appearances	29 appearances	None
Total	198 appearances	202 appearances	None

PRESIDENTIAL CAMPAIGN MEDIA EXPOSURE: 1960

3 TV Networks: Appearances of Presidential and
Vice Presidential Candidates on Programs Paid
for by Political Parties

Program Duration	Number of Programs:	
	Republican	Democratic
4 hours	1	
30 minutes	9	7
15 minutes	5	3
5 minutes	15	49

PRESIDENTIAL CAMPAIGN MEDIA EXPOSURE: 1960

Networks: Amount of Program Time and Number of
Appearances of Presidential and Vice Presidential Candidates

		AM Radio	
	Republican	Democratic	Other
Sustaining Time:			
Programs on which candidate's appearance was 5 minutes or longer:			
President	9 hrs. 18 mins.	9 hrs. 48 mins.	51 mins.
Vice President	1 hr.	1 hr.	None
Total	10 hrs. 18 mins.	10 hrs. 48 mins.	51 mins.
Non-Sustaining Time:			
Programs on which candidate's appearance was 5 minutes or longer:			
President	4 hrs. 4 mins.	57 mins.	None
Vice President	30 mins.	45 mins.	None
Total	4 hrs. 34 mins.	1 hr. 42 mins.	None
Programs on which the candidate's appearance was less than 5 minutes			
President	39 appearances	40 appearances	1 appearance
Vice President	7 appearances	7 appearances	None
Total	46 appearances	47 appearances	1 appearance

PRESIDENTIAL CAMPAIGN MEDIA EXPOSURE: 1960

Television: Programs on Which the Candidate's Appearance was
Less Than 5 Minutes

Candidates	Announcements[§]		Programs Exempt from the "Equal Time" Provisions[§§]	
	Number of Stations Reporting	Number of Announcements by Candidates	Number of Stations Reporting	Number of Times Candidates Appeared
President				
Republican				
ABC,CBS,MBS,NBC			409	7,158
All other programs	322	3,984	218	2,754
Democratic				
ABC,CBS,MBS,NBC			408	8,157
All other programs	309	5,076	232	2,740
Other				
ABC,CBS,MBS,NBC			6	11
All other programs			25	46
Vice President				
Republican				
ABC,CBS,MBS,NBC			394	3,611
All other programs	152	912	152	625
Democratic				
ABC,CBS,MBS,NBC			378	2,528
All other programs	49	992	152	547
Other				
ABC,CBS,MBS,NBC			2	7
All other programs			6	11

[§] No announcements were carried by the networks.
[§§] All appearances of Presidential and Vice Presidential candidates were
exempt from the "equal time" provisions.

PRESIDENTIAL CAMPAIGN MEDIA EXPOSURE: 1960

Television: Programs on Which the Candidate's
Appearance was 5 Minutes or Longer

Candidates	Programs Exempt from the "Equal Time" Provisions			
	Sustaining		Non-Sustaining	
	Number of Stations Reporting	Total Amount of Time Candidates Appeared	Number of Stations Reporting	Total Amount of Time Candidates Appeared
President				
Republican				
ABC,CBS,MBS,NBC	450	973:09	447	1,213:17
All other programs	75	45:11	215	175:00
Democratic				
ABC,CBS,MBS,NBC	447	1,002:35	449	1,387:12
All other programs	89	47:13	331	314:03
Other				
ABC,CBS,MBS,NBC	154	67:31		
All other programs	10	4:55	19	6:29
Vice President				
Republican				
ABC,CBS,MBS,NBC	233	133:29	426	648:19
All other programs	23	9:58	54	28:57
Democratic				
ABC,CBS,MBS,NBC	194	100:40	306	206:17
All other programs	15	6:49	63	51:34
Other				
ABC,CBS,MBS,NBC	15	5:00		
All other programs			5	1:15

PRESIDENTIAL CAMPAIGN MEDIA EXPOSURE: 1960

AM Radio: Programs on Which the Candidate's Appearance was
Less than 5 Minutes

Candidates	Announcements§		Programs Exempt from the "Equal Time" Provisions§§	
	Number of Stations Reporting	Number of Announcements by Candidates	Number of Stations Reporting	Number of Times Candidates Appeared
President				
Republican				
ABC,CBS,MBS,NBC			537	4,517
All other programs	384	13,376	210	2,754
Democratic				
ABC,CBS,MBS,NBC			449	4,451
All other programs	451	12,150	209	2,868
Other				
ABC,CBS,MBS,NBC			92	104
All other programs	2	154	18	28
Vice President				
Republican				
ABC,CBS,MBS,NBC			295	903
All other programs	119	2,854	116	648
Democratic				
ABC,CBS,MBS,NBC			296	693
All other programs	71	2,263	100	472
Other				
ABC,CBS,MBS,NBC			10	15
All other programs			6	8

§ No announcements were carried by the networks.
§§ All appearances of Presidential and Vice Presidential candidates were
exempt from the "equal time" provisions.

PRESIDENTIAL CAMPAIGN MEDIA EXPOSURE: 1960

AM Radio: Programs on Which the Candidate's
Appearance was 5 Minutes or Longer

Candidates	Programs Exempt from the "Equal Time" Provisions			
	Sustaining		Non-Sustaining	
	Number of Stations Reporting	Total Amount of Time Candidates Appeared	Number of Stations Reporting	Total Amount of Time Candidates Appeared
President				
Republican				
ABC,CBS,MBS,NBC	884	1,822:37	389	352:18
All other programs	201	137:05	178	117:16
Democratic				
ABC,CBS,MBS,NBC	882	1,866:15	371	189:40
All other programs	225	132:38	171	139:25
Other				
ABC,CBS,MBS,NBC	137	58:59		
All other programs	12	5:52	28	8:45
Vice President				
Republican				
ABC,CBS,MBS,NBC	279	151:50	185	91:26
All other programs	52	16:42	37	16:28
Democratic				
ABC,CBS,MBS,NBC	250	136:35	289	113:59
All other programs	56	28:20	53	33:19
Other				
ABC,CBS,MBS,NBC	7	2:15		
All other programs	5	1:57	20	10:04

PRESIDENTIAL CAMPAIGN MEDIA EXPOSURE: 1960

FM Radio: Programs on Which the Candidate's Appearance was
Less Than 5 Minutes

Candidates	Announcements[§]		Programs Exempt from the "Equal Time" Provisions[§§]	
	Number of Stations Reporting	Number of Announcements by Candidates	Number of Stations Reporting	Number of Times Candidates Appeared
President				
Republican				
ABC,CBS,MBS,NBC			123	907
All other programs	74	1,925	62	897
Democratic				
ABC,CBS,MBS,NBC			113	862
All other programs	73	1,834	61	891
Other				
ABC,CBS,MBS,NBC			30	38
All other programs			5	8
Vice President				
Republican				
ABC,CBS,MBS,NBC			66	188
All other programs	25	564	37	263
Democratic				
ABC,CBS,MBS,NBC			68	143
All other programs	9	231	36	186
Other				
ABC,CBS,MBS,NBC			3	5
All other programs				

§ No announcements were carried by the networks.
§§ All appearances of Presidential and Vice Presidential candidates were
exempt from the "equal time" provisions.

PRESIDENTIAL CAMPAIGN MEDIA EXPOSURE: 1960

FM Radio: Programs on Which the Candidate's
Appearance was 5 Minutes or Longer

| | Programs Exempt from the "Equal Time" Provisions | | | |
| | Sustaining | | Non-Sustaining | |
Candidates	Number of Stations Reporting	Total Amount of Time Candidates Appeared	Number of Stations Reporting	Total Amount of Time Candidates Appeared
President				
Republican				
ABC,CBS,MBS,NBC	199	382:20	76	56:16
All other programs	50	50:28	20	12:23
Democratic				
ABC,CBS,MBS,NBC	200	394:03	81	38:19
All other programs	65	53:50	24	12:39
Other				
ABC,CBS,MBS,NBC	38	15:20		
All other programs	3	1:22	11	4:05
Vice President				
Republican				
ABC,CBS,MBS,NBC	76	37:49	52	27:32
All other programs	12	3:29	8	3:35
Democratic				
ABC,CBS,MBS,NBC	70	36:47	69	29:43
All other programs	9	6:24	10	9:40
Other				
ABC,CBS,MBS,NBC	1	0:15		
All other programs			10	7:00

PRESIDENTIAL CAMPAIGN MEDIA EXPOSURE: 1960

Affiliates Broadcasting "Great Debates" Programs of
Major Presidential Candidates

| | 3 TV Networks "Great Debates" | | | |
	First	Second	Third	Fourth
TV Stations Carrying	472	468	471	468 [§]
TV Stations Not Carrying	10	11	8	11
TV Stations Not Replying	9	12	12	13

§ Includes one station which was not in operation during the first three debates.

| | 4 AM Networks "Great Debates" | | | |
	First	Second	Third	Fourth
AM Stations Carrying	851	831	856	800
AM Stations Not Carrying	208 [§]	221 [§]	198 [^]	250 [^^]
AM Stations Not Replying	23	30	28	32
Non-Affiliated AM Stations Carrying	45	44	44	42

§ Includes 68 "daytime only" stations.
§§ Includes 73 "daytime only" stations.
^ Inclues 72 "daytime only" stations.
^^ Includes 73 "daytime only" stations.

PRESIDENTIAL CAMPAIGN MEDIA EXPOSURE: 1964

Total Charges for Political Broadcasts[§]

	Total	Television 3 Networks	Stations
Primary and General Election – Total	$23,776,935	$4,063,640	$19,713,295
Republican	11,373,208	2,168,245	9,204,963
Democratic	11,911,916	1,895,395	10,016,521
Other	491,811		491,811
Primary – Total	6,280,530	256,629	6,023,901
Republican	1,942,098	256,629	1,685,469
Democratic	4,196,822		4,196,822
Other	141,610		141,610
General – Total	17,496,405	3,807,011	13,689,394
Republican	9,431,110	1,911,616	7,519,494
Democratic	7,715,094	1,895,395	5,819,699
Other	350,201		350,201

	Total	AM Radio 4 Networks	Stations
Primary and General Election – Total	$10,833,779	$121,705	$10,712,074
Republican	4,543,697	91,203	4,452,494
Democratic	5,929,209	30,502	5,898,707
Other	360,873		360,873
Primary – Total	3,726,195	2,340	3,723,855
Republican	942,232	2,340	939,892
Democratic	2,631,677		2,631,677
Other	152,286		152,286
General – Total	7,107,584	119,365	6,988,219
Republican	3,601,465	88,863	3,512,602
Democratic	3,297,532	30,502	3,267,030
Other	208,587		208,587

§ Before commissions and after discounts.

PRESIDENTIAL CAMPAIGN MEDIA EXPOSURE: 1964

Networks: Time Devoted to Appearances of Candidates
for President and Vice President[§]
(In Hours and Minutes)

	Primary				General Election			
	Repub-lican	Demo-cratic	All Other	Total	Repub-lican	Demo-cratic	All Other	Total
3 TV Networks								
Time Paid for by Candidates or Supporters	1:22			1:22	9:11	7:01		16:12
Time on Commercially Sponsored Programs	7:15	0:46		8:01	3:40	2:21	0:42	6:43
Sustaining Time	4:28	0:31		4:59	0:51	0:27		1:18
4 AM Radio Networks								
Time Paid for by Candidates or Supporters					1:00	1:00		2:00
Time on Commercially Sponsored Programs								
Sustaining Time	11:25	1:56		13:21	4:26	2:42	0:30	7:38

§ Does not include time for supporters.

PRESIDENTIAL CAMPAIGN MEDIA EXPOSURE: 1964

Networks: Clearances of TV Programs on Which Candidates
for President and Vice President Appeared

	Sustaining (Free) Programs		Programs Paid for by Candidates or Supporters	
	Primary	General Election	Primary	General Election
Number of Programs	17	7	3	101
Average Number of Stations Per Program	119	129	169	174
Percent of Total Stations§	60%	65%	85%	91%

§ Average number of stations carrying as a percentage of the average number
of stations offered the programs for sustaining programs and as a percentage
of the average number of stations ordered for programs paid for by candidates
or supporters.

PRESIDENTIAL CAMPAIGN MEDIA EXPOSURE: 1964

Programs Devoted to Presidential and Vice Presidential Contests

Television Stations: Network Programs Only[§]

	Primary		General Election		
	Rep.	Dem.	Rep.	Dem.	Other
1. Program time paid for by candidates or supporters:					
Number of stations reporting	301		517	513	
Amount of program time	275:10		2,523:43	1,389:17	
2. Program time free of charge to candidates or supporters:					
a. Sustaining time:					
Number of stations reporting	410	317	430	404	
Amount of program time	857:55	174:16	571:40	328:25	
b. Program time on commercially sponsored programs, e.g. "Meet the Press":					
Number of stations reporting	410	233	451	451	171
Amount of program time	1,321:59	335:17	1,276:43	858:07	44:37

	Republican	Total Democratic	Other
1. Program time paid for by candidates or supporters:			
Number of stations reporting	517	513	
Amount of program time	2,798:53	1,389:17	
2. Program time free of charge to candidates or supporters:			
a. Sustaining time:			
Number of stations reporting	436	455	
Amount of program time	1,429:35	502:41	
b. Program time on commercially sponsored programs, e.g. "Meet the Press":			
Number of stations reporting	461	456	171
Amount of program time	2,598:42	1,193:24	44:37

§ Program time is in hours and minutes; including appearances of supporters.

PRESIDENTIAL CAMPAIGN MEDIA EXPOSURE: 1964

Time Devoted to Appearances of Candidates for President and Vice President

Television Stations: Network Programs Only[§]

	Primary Campaign President	
	Republican	Democratic
A. Time paid for by candidates or supporters		
Paid Time:		
Number of stations reporting	294	12
Amount of program time	243:40	8:25
B. Program time free of charge to candidates and supporters (not paid for by candidates or their supporters)		
Sustaining time:		
Number of stations reporting	388	200
Amount of program time	572:19	72:56
Program time on commercially sponsored programs, e.g. "Meet the Press":		
Number of stations reporting	381	200
Amount of program time	207:43	18:11

[§] Does not include appearances of supporters; program time is in hours and minutes.

PRESIDENTIAL CAMPAIGN MEDIA EXPOSURE: 1964

Time Devoted to Appearances of Candidates for President and Vice President

Television Stations: Network Programs Only[§]

| | General Election Campaign | | | | |
| | President | | | Vice President | |
	Rep.	Dem.	Other	Rep.	Dem.
A. Time paid for by candidates or supporters					
Paid time:					
Number of stations reporting	512	509		423	325
Amount of program time	1,612:42	1,158:05		54:39	76:51
Paid participations:					
Number of stations reporting		258			
Number of participations		1,288			
B. Program time free of charge to candidates and supporters (not paid for by candidates or their supporters)					
Sustaining time:					
Number of stations reporting	350	326		166	102
Amount of program time	11:52	63:33		72:05	35:29
Program time on commercially sponsored programs, e.g. "Meet the Press":					
Number of stations reporting	356	350	161	395	368
Amount of program time	53:15	15:56	12:55	61:21	57:45

[§] Does not include appearances of supporters; program time is in hours and minutes.

PRESIDENTIAL CAMPAIGN MEDIA EXPOSURE: 1964

Programs Devoted to Presidential and Vice Presidential Contests

AM Radio Stations: Network Programs Only[§]

	Primary		General Election		
	Rep.	Dem.	Rep.	Dem.	Other
1. Program time paid for by candidates or supporters:					
Number of stations reporting			401	395	
Amount of program time			507:25	307:09	
2. Program time free of charge to candidates or supporters:					
a. Sustaining time:					
Number of stations reporting	616	422	679	633	288
Amount of program time	2,087:46	236:24	1,290:14	917:40	78:26
b. Program time on commercially sponsored programs, e.g. "Meet the Press":					
Number of stations reporting	209				
Amount of program time	83:40				

	Total		
	Republican	Democratic	Other
1. Program time paid for by candidates or supporters:			
Number of stations reporting	401	395	
Amount of program time	507:25	307:09	
2. Program time free of charge to candidates or supporters:			
a. Sustaining time:			
Number of stations reporting	717	664	
Amount of program time	3,378:00	1,154:04	
b. Program time on commercially sponsored programs, e.g. "Meet the Press":			
Number of stations reporting	209		
Amount of program time	83:40		

§ Program time is in hours and minutes; including appearances of supporters.

PRESIDENTIAL CAMPAIGN MEDIA EXPOSURE: 1964

Time Devoted to Appearances of Candidates for President and Vice President

AM Radio Stations: Network Programs Only[§]

	Primary Campaign President	
	Republican	Democratic
Program time free of charge to candidates and supporters (not paid for by candidates or their supporters)		
Sustaining time:		
Number of stations reporting	494	324
Amount of program time	899:59	26:06

	General Election Campaign				
	President			Vice President	
	Rep.	Dem.	Other	Rep.	Dem.
Time paid for by candidates or supporters					
Paid time:					
Number of stations reporting	259	190			132
Amount of program time	252:06	91:51			43:47
Program time free of charge to candidates and supporters (not paid for by candidates or their supporters)					
Sustaining time:					
Number of stations reporting	430	374	230	493	461
Amount of program time	251:44	170:07	72:31	333:51	202:31

§ Does not include appearances of supporters; program time is in hours and minutes.

PRESIDENTIAL CAMPAIGN MEDIA EXPOSURE: 1964

Charges for Program Time and Announcements Relating to Candidacy for President and Vice President

Television Stations: Non-Network Programs Only[§]

	Primary Campaigns Number of Stations Reporting	Charges	General Election Campaigns Number of Stations Reporting	Charges	Total Both Campaigns Number of Stations Reporting	Total Charges
Republican	161	$636,865	470	$3,204,686	479	$3,841,551
Democratic	50	244,748	386	1,870,112	395	2,114,860
Other	9	64,329	17	13,804	25	78,133
Total	191	945,942	489	5,088,602	495	6,034,544

AM Radio Stations: Non-Network Programs Only[§]

	Primary Campaigns Number of Stations Reporting	Charges	General Election Campaigns Number of Stations Reporting	Charges	Total Both Campaigns Number of Stations Reporting	Total Charges
Republican	653	$355,349	2,677	$1,163,599	2,765	$1,518,948
Democratic	206	165,559	2,017	877,859	2,070	1,043,418
Other	48	22,380	122	25,129	154	47,509
Total	805	543,288	2,948	2,066,587	3,023	2,609,875

§ Program time is in hours and minutes.

PRESIDENTIAL CAMPAIGN MEDIA EXPOSURE: 1964

Requests for Time by or on Behalf of Presidential and Vice Presidential
Candidates or Supporters and Time Offered by Station

Television Stations: Non-Network Programs Only[§]

	Primary Campaigns			General Election Campaigns		
	Rep.	Dem.	Other	Rep.	Dem.	Other
A. Broadcast time requested by or on behalf of candidates or supporters (including time for appearances of candidates' supporters)						
Paid time:						
Number of stations reporting	153	51	11	432	328	30
Amount of program time	357:02	91:00	8:50	859:58	403:38	16:31
Number of stations reporting	113	28	1	445	332	3
Number of announcements	5,020	768	1	32,092	15,243	38
Sustaining time:						
Number of stations reporting	8	2		31	25	5
Amount of program time	4:13	0:30		18:56	17:03	3:15
Time on commercially sponsored programs, e.g. "Meet the Press":						
Number of stations reporting	5	3	1	11	13	3
Amount of program time	15:48	4:21	0:05	23:03	10:09	0:32
B. Free time offered by station on own initiative, whether or not it was used						
For use by candidates at their discretion:						
Number of stations reporting	6	4		24	23	
Amount of program time	3:30	3:22		18:02	25:34	
For use in format determined by station:						
Number of stations reporting	19	11	1	65	67	5
Amount of program time	22:56	9:16	0:28	52:58	51:41	2:09

§ Program time is in hours and minutes.

PRESIDENTIAL CAMPAIGN MEDIA EXPOSURE: 1964

Time Devoted to Appearances of Presidential Candidates Only:
Primary Campaigns

Television Stations: Non-Network Programs Only[§]

	Republican	Democratic	Other
A. Time paid for by candidates or supporters			
Paid time:			
Number of stations reporting	129	48	7
Amount of program time	208:38	63:14	4:00
Paid announcements:			
Number of stations reporting	89	27	2
Number of announcements	3,998	767	8
B. Program time free of charge to candidates and supporters (not paid for by candidates or their supporters)			
Sustaining time:			
Number of stations reporting	23	12	3
Amount of program time	14:53	6:10	2:25
Program time on commercially sponsored programs, e.g. "Meet the Press":			
Number of stations reporting	7	7	3
Amount of program time	4:55	2:32	0:36

§ Does not include appearances of supporters; program time is in hours and minutes.

PRESIDENTIAL CAMPAIGN MEDIA EXPOSURE: 1964

Time Devoted to Appearances of
Presidential and Vice Presidential Candidates Only

General Election Campaigns

Television Stations: Non-Network Programs Only[§]

	President			Vice President		
	Rep.	Dem.	Other	Rep.	Dem.	Other
A. Time paid for by candidates or supporters						
Paid time:						
Number of stations reporting	305	183	12	58	105	1
Amount of program time	379:13	127:39	4:17	36:13	51:49	0:15
Paid announcements:						
Number of stations reporting	382	196	1	26	25	1
Number of announcements	24,792	4,508	5	994	452	77
B. Program time free of charge to candidates and supporters (not paid for by candidates or their supporters)						
Sustaining time:						
Number of stations reporting	51	51	6	19	15	4
Amount of program time	35:45	39:22	1:32	8:22	6:27	0:28
Program time on commercially sponsored programs, e.g. "Meet the Press":						
Number of stations reporting	13	12	3	9	17	2
Amount of program time	3:51	8:33	1:06	3:09	6:48	0:16

§ Does not include appearances of supporters; program time is in hours and minutes.

PRESIDENTIAL CAMPAIGN MEDIA EXPOSURE: 1964

Requests for Time by or on Behalf of Presidential and Vice Presidential
Candidates or Supporters and Time Offered by Station

AM Radio Stations: Non-Network Programs Only[§]

	Primary Campaigns			General Election Campaigns		
	Rep.	Dem.	Other	Rep.	Dem.	Other
A. Broadcast time requested by or on behalf of candidates or supporters (including time for appearances of candidates' supporters)						
Paid time:						
Number of stations reporting	175	103	25	1,316	816	79
Amount of program time	152:37	134:50	21:43	1,672:56	741:44	36:12
Number of stations reporting	619	81	14	2,506	1,845	29
Number of announcements	32,641	8,594	496	188,137	106,342	866
Sustaining time:						
Number of stations reporting	22	16	3	177	164	33
Amount of program time	16:26	11:11	0:43	139:25	115:08	18:30
Time on commercially sponsored programs, e.g. "Meet the Press":						
Number of stations reporting	11	4		35	24	9
Amount of program time	6:09	4:44		25:39	23:28	10:43
B. Free time offered by station on own initiative, whether or not it was used						
For use by candidates at their discretion:						
Number of stations reporting	26	24	9	123	122	15
Amount of program time	23:18	22:51	7:52	184:45	194:55	94:34
For use in format determined by station:						
Number of stations reporting	83	57	20	203	194	33
Amount of program time	81:12	43:28	15:36	165:53	163:38	28:24

§ Program time is in hours and minutes.

PRESIDENTIAL CAMPAIGN MEDIA EXPOSURE: 1964

Time Devoted to Appearances of Presidential Candidates Only:
Primary Campaigns

AM Radio Stations: Non-Network Programs Only[§]

	Republican	Democratic	Other
A. Time paid for by candidates or supporters			
Paid time:			
Number of stations reporting	119	104	23
Amount of program time	101:58	115:26	20:15
Paid announcements:			
Number of stations reporting	241	55	8
Number of announcements	13,284	10,484	207
B. Program time free of charge to candidates and supporters (not paid for by candidates or their supporters)			
Sustaining time:			
Number of stations reporting	64	36	6
Amount of program time	55:24	23:18	2:15
Program time on commercially sponsored programs, e.g. "Meet the Press":			
Number of stations reporting	19	13	4
Amount of program time	12:34	7:29	4:50

[§] Does not include appearances of supporters; program time is in hours and minutes.

PRESIDENTIAL CAMPAIGN MEDIA EXPOSURE: 1964

Time Devoted to Appearances of Presidential and Vice Presidential Candidates

General Election Campaigns

AM Radio Stations: Non-Network Programs Only[§]

	President			Vice President		
	Rep.	Dem.	Other	Rep.	Dem.	Other
A. Time paid for by candidates or supporters						
Paid time:						
Number of stations reporting	536	263	54	95	151	32
Amount of program time	560:19	259:28	16:40	63:46	87:44	10:15
Paid announcements:						
Number of stations reporting	804	352	5	40	56	3
Number of announcements	48,742	14,923	56	1,318	1,332	55
B. Program time free of charge to candidates and supporters (not paid for by candidates or their supporters)						
Sustaining time:						
Number of stations reporting	202	158	23	102	86	13
Amount of program time	150:41	123:07	13:52	53:26	47:18	5:45
Program time on commercially sponsored programs, e.g. "Meet the Press":						
Number of stations reporting	30	22	6	6	11	5
Amount of program time	25:54	13:14	5:40	3:41	7:59	2:49

[§] Does not include appearances of supporters; program time is in hours and minutes.

PRESIDENTIAL CAMPAIGN MEDIA EXPOSURE: 1968

Television: Total Charges for Political Broadcasts[§]

	Total	3 Networks	Stations
Primary and General Election Campaigns-Total	$37,977,729	$8,881,023	$29,096,706
Republican	18,704,302	5,197,057	13,507,245
Democratic	17,384,415	3,011,541	14,372,874
Other	1,889,012	672,425	1,216,587
Primary Campaigns-Total	10,890,702	1,518,783	9,371,919
Republican	3,521,430	1,007,759	2,513,671
Democratic	6,960,475	511,024	6,449,451
Other	408,797		408,797
General Election Campaigns-Total	27,087,027	7,362,240	19,724,787
Republican	15,182,872	4,189,298	10,993,574
Democratic	10,423,940	2,500,517	7,923,423
Other	1,480,215	672,425	807,790

§ Before commissions and after discounts. All figures on charges used in succeeding tables in this report are defined in same way.

PRESIDENTIAL CAMPAIGN MEDIA EXPOSURE: 1968

Radio: Total Charges for Political Broadcasts[§]

	Total	7 Networks[§§]	Stations[§§§]
Primary and General Election Campaigns-Total	$20,910,372	$691,740	$20,218,632
Republican	9,155,791	497,937	8,657,854
Democratic	10,481,234	177,803	10,303,431
Other	1,273,347	16,000	1,257,347
Primary Campaigns-Total	7,593,901	29,066	7,564,835
Republican	1,833,805	29,066	1,804,739
Democratic	5,457,185		5,457,185
Other	302,911		302,911
General Election Campaigns-Total	13,316,471	662,674	12,653,797
Republican	7,321,986	468,871	6,853,115
Democratic	5,024,049	177,803	4,846,246
Other	970,436	16,000	954,436

§ Before commissions and after discounts. All figures on charges used in succeeding tables in this report are defined in same way.
§§ Includes CBS, MBS, NBC and 4 networks of ABC.
§§§ Includes AM stations, FM stations associated with AM stations in same area and independent FM stations.

Program Time, Announcements, and Charges of Television and Radio Networks
to Candidates in Presidential and Vice Presidential Contests or Supporters[§]

| | Primary Campaigns | | | |
	Republican	Democratic	Other	Total
		Television		
1. Program time paid for by candidates or supporters	4:40	3:05		7:45
2. Charges for program time	$ 454,115	$338,680		$ 792,795
3. Number of announcements	21	11		32
4. Charges for announcements	$ 553,644	$172,344		$ 725,988
5. Total charges (lines 2&4)	$1,007,759	$511,024		$1,518,783
6. Program time free of charge to candidates or supporters				
a. Sustaining time	3:51	9:25		13:16
b. Time on commercially sponsored programs, e.g. "Meet the Press"	11:05	27:12	0:38	38:55
		Radio		
1. Program time paid for by candidates or supporters	2:13			2:13
2. Charges for program time	$ 29,066			$ 29,066
3. Total charges	$ 29,066			$ 29,066
4. Program time free of charge to candidates or supporters				
a. Sustaining time	10:01	20:35	0:53	31:29
b. Time on commercially sponsored programs, e.g. "Meet the Press"		0:50		0:50

[§] Includes appearances of both candidates and supporters; charges are in
dollars; program time is in hours and minutes.

Program Time, Announcements, and Charges of Television and Radio Networks
to Candidates in Presidential and Vice Presidential Contests or Supporters§
(continued)

	General Election Campaigns			
	Republican	Democratic	Other	Total

Television

1. Program time paid for by candidates or supporters	12:00	12:35	4:15	28:50
2. Charges for program time	$1,604,552	$1,656,204	$583,028	$3,843,784
3. Number of announcements	110	37	4	151
4. Charges for announcements	$2,584,746	$ 844,313	$ 89,397	$3,518,456
5. Total charges (lines 2&4)	$4,189,298	$2,500,917	$672,425	$7,362,640
6. Program time free of charge to candidates or supporters				
a. Sustaining time	1:05	0:39	1:17	3:01
b. Time on commercially sponsored programs, e.g. "Meet the Press"	9:37	14:07	8:19	32:03

Radio

1. Program time paid for by candidates or supporters	9:40	2:50	0:30	13:00
2. Charges for program time	$ 165,881	$ 37,801	$ 7,200	$ 210,882
3. Number of announcements	453	240	7	700
4. Charges for announcements	$ 302,990	$ 140,002	$ 8,800	$ 451,792
5. Total charges (lines 2&4)	$ 468,871	$ 177,803	$ 16,000	$ 662,674
6. Program time free of charge to candidates or supporters				
a. Sustaining time	6:41	10:56	6:40	24:17
b. Time on commercially sponsored programs, e.g. "Meet the Press"	0:50			0:50

§ Includes appearances of both candidates and supporters; charges are in
dollars; program time is in hours and minutes.

Program Time, Announcements, and Charges of Television and Radio Networks
to Candidates in Presidential and Vice Presidential Contests or Supporters[§]
(continued)

| | Combined Primary and General Election Campaigns | | | |
	Republican	Democratic	Other	Total
	Television			
1. Program time paid for by candidates or supporters	16:40	15:40	4:15	36:35
2. Charges for program time	$2,058,667	$1,994,884	$583,028	$4,636,579
3. Number of announcements	131	48	4	183
4. Charges for announcements	$3,138,390	$1,016,657	$ 89,397	$4,244,444
5. Total charges (lines 2&4)	$5,197,057	$3,011,541	$672,425	$8,881,023
6. Program time free of charge to candidates or supporters a. Sustaining time	4:56	10:04	1:17	16:17
b. Time on commercially sponsored programs, e.g. "Meet the Press"	20:42	41:19	8:57	70:58
	Radio			
1. Program time paid for by candidates or supporters	11:53	2:50	0:30	15:30
2. Charges for program time	$ 194,947	$ 37,801	$ 7,200	$ 239,948
3. Number of announcements	453	240	7	700
4. Charges for announcements	$ 302,990	$ 140,002	$ 8,800	$ 451,792
5. Total charges (lines 2&4)	$ 497,937	$ 177,803	$ 16,000	$ 691,740
6. Program time free of charge to candidates or supporters a. Sustaining time	16:42	31:31	7:33	55:46
b. Time on commercially sponsored programs, e.g. "Meet the Press"	0:50	0:50		1:40

[§] Includes appearances of both candidates and supporters; charges are in
dollars; program time is in hours and minutes.

PRESIDENTIAL CAMPAIGN MEDIA EXPOSURE: 1968

Charges for Program Time and Announcements Relating to
Candidacy for President and Vice President

Television Stations: Non-Network Programs Only

In Primary Campaigns	Number of Stations Reporting	Charges
Republican	171	$1,514,096
Democratic	263	2,886,537
Other	197	267,182
Total	371	4,667,815

In General Election Campaigns	Number of Stations Reporting	Charges
Republican	400	$4,817,814
Democratic	433	1,973,560
Other	325	484,136
Total	507	7,275,510

PRESIDENTIAL CAMPAIGN MEDIA EXPOSURE: 1968

Charges for Program Time and Announcements Relating to
Candidacy for President and Vice President

All Radio Stations: Non-Network Programs Only[§]

In Primary Campaigns	Number of Stations Reporting	Charges
Republican	439	$ 436,172
Democratic	918	1,392,340
Other	319	72,898
Total	1,247	1,901,410

In General Election Campaigns	Number of Stations Reporting	Charges
Republican	2,052	$3,121,970
Democratic	1,815	1,490,997
Other	1,589	463,204
Total	2,913	5,076,171

§ Includes AM stations, FM stations associated with AM stations in same area, and independent FM stations.

PRESIDENTIAL CAMPAIGN MEDIA EXPOSURE: 1968

Average Number of Stations Ordered and Carrying Network Programs
on Which Candidates in Presidential and Vice Presidential Contests Appeared[§]

| | Primary Campaigns | | | |
	Republican	Democratic	Other	Total
Television[§§]				
Program Time Paid for by Candidates or Supporters				
Average number of stations ordered per program	196	199		197
Average number of stations carrying programs	181	172		180
Sustaining Time				
Average number of stations carrying programs	158	158		158
Time on Commercially Sponsored Programs, e.g. "Meet the Press"				
Average number of stations ordered per program	208	210	210	210
Average number of stations carrying programs	165	173	181	171
Radio[§§]				
Program Time Paid for by Candidates or Supporters				
Average number of stations ordered per program	232			232
Average number of stations carrying programs	184			184
Sustaining Time				
Average number of stations carrying programs	116	156	158	145

§ Does not include appearances of supporters.
§§ The number of stations in the 3 TV network line-ups averaged 213 during the period under consideration compared with 282 stations in the 7 radio network line-ups.

Average Number of Stations Ordered and Carrying Network Programs
on Which Candidates in Presidential and Vice Presidential Contests Appeared[§]
(continued)

	General Campaigns			
	Republican	Democratic	Other	Total
Television[§§]				
Program Time Paid for by Candidates or Supporters				
Average number of stations ordered per program	193	188	193	191
Average number of stations carrying programs	178	176	174	177
Sustaining Time				
Average number of stations carrying programs	144	162	170	156
Time on Commercially Sponsored Programs, e.g. "Meet the Press"				
Average number of stations ordered per program	202	200	190	197
Average number of stations carrying programs	164	146	157	154
Radio[§§]				
Program Time Paid for by Candidates or Supporters				
Average number of stations ordered per program	227	94	243	219
Average number of stations carrying programs	165	84	204	161
Sustaining Time				
Average number of stations carrying programs	156	151	163	157

§ Does not include appearances of supporters.
§§ The number of stations in the 3 TV network line-ups averaged 213 during the period under consideration compared with 282 stations in the 7 radio network line-ups.

Average Number of Stations Ordered and Carrying Network Programs
on Which Candidates in Presidential and Vice Presidential Contests Appeared[§]
(continued)

	Combined Primary and General Election Campaigns			
	Republican	Democratic	Other	Total
	Television[§§]			
Program Time Paid for by Candidates or Supporters				
Average number of stations ordered per program	194	192	193	193
Average number of stations carrying programs	179	174	174	177
Sustaining Time				
Average number of stations carrying programs	154	158	170	158
Time on Commercially Sponsored Programs, e.g. "Meet the Press"				
Average number of stations ordered per program	205	207	194	204
Average number of stations carrying programs	164	164	161	164
	Radio[§§]			
Program Time Paid for by Candidates or Supporters				
Average number of stations ordered per program	227	94	243	220
Average number of stations carrying programs	116	84	204	162
Sustaining Time				
Average number of stations carrying programs	129	155	162	150

§ Does not include appearances of supporters.
§§ The number of stations in the 3 TV network line-ups averaged 213 during
the period under consideration compared with 282 stations in the 7 radio
network line-ups.

PRESIDENTIAL CAMPAIGN MEDIA EXPOSURE: 1968

Network Time Devoted to Appearances of Candidates in Presidential and Vice Presidential Contests[§]

| | Primary Campaigns | | | |
	Republican	Democratic	Other	Total
Television				
Program Time Paid for by Candidates or Supporters	4:32	3:00		7:32
Sustaining Time	3:32	9:16		12:48
Time on Commercially Sponsored Programs, e.g., "Meet the Press"	7:05	19:16	0:38	26:49
Radio				
Program Time Paid for by Candidates or Supporters	2:13			2:13
Sustaining Time	6:47	17:49	0:53	25:29
General Election Campaigns				
Television				
Program Time Paid for by Candidates or Supporters	10:54	9:25	4:10	24:29
Sustaining Time	1:03	0:08	1:17	2:28
Time on Commercially Sponsored Programs, e.g., "Meet the Press"	4:51	8:58	8:06	21:55
Radio				
Program Time Paid for by Candidates or Supporters	9:40	1:15	0:30	11:25
Sustaining Time	3:57	7:36	6:40	18:13

[§] Does not include appearances of supporters; time is in hours and minutes.

PRESIDENTIAL CAMPAIGN MEDIA EXPOSURE: 1968

Network Time Devoted to Appearances of Candidates
in Presidential and Vice Presidential Contests[§]
(continued)

	Combined Primary and General Election Campaigns			
	Republican	Democratic	Other	Total
Television				
Program Time Paid for by Candidates or Supporters	15:26	12:25	4:10	32:01
Sustaining Time	4:35	9:24	1:17	15:16
Time on Commercially Sponsored Programs, e.g., "Meet the Press"	11:56	28:14	8:44	48:44
Radio				
Program Time Paid for by Candidates or Supporters	11:53	1:15	0:30	13:38
Sustaining Time	10:44	25:25	7:33	43:42

§ Does not include appearances of supporters; time is in hours and minutes.

Presidential Campaign Media Exposure

NOTE

The data in Part VI, Section B was compiled and supplied by the A. C. Nielsen Company. All data are derived from Nielsen Television Index "National Nielsen TV Ratings" reports estimating audiences to commercial (sponsored) programming of the National television networks. Nielsen Television Index provides reports of research conducted during forty-eight weeks each year. Thus, the material to follow includes all available information but may not reflect all network political telecasting for the campaign period. The data are estimates only, subject to definitions and reminders, qualifications and limitations set forth in the Nielsen reports from which they are cited. The use of mathematical terms herewith should not be regarded as a representation by Nielsen that such estimates are exact to precise mathematical values. To aid in the use of the data in this section, included in the following are the annual estimates of total United States television households. (Figures to be read as millions.)

July,	1952	17,259	Jan.,	1962	49,000
July,	1953	23,395	Sept.,	1962	49,800
July,	1954	28,220	Sept.,	1963	51,260
July,	1955	32,320	Sept.,	1964	52,600
July,	1956	36,500	Sept.,	1965	53,800
July,	1957	40,300	Sept.,	1966	54,900
July,	1958	43,000	Sept.,	1967	56,000
July,	1959	44,500	Sept.,	1968	57,000
Jan.,	1960	45,200	Sept.,	1969	58,500
Jan.,	1961	46,900	Sept.,	1970	60,100

DEFINITIONS

NIELSEN AVERAGE AUDIENCE. Number of TV households tuned to the program during the average minute, reported in two ways:

(a) In percent of U.S. TV households.
(b) In terms of the projected number of households reached, rounded to the nearest 10,000 households.

These data are particularly useful (a) to afford a convenient estimate of the audience to a single commercial, (b) to compare programs having different durations. Note that Nielsen Average Audience is based on each sample household's record of viewing activity during the entire program, not just one selected minute.

SHARE OF AUDIENCE. Audience during the average minute of the program, in percent of households using television at the time of the program's principal telecast in the Eastern, Central, and Pacific Time Zones. (Mountain Time Zone households located in the Nielsen Pacific Territory are included with Pacific Time Zone households. All other MTZ households are included with Central Time Zone households.) Share of Audience makes it possible to compare programs telecast at times when TV usage levels are different—*e.g.*, different hours of the day of different seasons of the year.

Share of Audience is also reported by half-hour program segments, corresponding to Average Audience by half-hours.

Section B/*Network Television Programs and*
Spot Announcements
1952-1968

PRESIDENTIAL CAMPAIGN MEDIA EXPOSURE

Network Television Programs and Spot Announcements: 1952

Date	Network	Time	Person Appearing
8/ 8/52	ABC	8:00 - 8:15 PM	Stevenson
9/ 1/52	CBS	1:00 - 1:30 PM	Stevenson
9/ 4/52	NBC	9:30 - 10:00 PM	Eisenhower
9/ 5/52	ABC	9:00 - 9:30 PM	Stevenson
9/ 9/52	CBS	10:30 - 11:00 PM	Stevenson
9/15/52	NBC	10:30 - 11:00 PM	Stevenson
9/17/52	NBC	10:00 - 10:30 PM	Robert Taft
9/17/52	ABC	11:30 - 12:00 MID	Nixon
9/19/52	NBC	10:45 - 11:15 PM	Eisenhower
9/23/52	NBC	9:30 - 10:00 PM	Nixon
9/23/52	CBS	10:00 - 10:30 PM	Stevenson
9/24/52	NBC	7:15 - 7:30 PM	Dewey
9/25/52	ABC	7:00 - 7:15 PM	Rep. Press Interview
9/25/52	DUM	9:30 - 10:00 PM	Eisenhower
9/29/52	NBC	10:30 - 11:00 PM	Stevenson
9/30/52	NBC	10:30 - 11:00 PM	Clare Luce
10/ 2/52	CBS	7:15 - 7:30 PM	Dewey
10/ 3/52	ABC	9:00 - 9:30 PM	Stevenson
10/ 7/52	CBS	10:30 - 11:00 PM	Stevenson
10/ 8/52	ABC	7:15 - 7:30 PM	Dewey
10/ 9/52	DUM	10:30 - 11:00 PM	Stevenson
10/13/52	CBS	8:00 - 8:30 PM	Nixon
10/14/52	DUM	10:30 - 11:00 PM	Stevenson
10/16/52	DUM	10:30 - 11:00 PM	Stevenson
10/18/52	CBS	9:30 - 10:00 PM	Hoover
10/19/52	CBS	5:30 - 6:00 PM	W. Reuther
10/21/52	NBC	9:30 - 10:00 PM	Stevenson
10/21/52	CBS	10:30 - 10:45 PM	Philip Murray
10/22/52	CBS	8:30 - 9:00 PM	Truman
10/23/52	NBC	9:00 - 9:30 PM	Stevenson
10/23/52	DUM	10:30 - 11:00 PM	Alben Barkley
10/24/52	NBC	9:00 - 9:30 PM	Eisenhower
10/25/52	DUM	10:30 - 11:00 PM	Stevenson
10/26/52	CBS§	5:30 - 6:00 PM	W. Reuther
10/26/52	ABC	6:00 - 6:30 PM	Clare Luce
10/27/52	ABC	9:30 - 10:00 PM	J. McCarthy
10/28/52	NBC	9:00 - 9:30 PM	Eisenhower
10/28/52	NBC	10:30 - 11:00 PM	Stevenson
10/29/52	CBS	8:30 - 9:00 PM	Nixon
10/29/52	ABC	10:15 - 10:30 PM	For Stevenson
10/29/52	CBS	10:00 - 10:45 PM	For Eisenhower
10/29/52	NBC	10:30 - 11:00 PM	Truman

§ Average of two telecasts.

Sponsor	Type	Average Audience		
		% Total U.S.	Homes Reached	% Share of Audience
Stevenson - Sparkman Club	15 Min. Speech	3.7	672	18.5
Democratic Nat'l. Commit.	30 Min. Speech	6.5	1,193	39.9
Republican Nat'l. Commit.	30 Min. Speech	25.8	4,735	45.5
Volunteers for Stevenson	30 Min. Speech	14.7	2,698	32.2
Democratic Nat'l. Commit.	30 Min. Speech	13.6	2,496	38.2
Volunteers for Stevenson	30 Min. Speech	12.0	2,245	27.9
Republican Sen. Commit.	30 Min. Speech	2.3	430	6.5
Republican Nat'l. Commit.	30 Min. Speech	3.9	730	25.6
Republican Nat'l. Commit.	30 Min. Speech	21.5	4,023	45.0
Republican Nat'l. Commit.	30 Min. Speech	44.4	8,308	68.8
Volunteers for Stevenson	30 Min. Speech	24.7	4,622	45.8
N.Y. State Rep. Commit.	15 Min. Speech	Insufficient for Reporting		
Republican Nat'l. Commit.	15 Min. Speech	Insufficient for Reporting		
Republican Nat'l. Commit.	30 Min. Speech	25.0	4,678	40.9
Volunteers for Stevenson	30 Min. Speech	12.4	2,320	34.0
Republican Nat'l. Commit.	30 Min. Speech	14.1	2,638	40.2
N.Y. State Rep. Commit.	15 Min. Speech	Insufficient for Reporting		
Volunteers for Stevenson	30 Min. Speech	16.3	3,050	29.9
Democratic Nat'l. Commit.	30 Min. Speech	13.3	2,489	35.6
N.Y. State Rep. Commit.	15 Min. Speech	Insufficient for Reporting		
Democratic Nat'l. Commit.	30 Min. Speech	12.4	2,320	36.3
Republican Nat'l. Commit.	30 Min. Speech	22.2	4,246	41.0
Stevenson - Sparkman Club	30 Min. Speech	14.4	2,754	33.8
Stevenson - Sparkman Club	30 Min. Speech	10.7	2,046	39.4
Nat'l. Rep. Sen. Commit.	30 Min. Speech	16.5	3,156	32.6
United Auto Workers	30 Min. Speech	2.7	516	11.7
Democratic Nat'l. Commit.	30 Min. Speech	22.7	4,341	42.5
CIO Committee	15 Min. Speech	6.6	1,262	23.1
Stevenson - Sparkman Club	30 Min. Speech	28.4	5,431	50.4
N.Y. Fund for Stevenson	30 Min. Speech	17.1	3,270	47.5
Democratic Nat'l. Commit.	30 Min. Speech	Data Not Available		
Republican Nat'l. Commit.	30 Min. Speech	21.3	4,074	36.2
Democratic Nat'l. Commit.	30 Min. Speech	Data Not Available		
United Auto Workers	30 Min. Speech	2.6	497	11.0
Rep. Congressional Commit.	30 Min. Speech	5.4	1,033	17.8
McCarthy Dinner Commit.	30 Min. Speech	24.3	4,647	43.0
Republican Sen. Commit.	30 Min. Speech	25.9	4,953	44.6
Volunteers for Stevenson	30 Min. Speech	9.4	1,798	31.7
Republican Sen. Commit.	30 Min. Speech	27.8	5,317	47.7
Ladies Garment Workers	15 Min. Speech	4.0	765	13.8
Rep. Congressional Commit.	45 Min. Speech	20.9	3,997	43.7
Labor League - Education	30 Min. Speech	Insufficient for Reporting		

Network Television Programs and Spot Announcements: 1952
(continued)

Date	Network	Time	Person Appearing
10/30/52	NBC	10:00 – 10:30 PM	Eisenhower
10/31/52	NBC	1:00 – 1:30 PM	Eisenhower
10/31/52	ABC	7:00 – 7:15 PM	Wayne Morse
10/31/52	NBC	9:30 – 10:00 PM	Stevenson
11/ 1/52	NBC	10:00 – 10:30 PM	Eisenhower
11/ 1/52	NBC	10:30 – 11:00 PM	Stevenson
11/ 2/52	CBS§	5:30 – 6:00 PM	W. Reuther
11/ 2/52	NBC	10:30 – 11:00 PM	Gen. Wedemeyer
11/ 3/52	NBC	11:00 – 11:30 AM	Alben Barkley
11/ 3/52	CBS	12:30 – 12:45 PM	Eisenhower
11/ 3/52	NBC	4:45 – 5:00 PM	Eisenhower
11/ 3/52	NBC	10:00 – 10:30 PM	Eisenhower
11/ 3/52	ABC	10:00 – 10:30 PM	Eisenhower
11/ 3/52	NBC	10:30 – 11:00 PM	For Stevenson
11/ 3/52	ABC	10:30 – 11:00 PM	For Stevenson
11/ 3/52	CBS	10:30 – 11:00 PM	For Stevenson
11/ 3/52	ABC	11:00 – 12:00 MID	Eisenhower & Nixon
11/ 3/52	CBS	11:00 – 12:00 MID	Eisenhower & Nixon
11/ 3/52	NBC	11:00 – 12:00 MID	Eisenhower & Nixon

§ Average of two telecasts.

Sponsor	Type	Average Audience		
		% Total U.S.	Homes Reached	% Share of Audience
Republican Nat'l. Commit.	30 Min. Speech	21.6	4,131	43.9
Republican Sen. Commit.	30 Min. Speech	1.1	210	19.0
Volunteers for Stevenson	15 Min. Speech	4.6	880	17.7
Democratic Nat'l. Commit.	30 Min. Speech	14.8	2,830	34.0
Rep. Congressional Commit.	30 Min. Speech	25.9	4,953	50.2
Volunteers for Stevenson	30 Min. Speech	13.0	2,486	36.3
United Auto Workers	30 Min. Speech	2.6	497	11.0
Republican Sen. Commit.	30 Min. Speech	8.8	1,683	31.0
Volunteers for Stevenson	30 Min. Speech	5.8	1,109	51.3
Republican Nat'l. Commit.	15 Min. Speech	8.4	1,606	65.7
Republican Nat'l. Commit.	15 Min. Speech	12.6	2,410	47.1
Citizens for Eisenhower	30 Min. Speech	22.3	4,265	54.9
Citizens for Eisenhower	30 Min. Speech	5.9	1,128	17.7
Democratic Nat'l. Commit.	30 Min. Speech	19.9	3,806	52.5
Stevenson – Sparkman Club	30 Min. Speech	3.1	593	14.3
Stevenson – Sparkman Club	30 Min. Speech	14.3	2,735	39.7
Citizens for Eisenhower	60 Min. Speech	2.6	497	14.7
Citizens for Eisenhower	60 Min. Speech	8.0	1,530	31.9
Citizens for Eisenhower	60 Min. Speech	18.6	3,557	58.2

PRESIDENTIAL CAMPAIGN MEDIA EXPOSURE

Network Television Programs and Spot Announcements: 1956

Date	Network	Time	Person Appearing
9/10/56	NBC	7:00 – 7:30 PM	Political Telecast
9/13/56	ABC	9:30 – 10:00 PM	Stevenson
9/13/56	CBS	9:30 – 10:00 PM	Stevenson
9/13/56	NBC	9:30 – 10:00 PM	Stevenson
9/17/56	NBC	7:00 – 7:30 PM	Democrat
9/19/56	CBS	9:30 – 10:00 PM	Eisenhower
9/23/56	ABC	9:55 – 10:00 PM	Stevenson
9/24/56	ABC§§	3:00 – 3:05 PM	Democrat
9/24/56	NBC	10:25 – 10:30 PM	Stevenson
9/25/56	CBS	7:55 – 8:00 PM	Stevenson
9/25/56	CBS^	9:30 – 10:00 PM	Eisenhower
9/26/56	ABC§§	3:00 – 3:05 PM	Democrat
9/26/56	CBS	7:00 – 7:15 PM	Jacob Javits
9/26/56	ABC§	8:55 – 9:00 PM	Stevenson
9/26/56	CBS§	9:55 – 10:00 PM	Stevenson
9/26/56	NBC	9:55 – 10:00 PM	Stevenson
9/28/56	ABC§§	3:00 – 3:05 PM	Stevenson
9/28/56	CBS	8:30 – 9:00 PM	Stevenson
9/29/56	ABC	10:25 – 10:30 PM	Stevenson
9/30/56	NBC	9:55 – 10:00 PM	Stevenson
9/30/56	CBS	10:25 – 10:30 PM	Stevenson
10/ 1/56	ABC§§	3:00 – 3:05 PM	Stevenson
10/ 1/56	CBS^	9:30 – 10:00 PM	Eisenhower
10/ 2/56	ABC§§	3:00 – 3:05 PM	Stevenson
10/ 2/56	CBS	7:00 – 7:15 PM	Robert Wagner
10/ 2/56	CBS	9:55 – 10:00 PM	John Kennedy
10/ 3/56	ABC§	8:55 – 9:00 PM	Stevenson
10/ 3/56	CBS§	8:55 – 9:00 PM	Stevenson
10/ 3/56	ABC	10:50 – 11:05 PM	Dewey
10/ 4/56	NBC	8:30 – 9:00 PM	Nixon
10/ 5/56	NBC	9:55 – 10:00 PM	Stevenson
10/ 6/56	NBC	9:55 – 10:00 PM	Humphrey
10/ 8/56	CBS	8:55 – 9:00 PM	Leader
10/ 8/56	ABC	10:25 – 10:30 PM	Stevenson
10/ 9/56	CBS	7:00 – 7:15 PM	Jacob Javits
10/ 9/56	NBC	9:00 – 9:30 PM	Eisenhower
10/ 9/56	CBS	10:25 – 10:30 PM	Stevenson
10/ 9/56	NBC	10:25 – 10:30 PM	Stevenson
10/10/56	CBS	10:55 – 11:00 PM	Stevenson
10/11/56	NBC	6:30 – 6:45 PM	Dewey

^ Average of two telecasts.
§ Average of two spots.
§§Average of five spots.

238

Sponsor	Type	% Total U.S.	Average Audience Homes Reached	% Share of Audience
N.Y. Democratic Commit.	30 Min. Speech	Insufficient for Reporting		
Democratic Nat'l. Commit.	30 Min. Speech	3.9	1,470	10.0
Democratic Nat'l. Commit.	30 Min. Speech	13.4	5,052	29.2
Democratic Nat'l. Commit.	30 Min. Speech	13.1	4,939	27.2
N.Y. Democratic Commit.	30 Min. Speech	Insufficient for Reporting		
Republican Nat'l. Commit.	30 Min. Speech	13.2	4,976	25.0
Democratic Nat'l. Commit.	Spot	7.9	2,978	15.4
Democratic Nat'l. Commit.	Spot	.8	302	7.9
Democratic Nat'l. Commit.	Spot	17.5	6,598	34.3
Democratic Nat'l. Commit.	Spot	14.1	5,316	33.5
Republican Nat'l. Commit.	30 Min. Speech	18.6	7,012	30.3
Democratic Nat'l. Commit.	Spot	.8	302	7.9
N.Y. Republican Commit.	15 Min. Speech	Insufficient for Reporting		
Volunteers for Stev. Kef.	Spot	4.7	1,772	10.9
Democratic Nat'l. Commit.	Spot	18.4	6,937	31.7
Democratic Nat'l. Commit.	Spot	16.6	6,258	28.3
Democratic Nat'l. Commit.	Spot	.8	302	7.9
Democratic Nat'l. Commit	30 Min. Speech	8.9	3,355	17.1
Democratic Nat'l. Commit	Spot	4.3	1,621	10.3
Democratic Nat'l. Commit.	Spot	11.0	4,147	18.4
Democratic Nat'l. Commit.	Spot	24.5	9,237	44.1
Democratic Nat'l. Commit.	Spot	.8	302	7.9
Republican Nat'l. Commit.	30 Min. Speech	18.6	7,012	30.3
Democratic Nat'l. Commit.	Spot	.8	9,237	44.1
Citizens Committee	15 Min. Speech	Insufficient for Reporting		
Democratic Nat'l. Commit.	Spot	21.1	7,955	37.5
Volunteers for Stev. Kef.	Spot	4.7	1,772	10.9
Democratic Nat'l. Commit.	Spot	18.4	6,937	31.7
Rep. Nat'l. Cong. Commit.	15 Min. Speech	6.9	2,601	17.1
Republican Nat'l. Commit.	30 Min. Speech	13.7	5,165	22.9
Democratic Nat'l. Commit.	Spot	15.6	5,881	25.9
Democratic Nat'l. Commit.	Spot	15.8	5,957	25.4
Stevenson-Kefauver Commit.	Spot	24.9	9,387	41.7
Stevenson-Kefauver Commit.	Spot	9.3	3,506	19.3
N.Y. Republican Commit.	15 Min. Speech	Insufficient for Reporting		
Rep. Nat'l. Cong. Commit.	30 Min. Speech	15.8	5,957	23.3
Democratic Nat'l. Commit.	Spot	26.7	10,066	45.6
Democratic Nat'l. Commit.	Spot	12.0	4,524	21.4
Democratic Nat'l. Commit.	Spot	12.3	4,637	29.8
N.Y. Republican Commit.	15 Min. Speech	Insufficient for Reporting		

Network Television Programs and Spot Announcements: 1956
(continued)

Date	Network	Time	Person Appearing
10/11/56	NBC	9:00 – 9:30 PM	Stevenson
10/12/56	ABC§§	3:00 – 3:05 PM	Democrat
10/12/56	CBS	7:00 – 7:15 PM	Robert Wagner
10/12/56	NBC	9:00 – 9:30 PM	Eisenhower
10/13/56	ABC	9:55 – 10:00 PM	Mike Monroney
10/13/56	CBS	10:00 – 10:30 PM	President's Birthday
10/13/56	NBC§	10:55 – 11:00 PM	Stevenson
10/14/56	ABC	8:25 – 8:30 PM	Stevenson
10/15/56	CBS§	1:00 – 1:05 PM	Democrat
10/15/56	ABC§§	3:00 – 3:05 PM	Democrat
10/15/56	NBC§	3:55 – 4:00 PM	Democrat
10/15/56	NBC	9:25 – 9:30 PM	Eisenhower
10/15/56	ABC	10:25 – 10:30 PM	Eisenhower
10/15/56	NBC	10:25 – 10:30 PM	Chester Bowles
10/15/56	ABC	10:30 – 11:00 PM	Stevenson
10/16/56	CBS§	1:00 – 1:05 PM	Democrat
10/16/56	ABC§§	3:00 – 3:05 PM	Democrat
10/16/56	NBC§	3:55 – 4:00 PM	Democrat
10/16/56	CBS	7:55 – 8:00 PM	Eisenhower
10/16/56	ABC	8:30 – 9:00 PM	Dewey
10/16/56	ABC	9:00 – 9:30 PM	Kefauver
10/16/56	NBC	10:25 – 10:30 PM	Charles Wilson
10/17/56	ABC§§	3:00 – 3:05 PM	Democrat
10/17/56	CBS	7:00 – 7:15 PM	Decision for Tomorrow
10/17/56	NBC	7:15 – 7:30 PM	Averell Harriman
10/17/56	CBS	9:00 – 9:30 PM	Nixon
10/17/56	CBS	9:55 – 10:00 PM	John F. Dulles
10/17/56	NBC	9:55 – 10:00 PM	Kefauver
10/17/56	ABC	10:50 – 10:55 PM	Mitchell
10/18/56	ABC§§	3:00 – 3:05 PM	Democrat
10/18/56	NBC	10:55 – 11:00 PM	Stevenson
10/18/56	CBS	10:55 – 11:00 PM	Robert Meyner
10/18/56	ABC	11:30 – 12:00 MID	Eisenhower
10/19/56	NBC	8:55 – 9:00 PM	Eugene Folsom
10/19/56	ABC	9:25 – 9:30 PM	Stevenson
10/20/56	CBS	8:55 – 9:00 PM	Kefauver
10/20/56	NBC§	8:55 – 9:00 PM	Stevenson
10/20/56	NBC	10:55 – 11:00 PM	Nixon
10/29/56	NBC	10:30 – 10:45 AM	Mrs. Roosevelt

§ Average of two spots.
§§ Average of five spots.

Sponsor	Type	Average Audience		
		% Total U.S.	Homes Reached	% Share of Audience
Democratic Nat'l. Commit.	30 Min. Speech	10.2	3,845	17.5
Democratic Nat'l. Commit.	Spot	.8	302	8.2
Citizens Committee	15 Min. Speech	Insufficient for Reporting		
Citizens for Eisenhower	30 Min. Speech	11.7	4,411	20.7
Stevenson-Kefauver Commit.	Spot	10.2	3,845	19.5
Nat'l. Ike Day Commit.	30 Min. Speech	22.7	8,558	37.5
Democratic Nat'l. Commit.	Spot	18.8	7,088	32.6
Democratic Nat'l. Commit.	Spot	4.6	1,734	9.4
Democratic Nat'l. Commit.	Spot	6.3	2,375	51.1
Democratic Nat'l. Commit.	Spot	.8	302	8.2
Democratic Nat'l. Commit.	Spot	3.9	1,470	30.6
Republican Nat'l. Commit.	Spot	13.2	4,976	19.7
Republican Nat'l. Commit.	Spot	8.4	3,167	19.0
Democratic Nat'l. Commit.	Spot	11.3	4,260	20.9
Stevenson-Kefauver Commit.	30 Min. Speech	2.4	905	7.3
Democratic Nat'l. Commit.	Spot	6.3	2,375	51.1
Democratic Nat'l. Commit.	Spot	.8	302	8.2
Democratic Nat'l. Commit.	Spot	3.9	1,470	30.6
Repub. Nat'l. Sen. Commit.	Spot	11.9	4,486	34.3
Rep. Nat'l. Cong. Commit.	30 Min. Speech	4.3	1,621	10.9
Stevenson-Kefauver Commit.	30 Min. Speech	4.3	1,621	8.8
Repub. Nat'l. Sen. Commit.	Spot	15.2	5,730	25.7
Democratic Nat'l. Commit.	Spot	.8	302	8.2
N.Y. Ctzns. for Ike & Dick	15 Min. Speech	Insufficient for Reporting		
N.Y. Democratic Commit.	15 Min. Speech	Insufficient for Reporting		
Republican Nat'l. Commit.	30 Min. Speech	15.5	5,844	24.9
Rep. Nat'l. Cong. Commit.	Spot	16.4	6,183	30.7
Democratic Nat'l. Commit.	Spot	16.5	6,221	29.2
Rep. Nat'l. Cong. Commit.	Spot	6.0	2,262	14.9
Democratic Nat'l. Commit.	Spot	.8	302	8.2
Stevenson-Kefauver Commit.	Spot	14.3	5,391	28.7
Stevenson-Kefauver Commit.	Spot	13.4	5,052	30.1
Rep. Nat'l. Cong. Commit.	30 Min. Speech	5.2	1,960	17.9
Rep. Nat'l. Cong. Commit.	Spot	11.9	4,486	21.6
Stevenson-Kefauver Commit.	Spot	5.9	2,224	16.9
Stevenson-Kefauver Commit.	Spot	26.3	9,915	41.0
Democratic Nat'l. Commit.	Spot	18.8	7,088	32.6
Rep. Nat'l. Sen. Commit.	Spot	17.6	6,635	34.7
Stevenson-Kefauver Commit.	15 Min. Speech	2.4	905	18.8

Network Television Programs and Spot Announcements: 1956
(continued)

Date	Network	Time	Person Appearing
10/29/56	NBC§§	3:55 - 4:00 PM	Democrat
10/29/56	ABC	8:30 - 9:00 PM	Stevenson
10/29/56	CBS	8:55 - 9:00 PM	Hoover
10/29/56	CBS	10:00 - 10:45 PM	Stevenson
10/29/56	NBC	10:25 - 10:30 PM	Citizens for Eisenhower
10/29/56	CBS	10:55 - 11:00 PM	Dr. Spock
10/30/56	ABC§	3:00 - 3:05 PM	Democrat
10/30/56	CBS	3:25 - 3:30 PM	Jones
10/30/56	NBC§§	3:55 - 4:00 PM	Democrat
10/30/56	NBC	8:25 - 8:30 PM	Dewey
10/30/56	CBS	9:25 - 9:30 PM	Stephans
10/30/56	NBC	10:25 - 10:30 PM	Stevenson
10/30/56	CBS	11:55 - 12:00 N	Stengel
10/31/56	CBS	8:55 - 9:00 PM	Interviews
10/31/56	NBC	9:55 - 10:00 PM	Mitchell
10/31/56	NBC	10:25 - 10:30 PM	Stevenson
11/ 1/56	CBS	1:55 - 2:00 PM	Mrs. Williams
11/ 1/56	ABC§	3:00 - 3:05 PM	Democrat
11/ 1/56	CBS	3:25 - 3:30 PM	Lamkin
11/ 1/56	CBS	9:25 - 9:30 PM	Interviews
11/ 1/56	NBC	9:30 - 10:00 PM	Eisenhower
11/ 1/56	NBC	10:55 - 11:00 PM	Nixon
11/ 1/56	CBS	11:00 - 11:15 PM	Stevenson
11/ 2/56	CBS	11:55 - 12:00 N	Lord
11/ 2/56	CBS	3:25 - 3:30 PM	Clinton Anderson
11/ 2/56	ABC	6:45 - 7:00 PM	Robert Wagner
11/ 2/56	CBS	7:00 - 7:15 PM	Dewey
11/ 2/56	NBC	8:55 - 9:00 PM	Stevenson
11/ 2/56	CBS	9:30 - 10:00 PM	Nixon
11/ 2/56	NBC	9:55 - 10:00 PM	Dewey
11/ 2/56	CBS	10:55 - 11:00 PM	Stephans
11/ 3/56	CBS	7:25 - 7:30 PM	Stephans
11/ 3/56	NBC	9:55 - 10:00 PM	Citizens for Eisenhower
11/ 3/56	ABC	9:55 - 10:00 PM	Thomas Finletter
11/ 3/56	NBC	10:30 - 11:00 PM	Arthur Larson
11/ 3/56	NBC	11:00 - 11:30 PM	Stevenson
11/ 5/56	NBC§§§	3:55 - 4:00 PM	Democrat
11/ 5/56	NBC	6:30 - 6:45 PM	Jacob Javits

§ Average of two spots.
§§ Average of three spots.

242

Sponsor	Type	Average Audience		
		% Total U.S.	Homes Reached	% Share of Audience
Democratic Nat'l. Commit.	Spot	5.8	2,187	31.6
Democratic Nat'l. Commit.	30 Min. Speech	8.1	3,054	13.9
Repub. Nat'l. Sen. Commit.	Spot	30.5	11,499	48.3
Democratic Nat'l. Commit.	45 Min. Speech	16.1	6,070	29.2
Citizens for Eisenhower	Spot	11.8	4,449	23.1
Stevenson-Kefauver Commit.	Spot	11.9	4,486	27.2
Stevenson-Kefauver Commit.	Spot	1.4	528	11.2
Repub. Nat'l. Sen. Commit.	Spot	7.2	2,903	40.2
Democratic Nat'l. Commit.	Spot	5.8	2,187	31.6
Rep. Nat'l. Cong. Commit.	Spot	15.9	5,994	19.8
Citizens for Eisenhower	Spot	17.8	6,711	29.2
Stevenson-Kefauver Commit.	Spot	10.6	3,996	19.6
Volunteers for Stev. Kef.	Spot.	6.3	2,375	44.0
Citizens for Eisenhower	Spot	22.0	8,294	36.2
Repub. Nat'l. Sen. Commit.	Spot	14.6	5,504	25.4
Stevenson-Kefauver Commit.	Spot	10.6	3,996	19.6
Stevenson-Kefauver Commit.	Spot	6.0	2,262	37.0
Stevenson-Kefauver Commit.	Spot	1.4	528	11.2
Repub. Nat'l. Sen. Commit.	Spot	6.9	2,601	43.0
Citizens for Eisenhower	Spot	26.5	9,991	30.8
Rep. Nat'l. Cong. Commit.	30 Min. Speech	20.2	7,615	32.0
Rep. Nat'l. Cong. Commit.	Spot	9.7	3,657	20.9
Liberal Party	15 Min. Speech	Insufficient for Reporting		
Repub. Nat'l. Sen. Commit.	Spot	6.5	2,451	43.9
Stevenson-Kefauver Commit.	Spot	5.6	2,111	30.7
N.Y. State Labor Comm.	15 Min. Speech	Insufficient for Reporting		
Republican State Commit.	15 Min. Speech	Insufficient for Reporting		
Stevenson-Kefauver Commit.	Spot	15.1	5,693	25.3
Rep. Nat'l. Cong. Commit.	30 Min. Speech	12.4	4,675	22.0
Citizens for Eisenhower	Spot	20.4	7,691	36.6
Citizens for Eisenhower	Spot	12.3	4,637	35.0
Citizens for Eisenhower	Spot	9.9	3,732	28.7
Citizens for Eisenhower	Spot	14.6	5,504	23.3
Volunteers for Stev. Kef.	Spot	9.5	3,582	19.2
Republican Nat'l. Commit.	30 Min. Speech	8.8	3,318	16.5
Stevenson-Kefauver Commit.	30 Min. Speech	7.5	2,828	21.0
Democratic Nat'l. Commit.	Spot	5.8	2,187	31.6
Citizens for Javits	15 Min. Speech	Insufficient for Reporting		

PRESIDENTIAL CAMPAIGN MEDIA EXPOSURE

Network Television Programs and Spot Announcements: 1956
(continued)

Date	Network	Time	Person Appearing
11/ 5/56	ABC	6:45 – 7:00 PM	Dewey
11/ 5/56	CBS	7:00 – 7:15 PM	Robert Wagner
11/ 5/56	NBC	8:55 – 9:00 PM	Dewey
11/ 5/56	ABC	11:00 – 12:00 MID	Eisenhower & Nixon
11/ 5/56	CBS	11:00 – 12:00 MID	Eisenhower & Nixon
11/ 5/56	NBC	11:00 – 12:00 MID	Eisenhower & Nixon

Sponsor	Type	Average Audience		
		% Total U.S.	Homes Reached	% Share of Audience
N.Y. Republican Commit.	15 Min. Speech	Insufficient for Reporting		
Democratic State Commit.	15 Min. Speech	Insufficient for Reporting		
Repub. Nat'l. Sen. Commit.	Spot	11.0	4,147	19.1
Citizens for Eisenhower	60 Min. Speech	2.4	905	12.8
Citizens for Eisenhower	60 Min. Speech	9.0	3,393	35.1
Citizens for Eisenhower	60 Min. Speech	7.8	2,941	29.8

PRESIDENTIAL CAMPAIGN MEDIA EXPOSURE

Network Television Programs and Spot Announcements: 1960

Date	Network	Time	Person Appearing
9/20/60	ABC	8:30 – 9:00 PM	Kennedy
10/ 3/60	CBS	8:30 – 9:00 PM	Lodge
10/10/60	NBC	8:30 – 9:00 PM	Republican
10/16/60	CBS	10:55 – 11:00 PM	Democrat
10/24/60	CBS[§]	1:55 – 2:00 PM	Democrat
10/24/60	ABC[§]	2:25 – 2:30 PM	Republican
10/24/60	CBS[§]	2:55 – 3:00 PM	Democrat
10/24/60	CBS	7:55 – 8:00 PM	Democrat
10/24/60	NBC	8:25 – 8:30 PM	Democrat
10/25/60	NBC	11:25 – 11:30 AM	Republican
10/25/60	NBC	11:55 – 12:00 N	Democrat
10/25/60	ABC[§§]	2:25 – 2:30 PM	Democrat
10/25/60	CBS	4:55 – 5:00 PM	Republican
10/25/60	NBC	8:25 – 8:30 PM	Democrat
10/25/60	CBS	9:00 – 9:30 PM	Nixon
10/25/60	CBS	9:55 – 10:00 PM	Republican
10/26/60	ABC[§]	2:25 – 2:30 PM	Republican
10/26/60	CBS	3:55 – 4:00 PM	Democrat
10/26/60	CBS	9:55 – 10:00 PM	Democrat
10/26/60	NBC[§]	9:55 – 10:00 PM	Republican
10/27/60	ABC[§§]	2:25 – 2:30 PM	Democrat
10/27/60	CBS[§]	2:55 – 3:00 PM	Democrat
10/27/60	CBS	8:25 – 8:30 PM	Democrat
10/27/60	NBC[§]	9:55 – 10:00 PM	Republican
10/28/60	NBC	10:55 – 11:00 AM	Democrat
10/28/60	NBC[§]	12:25 – 12:30 PM	Republican
10/28/60	ABC	12:55 – 1:00 PM	Republican
10/28/60	NBC	2:25 – 2:30 PM	Democrat
10/28/60	CBS[§]	4:55 – 5:00 PM	Democrat
10/28/60	NBC	8:25 – 8:30 PM	Democrat
10/28/60	NBC	9:55 – 10:00 PM	Democrat
10/28/60	ABC	10:00 – 10:30 PM	Eisenhower
10/29/60	ABC	9:55 – 10:00 PM	Republican
10/30/60	CBS	9:55 – 10:00 PM	Democrat
10/31/60	NBC	11:25 – 11:30 AM	Democrat
10/31/60	ABC[§]	12:55 – 1:00 PM	Republican
10/31/60	NBC[§]	3:55 – 4:00 PM	Democrat
10/31/60	NBC	8:25 – 8:30 PM	Republican
10/31/60	NBC	8:30 – 9:00 PM	Kennedy
11/ 1/60	NBC[§]	8:55 – 9:00 AM	Republican
11/ 1/60	NBC[§]	12:25 – 12:30 PM	Republican

§ Average of two spots.
§§ Average of three spots.

246

Sponsor	Type	% Total U.S.	Average Audience Homes Reached	% Share of Audience
Ctzns. for Kennedy–Johnson	30 Min. Speech	11.8	5,334	20.2
Republican Nat'l. Commit.	30 Min. Speech	11.6	5,243	17.9
Volunteers for Nixon–Lodge	30 Min. Speech	15.2	6,870	23.2
Democratic Nat'l. Commit.	Spot	17.5	7,910	39.9
Democratic Nat'l. Commit.	Spot	7.0	3,164	32.3
Independent TV Commit.	Spot	3.5	1,582	19.8
Ctzns. for Kennedy–Johnson	Spot	6.1	2,757	34.5
Ctzns. for Kennedy–Johnson	Spot	13.1	5,921	21.7
Democratic Nat'l. Commit.	Spot	14.3	6,464	22.9
Republican Nat'l. Commit.	Spot	7.5	3,390	45.7
Democratic Nat'l. Commit.	Spot	7.2	3,254	42.9
Ctzns. for Kennedy–Johnson	Spot	3.8	1,718	20.0
Independent TV Commit.	Spot	7.3	3,300	30.3
Ctzns. for Kennedy–Johnson	Spot	16.4	7,413	25.8
Rep. Nat'l. Cong. Commit.	30 Min. Speech	17.1	7,729	26.7
Independent TV Commit.	Spot	18.1	8,181	28.7
Independent TV Commit.	Spot	3.5	1,582	19.8
Ctzns. for Kennedy–Johnson	Spot	6.8	3,074	33.8
Ctzns. for Kennedy–Johnson	Spot	14.7	6,644	24.5
Republican Nat'l. Commit.	Spot	16.4	7,413	26.1
Ctzns. for Kennedy–Johnson	Spot	3.8	1,718	20.0
Ctzns. for Kennedy–Johnson	Spot	6.1	2,757	34.5
Ctzns. for Kennedy–Johnson	Spot	7.2	3,254	12.0
Republican Nat'l. Commit.	Spot	16.4	7,413	26.1
Democratic Nat'l. Commit.	Spot	6.2	2,802	40.0
Independent TV Commit.	Spot	6.9	3,119	30.8
Independent TV Commit.	Spot	2.9	1,311	14.1
Democratic Nat'l. Commit.	Spot	3.5	1,582	20.2
Ctzns. for Kennedy–Johnson	Spot	7.7	3,480	29.2
Democratic Nat'l. Commit.	Spot	14.6	6,599	25.7
Democratic Nat'l. Commit.	Spot	13.3	6,012	22.4
Volunteers for Nixon–Lodge	30 Min. Speech	17.9	8,091	33.4
Independent TV Commit.	Spot	11.0	4,972	17.8
Ctzns. for Kennedy–Johnson	Spot	19.7	8,904	32.3
Ctzns. for Kennedy–Johnson	Spot	8.6	3,887	43.2
Rep. Nat'l. Cong. Commit.	Spot	3.3	1,492	13.6
Ctzns. for Kennedy–Johnson	Spot	5.6	2,531	25.7
Independent TV Commit.	Spot	10.1	4,565	16.9
Democratic Nat'l. Commit.	30 Min. Speech	13.2	5,966	21.6
Republican Nat'l. Commit.	Spot	5.1	2,305	37.2
Independent TV Commit.	Spot	6.9	3,119	30.8

PRESIDENTIAL CAMPAIGN MEDIA EXPOSURE

Network Television Programs and Spot Announcements: 1960
(continued)

Date	Network	Time	Person Appearing
11/ 1/60	ABC§	12:55 – 1:00 PM	Democrat
11/ 1/60	CBS§	1:55 – 2:00 PM	Democrat
11/ 1/60	ABC§	2:25 – 2:30 PM	Republican
11/ 1/60	CBS	8:00 – 8:30 PM	Anderson
11/ 1/60	NBC	8:25 – 8:30 PM	Democrat
11/ 1/60	CBS	9:55 – 10:00 PM	Democrat
11/ 2/60	NBC	11:25 – 11:30 AM	Republican
11/ 2/60	NBC	11:55 – 12:00 N	Democrat
11/ 2/60	CBS	3:00 – 3:30 PM	Kennedys & H. Fonda
11/ 2/60	NBC	3:25 – 3:30 PM	Democrat
11/ 2/60	NBC	8:30 – 9:00 PM	Republican
11/ 2/60	NBC§	9:55 – 10:00 PM	Democrat
11/ 2/60	CBS	9:55 – 10:00 PM	Republican
11/ 2/60	CBS	10:55 – 11:00 PM	Democrat
11/ 3/60	NBC§	8:55 – 9:00 AM	Republican
11/ 3/60	ABC§	12:55 – 1:00 PM	Republican
11/ 3/60	CBS	1:55 – 2:00 PM	Republican
11/ 3/60	ABC§§	2:25 – 2:30 PM	Democrat
11/ 3/60	CBS§	4:55 – 5:00 PM	Democrat
11/ 3/60	NBC	8:25 – 8:30 PM	Democrat
11/ 3/60	CBS	8:25 – 8:30 PM	Republican
11/ 3/60	NBC§	9:55 – 10:00 PM	Democrat
11/ 3/60	NBC	10:25 – 10:30 PM	Republican
11/ 4/60	NBC	10:55 – 11:00 AM	Republican
11/ 4/60	ABC§	12:55 – 1:00 PM	Democrat
11/ 4/60	ABC§	2:25 – 2:30 PM	Republican
11/ 4/60	NBC§	3:55 – 4:00 PM	Democrat
11/ 4/60	CBS	3:55 – 4:00 PM	Republican
11/ 4/60	NBC	8:25 – 8:30 PM	Democrat
11/ 4/60	NBC	9:00 – 9:30 PM	Eisenhower
11/ 4/60	NBC	9:30 – 10:00 PM	**Kennedy**
11/ 5/60	CBS	9:30 – 10:00 PM	Kennedy
11/ 5/60	ABC	9:45 – 10:00 PM	Nixon
11/ 5/60	CBS	10:00 – 10:30 PM	Nixon
11/ 6/60	CBS	9:00 – 9:30 PM	Nixon
11/ 7/60	NBC	8:55 – 9:00 AM	Republican
11/ 7/60	NBC	11:25 – 11:30 AM	Republican
11/ 7/60	NBC	11:55 – 12:00 N	Democrat
11/ 7/60	ABC	12:55 – 1:00 PM	Republican

§ Average of two spots.
§§ Average of three spots.

Sponsor	Type	Average Audience % Total U.S.	Homes Reached	% Share of Audience
Ctzns. for Kennedy-Johnson	Spot	3.4	1,537	14.2
Democratic Nat'l. Commit.	Spot	7.0	3,164	32.3
Rep. Nat'l. Cong. Commit.	Spot	4.1	1,853	20.5
Independent TV Commit.	30 Min. Speech	9.9	4,475	16.2
Republican Committee				
Ctzns. for Kennedy-Johnson	Spot	16.0	7,232	26.1
Ctzns. for Kennedy-Johnson	Spot	17.6	7,955	29.3
Independent TV Commit.	Spot	9.5	4,294	50.0
Ctzns. for Kennedy-Johnson	Spot	9.0	4,068	45.0
Ctzns. for Kennedy-Johnson	30 Min. Speech	7.9	3,571	42.2
Ctzns. for Kennedy-Johnson	Spot	5.2	2,350	27.5
Repub. Nat'l. Sen. Commit.	30 Min. Speech	20.7	9,356	32.1
Ctzns. for Kennedy-Johnson	Spot	16.4	7,413	27.4
Rep. Nat'l. Cong. Commit.	Spot	15.1	6,825	25.3
Democratic Nat'l. Commit.	Spot	9.0	4,068	23.2
Republican Nat'l. Commit.	Spot	5.1	2,305	37.2
Rep. Nat'l. Cong. Commit.	Spot	3.3	1,492	13.6
Rep. Nat'l. Cong. Commit.	Spot	7.5	3,390	33.8
Ctzns. for Kennedy-Johnson	Spot	3.8	1,718	20.0
Ctzns. for Kennedy-Johnson	Spot	7.7	3,480	29.2
Ctzns. for Kennedy-Johnson	Spot	14.7	6,644	24.1
Rep. Nat'l. Cong. Commit.	Spot	12.0	5,424	19.7
Ctzns. for Kennedy-Johnson	Spot	16.4	7,413	27.4
Independent TV Commit.	Spot	13.7	6,192	25.5
Independent TV Commit.	Spot	6.3	2,848	40.9
Ctzns. for Kennedy-Johnson	Spot	3.4	1,537	14.2
Rep. Nat'l. Cong. Commit.	Spot	4.1	1,853	20.5
Ctzns. for Kennedy-Johnson	Spot	5.6	2,531	25.7
Rep. Nat'l. Cong. Commit.	Spot	7.5	3,390	35.4
Ctzns. for Kennedy-Johnson	Spot	9,1	4,113	15.6
Republican Nat'l. Commit.	30 Min. Speech	10.7	4,836	17.7
Dem. Party-Cook County	30 Min. Speech	11.8	5,334	20.5
Ctzns. for Kennedy-Johnson	30 Min. Speech	20.0	9,040	32.3
Rep. Nat'l. Cong. Commit.	15 Min. Speech	16.3	7,368	26.6
Rep. Nat'l. Cong. Commit.	30 Min. Speech	21.2	9,582	37.0
Independent TV Commit.	30 Min. Speech	16.3	7,368	25.4
Republican Nat'l. Commit.	Spot	4.7	2,124	40.2
Republican Nat'l. Commit.	Spot	8.6	3,887	43.4
Ctzns. for Kennedy-Johnson	Spot	8.5	3,842	41.9
Rep. Nat'l. Cong. Commit.	Spot	3.7	1,672	14.0

PRESIDENTIAL CAMPAIGN MEDIA EXPOSURE

Network Television Programs and Spot Announcements: 1960
(continued)

Date	Network	Time	Person Appearing
11/ 7/60	ABC	2:00 - 6:00 PM	Republicans
11/ 7/60	NBC	3:25 - 3:30 PM	Democrat
11/ 7/60	ABC	6:00 - 6:30 PM	Kennedy
11/ 7/60	ABC	6:30 - 6:45 PM	Dewey
11/ 7/60	CBS	6:30 - 6:45 PM	Kennedy-Hodges
11/ 7/60	NBC	7:00 - 7:15 PM	Kennedy-Hodges
11/ 7/60	NBC	8:25 - 8:30 PM	Democrat
11/ 7/60	CBS	10:30 - 11:00 PM	Republican
11/ 7/60	CBS	11:00 - 11:30 PM	Kennedys & Johnson
11/ 7/60	ABC	11:00 - 11:30 PM	Nixon
11/ 7/60	NBC	11:00 - 11:30 PM	Republican
11/ 7/60	NBC	11:30 - 12:00 MID	Walter Judd
	3 Networks Combined		
9/26/60	ABC,CBS,NBC	9:30 - 10:30 PM	Kennedy-Nixon
10/ 7/60	ABC,CBS,NBC	7:30 - 8:30 PM	Kennedy-Nixon
10/13/60	ABC,CBS,NBC	7:30 - 8:30 PM	Kennedy-Nixon

Sponsor	Type	Average Audience		
		% Total U.S.	Homes Reached	% Share of Audience
Independent TV Commit.	4 Hr. Telethon	7.2	3,254	26.7
Republican Nat'l. Commit.				
Volunteers for Nixon-Lodge				
Rep. Nat'l. Cong. Commit.				
Nat'l. Sen. Cong. Commit.				
Ctzns. for Kennedy-Johnson	Spot	7.1	3,209	28.7
Ctzns. for Kennedy-Johnson	30 Min. Speech	8.5	3,842	21.4
Repub. Nat'l. Sen. Commit.	15 Min. Speech	5.1	2,305	11.5
Ctzns. for Kennedy-Johnson	15 Min. Speech	9.9	4,475	20.0
Ctzns. for Kennedy-Johnson	15 Min. Speech	8.5	3,842	17.4
Ctzns. for Kennedy-Johnson	Spot	13.1	5,921	19.9
Independent TV Commit. &	30 Min. Speech	12.4	5,605	27.9
Volunteers for Nixon				
Ctzns. for Kennedy-Johnson	30 Min. Speech	17.7	8,000	51.0
Republican Nat'l. Commit.	30 Min. Speech	5.6	2,531	16.1
Volunteers for Nixon-Lodge	30 Min. Speech	5.1	2,305	14.7
Volunteers for Nixon-Lodge	30 Min. Speech	4.0	1,808	17.9
Great Debates - Free Time	60 Min. Debate	59.5	26,894	89.7
Great Debates - Free Time	60 Min. Debate	53.1	24,001	89.2
Great Debates - Free Time	60 Min. Debate	55.0	24,860	87.0

PRESIDENTIAL CAMPAIGN MEDIA EXPOSURE

Network Television Programs and Spot Announcements: 1964

Date	Network	Time	Person Appearing
9/14/64	CBS	2:25 - 2:30 PM	Republican
9/17/64	NBC	8:55 - 9:00 AM	Republican
9/18/64	CBS	9:30 - 10:00 PM	Goldwater
9/22/64	CBS	4:25 - 4:30 PM	Republican
9/22/64	NBC	9:30 - 10:00 PM	Conversation at Gettysburg
9/23/64	NBC	8:55 - 9:00 AM	Republican
9/25/64	NBC	11:25 - 11:30 AM	Democrat
9/29/64	NBC	12:25 - 12:30 PM	Democrat
9/30/64	NBC	8:55 - 9:00 AM	Republican
9/30/64	CBS	2:25 - 2:30 PM	Republican
9/30/64	NBC	3:55 - 4:00 PM	Democrat
10/ 1/64	CBS	3:55 - 4:00 PM	Democrat
10/ 5/64	NBC	11:25 - 11:30 AM	Democrat
10/ 5/64	NBC	11:55 - 12:00 N	Republican
10/ 6/64	NBC	8:55 - 9:00 AM	Republican
10/ 6/64	NBC	11:55 - 12:00 N	Democrat
10/ 6/64	CBS	3:55 - 4:00 PM	Democrat
10/ 6/64	NBC	9:30 - 10:00 PM	America Asks Goldwater
10/ 7/64	CBS	9:30 - 10:00 PM	Johnson
10/ 8/64	CBS	2:55 - 3:00 PM	Republican
10/ 9/64	ABC	9:30 - 10:00 PM	Real Job-Presidency
10/10/64	ABC	10:25 - 10:30 PM	Republican
10/11/64	ABC	10:55 - 11:00 PM	Democrat
10/11/64	CBS	10:55 - 11:00 PM	Democrat
10/12/64	NBC	8:55 - 9:00 AM	Republican
10/12/64	NBC	12:25 - 12:30 PM	Democrat
10/13/64	NBC	12:25 - 12:30 PM	Republican
10/13/64	CBS	2:55 - 3:00 PM	Democrat
10/13/64	NBC	9:30 - 10:00 PM	Milwaukee Rally
10/15/64	CBS	4:25 - 4:30 PM	Democrat
10/15/64	CBS	9:00 - 9:25 PM	Johnson
10/15/64	CBS§	9:25 - 9:30 PM	Republican
10/16/64	CBS	3:55 - 4:00 PM	Republican
10/16/64	CBS§	9:25 - 9:30 PM	Republican
10/18/64	NBC	3:30 - 5:00 PM	Golden Shower-Goldwater
10/18/64	CBS	10:55 - 11:00 PM	Republican
10/19/64	CBS	1:55 - 2:00 PM	Democrat
10/19/64	CBS	4:25 - 4:30 PM	Republican
10/19/64	CBS	7:55 - 8:00 PM	Republican

§ Average of two spots.

Sponsor	Type	% Total U.S.	Average Audience Homes Reached	% Share of Audience
Republican Nat'l. Commit.	Spot	9.1	4,790	40.8
Republican Nat'l. Commit.	Spot	2.9	1,530	22.5
Goldwater-Miller Commit.	30 Min. Speech	10.1	5,310	17.7
Republican Nat'l. Commit.	Spot	7.5	3,950	29.9
Republican Nat'l. Commit.	30 Min. Speech	8.6	4,520	13.2
Republican Nat'l. Commit.	Spot	4.6	2,420	34.6
Democratic Nat'l. Commit.	Spot	6.9	3,630	45.1
Democratic Nat'l. Commit.	Spot	6.9	3,630	26.3
Republican Nat'l. Commit.	Spot	3.4	1,790	28.8
Republican Nat'l. Commit.	Spot	10.5	5,520	45.3
Democratic Nat'l. Commit.	Spot	7.5	3,950	30.1
Democratic Nat'l. Commit	Spot	8.8	4,630	34.5
Democratic Nat'l. Commit.	Spot	6.6	3,470	37.7
Republican Nat'l. Commit.	Spot	6.4	3,370	33.2
Republican Nat'l. Commit.	Spot	4.2	2,210	28.6
Democratic Nat'l. Commit.	Spot	5.8	3,050	32.2
Democratic Nat'l. Commit.	Spot	10.0	5,260	38.9
Republican Nat'l. Commit.	30 Min. Speech	8.4	4,420	13.6
Johnson for Pres. Commit.	30 Min. Speech	13.2	6,940	21.9
Republican Nat'l. Commit.	Spot	6.6	3,470	20.7
Goldwater-Miller Commit.	30 Min. Speech	6.6	3,470	10.9
Republican Nat'l. Commit.	Spot	11.3	5,940	18.8
Democratic Nat'l. Commit.	Spot	14.3	7,520	27.1
Democratic Nat'l. Commit.	Spot	14.8	7,780	28.0
TV for Goldwater-Miller	Spot	3.6	1,890	24.3
Johnson for Pres. Commit.	Spot	6.6	3,470	22.1
TV for Goldwater-Miller	Spot	5.8	3,050	24.7
Democratic Nat'l. Commit.	Spot	8.9	4,680	38.0
Women Voters for Goldwater	30 Min. Speech	8.3	4,370	13.2
Democratic Nat'l. Commit.	Spot	6.4	3,370	17.4
Johnson for Pres. Commit.	30 Min. Speech	13.4	7,050	19.9
Republican Nat'l. Commit.	Spot	13.3	7,000	20.6
Republican Nat'l. Commit.	Spot	9.6	5,050	40.0
Republican Nat'l. Commit.	Spot	13.3	7,000	20.6
TV for Goldwater-Miller	90 Min. Speech	4.0	2,100	13.2
Republican Nat'l. Commit.	Spot	16.3	8,570	34.1
Democratic Nat'l. Commit.	Spot	12.5	6,580	45.8
Republican Nat'l. Commit.	Spot	9.4	4,940	30.1
Republican Nat'l. Commit.	Spot	18.8	9,890	29.1

Network Television Programs and Spot Announcements: 1964
(continued)

Date	Network	Time	Person Appearing
10/19/64	CBS	8:25 – 8:30 PM	Democrat
10/20/64	NBC§	8:55 – 9:00 AM	Republican
10/20/64	CBS	9:25 – 9:30 PM	Democrat
10/20/64	CBS	9:30 – 10:00 PM	Goldwater
10/21/64	NBC	3:55 – 4:00 PM	Democrat
10/21/64	ABC	10:30 – 11:00 PM	Goldwater-Miller
10/21/64	CBS	10:55 – 11:00 PM	Republican
10/22/64	NBC§	8:55 – 9:00 AM	Republican
10/22/64	NBC	11:55 – 12:00 N	Democrat
10/22/64	NBC	2:00 – 2:30 PM	Republican
10/22/64	NBC	3:55 – 4:00 PM	Republican
10/22/64	CBS§§	9:25 – 9:30 PM	Democrat
10/22/64	ABC	10:00 – 10:30 PM	In a Free Society
10/23/64	NBC	11:30 – 12:00 N	Brunch with Barry
10/23/64	CBS§§	9:25 – 9:30 PM	Democrat
10/24/64	CBS	8:25 – 8:30 PM	Democrat
10/24/64	NBC	8:30 – 9:00 PM	Democrat
10/24/64	ABC	9:25 – 9:30 PM	Republican
10/24/64	ABC	10:25 – 10:30 PM	Democrat
10/25/64	CBS	8:55 – 9:00 PM	Republican
10/25/64	CBS	10:25 – 10:30 PM	Democrat
10/25/64	ABC	10:55 – 11:00 PM	Democrat
10/26/64	NBC	8:55 – 9:00 AM	Republican
10/26/64	CBS	1:55 – 2:00 PM	Democrat
10/26/64	CBS	7:55 – 8:00 PM	Democrat
10/26/64	CBS	8:25 – 8:30 PM	Republican
10/27/64	NBC	12:25 – 12:30 PM	Democrat
10/27/64	CBS	1:55 – 2:00 PM	Republican
10/27/64	CBS	9:25 – 9:30 PM	Republican
10/27/64	NBC	9:30 – 10:00 PM	Time for Choosing
10/28/64	NBC	11:55 – 12:00 N	Republican
10/28/64	CBS	2:25 – 2:30 PM	Democrat
10/28/64	NBC	3:30 – 4:00 PM	Republican
10/28/64	CBS	8:30 – 9:00 PM	Johnson
10/28/64	CBS	10:55 – 11:00 PM	Democrat
10/29/64	NBC	8:55 – 9:00 AM	Republican

§ Average of two spots.
§§ Average of three spots.

Sponsor	Type	Average Audience % Total U.S.	Homes Reached	% Share of Audience
Democratic Nat'l. Commit.	Spot	20.1	10,570	29.6
TV for Goldwater-Miller	Spot	2.9	1,530	22.3
Democratic Nat'l. Commit.	Spot	17.5	9,210	27.3
TV for Goldwater-Miller	30 Min. Speech	13.1	6,890	20.8
Democratic Nat'l. Commit.	Spot	7.6	4,000	30.0
TV for Goldwater-Miller	30 Min. Speech	6.0	3,160	12.2
Republican Nat'l. Commit.	Spot	13.6	7,150	28.9
TV for Goldwater-Miller	Spot	2.9	1,530	22.3
Democratic Nat'l. Commit.	Spot	5.5	2,890	29.4
Ctzns. for Goldwater-Miller	30 Min. Speech	4.2	2,210	18.4
TV for Goldwater-Miller	Spot	5.2	2,740	19.9
Democratic Nat'l. Commit.	Spot	17.5	9,210	27.3
Republican Nat'l. Commit.	30 Min. Speech	9.2	4,840	18.0
Nat'l. Fed. Rep. Women Womens Div.-RNC Women for Goldw.-Miller Women Voters/Goldwater	30 Min. Speech	5.1	2,680	26.7
Democratic Nat'l. Commit.	Spot	17.5	9,210	27.3
Democratic Nat'l. Commit.	Spot	19.5	10,260	32.0
Women's Apparel Indep. Commit./LBJ	30 Min. Speech	8.3	4,370	13.4
TV for Goldwater-Miller	Spot	19.5	10,260	31.5
Democratic Nat'l. Commit.	Spot	7.9	4,160	13.1
Republican Nat'l. Commit.	Spot	20.9	10,990	30.9
Democratic Nat'l. Commit.	Spot	18.9	9,940	33.2
Democratic Nat'l. Commit.	Spot	9.9	5,210	21.2
Republican Nat'l. Commit.	Spot	3.1	1,630	23.5
Democratic Nat'l. Commit.	Spot	13.0	6,840	52.8
Democratic Nat'l. Commit.	Spot	17.3	9,100	26.6
Republican Nat'l. Commit.	Spot	20.3	10,680	29.5
Democratic Nat'l. Commit.	Spot	6.2	3,260	25.7
Republican Nat'l. Commit.	Spot	12.7	6,680	51.2
Republican Nat'l. Commit.	Spot	23.7	12,470	35.6
Reagan-Goldw. TV Commit.	30 Min. Speech	8.1	4,260	13.0
Republican Nat'l. Commit.	Spot	6.1	3,210	30.5
Democratic Nat'l. Commit.	Spot	9.8	5,150	45.2
Republican Nat'l. Commit.	30 Min. Speech	4.0	2,100	16.9
Johnson for Pres. Commit.	30 Min. Speech	10.2	5,370	15.8
Democratic Nat'l. Commit.	Spot	12.1	6,360	27.2
TV for Goldwater-Miller	Spot	4.3	2,260	28.1

Network Television Programs and Spot Announcements: 1964
(continued)

Date	Network	Time	Person Appearing
10/29/64	NBC	11:25 - 11:30 AM	Democrat
10/29/64	CBS	3:55 - 4:00 PM	Republican
10/29/64	CBS	9:30 - 10:00 PM	Goldwater
10/29/64	ABC	10:55 - 11:00 PM	Democrat
10/29/64	NBC§	11:15 - 11:30 PM	Republican
10/30/64	NBC	12:25 - 12:30 PM	Republican
10/30/64	CBS	1:30 - 2:00 PM	Goldwater
10/30/64	CBS	2:55 - 3:00 PM	Republican
10/30/64	CBS	4:25 - 4:30 PM	Democrat
10/30/64	CBS	9:25 - 9:30 PM	Democrat
10/30/64	NBC§	11:15 - 11:30 PM	Republican
10/31/64	NBC	8:00 - 9:00 PM	Time for Choosing
10/31/64	CBS	8:25 - 8:30 PM	Republican
10/31/64	ABC	9:25 - 9:30 PM	Democrat
10/31/64	ABC	10:25 - 10:30 PM	Republican
11/ 1/64	NBC	5:00 - 5:30 PM	Ronald Reagan
11/ 1/64	ABC	5:00 - 5:30 PM	Sorry, Senator Goldwater
11/ 1/64	ABC	5:30 - 6:00 PM	Brunch with Barry
11/ 1/64	CBS	8:55 - 9:00 PM	Democrat
11/ 1/64	CBS	10:25 - 10:30 PM	Republican
11/ 1/64	CBS	10:30 - 11:00 PM	Johnson
11/ 2/64	NBC	8:55 - 9:00 AM	Republican
11/ 2/64	NBC	11:55 - 12:00 N	Democrat
11/ 2/64	CBS	1:55 - 2:00 PM	Republican
11/ 2/64	CBS	2:00 - 2:30 PM	Johnson
11/ 2/64	CBS	2:55 - 3:00 PM	Democrat
11/ 2/64	NBC	3:55 - 4:00 PM	Republican
11/ 2/64	CBS	8:00 - 8:30 PM	Johnson
11/ 2/64	CBS	9:30 - 10:00 PM	Goldwater
11/ 2/64	ABC	9:30 - 10:00 PM	Democrat
11/ 2/64	NBC	10:00 - 10:30 PM	Pre-Election Special
11/ 2/64	ABC	10:00 - 10:30 PM	Republican
11/ 2/64	NBC	10:30 - 11:00 PM	Pre-Election Special
11/ 3/64	NBC	8:55 - 9:00 AM	Democrat

§ Average of two telecasts.

Sponsor	Type	% Total U.S.	Average Audience Homes Reached	% Share of Audience
Democratic Nat'l. Commit.	Spot	7.7	4,050	40.5
Republican Nat'l. Commit.	Spot	10.0	5,260	38.8
TV for Goldwater-Miller	30 Min. Speech	11.5	6,050	19.2
Democratic Nat'l. Commit.	Spot	9.3	4,890	20.9
TV for Goldwater-Miller	15 Min. Speech	4.3	2,260	13.5
Republican Nat'l. Commit.	Spot	5.2	2,740	22.3
Republican Nat'l. Commit.	30 Min. Speech	8.4	4,420	37.7
Republican Nat'l. Commit.	Spot	9.5	5,000	41.7
Democratic Nat'l. Commit.	Spot	7.5	3,950	27.8
Democratic Nat'l. Commit.	Spot	17.8	9,360	31.0
TV for Goldwater-Miller	15 Min. Speech	4.3	2,260	13.5
TV for Goldwater-Miller	60 Min. Speech	7.7	4,050	14.2
Republican Nat'l. Commit.	Spot	20.2	10,630	37.8
Democratic Nat'l. Commit.	Spot	14.4	7,570	25.2
Republican Nat'l. Commit.	Spot	10.3	5,420	18.7
TV for Goldwater-Miller	30 Min. Speech	5.7	3,000	17.1
Scientists, Engineers, Physicists for Johnson	30 Min. Speech	3.3	1,740	10.4
TV for Goldwater-Miller	30 Min. Speech	2.3	1,210	6.3
Democratic Nat'l. Commit.	Spot	22.1	11,620	32.8
Republican Nat'l. Commit.	Spot	16.4	8,630	31.0
Johnson for Pres. Commit.	30 Min. Speech	12.2	6,420	28.8
Republican Nat'l. Commit.	Spot	4.8	2,520	32.9
Democratic Nat'l. Commit.	Spot	5.2	2,740	28.0
Republican Nat'l. Commit.	Spot	11.2	5,890	47.9
Women's Apparel Indep. Commit./LBJ	30 Min. Speech	9.5	5,000	44.4
Democratic Nat'l. Commit.	Spot	10.4	5,470	44.3
Republican Nat'l. Commit.	Spot	6.8	3,580	26.5
President's Club-Johnson	30 Min. Speech	13.0	6,840	19.7
Republican Nat'l. Commit.	30 Min. Speech	14.7	7,730	25.6
Democratic Nat'l. Commit.	30 Min. Speech	10.2	5,370	17.8
Johnson for Pres. Commit.	30 Min. Speech	12.4	6,520	25.2
TV for Goldwater-Miller	30 Min. Speech	8.6	4,520	17.5
TV for Goldwater-Miller	30 Min. Speech	8.9	4,680	21.1
Democratic Nat'l. Commit.	Spot	4.1	2,160	26.5

PRESIDENTIAL CAMPAIGN MEDIA EXPOSURE

Network Television Programs and Spot Announcements: 1968

Date	Network	Time	Person Appearing
8/21/68	NBC	8:55 - 9:00 PM	Nixon-Agnew
8/23/68	CBS	8:30 - 9:00 PM	Nixon-Agnew
8/23/68	NBC§	8:55 - 9:00 PM	Nixon-Agnew
8/23/68	NBC	9:30 - 10:00 PM	Nixon-Agnew
9/ 3/68	NBC	7:30 - 8:00 PM	George Wallace
9/ 7/68	ABC	9:25 - 9:30 PM	Nixon-Agnew
9/ 9/68	ABC	9:00 - 9:30 PM	George Wallace
9/10/68	NBC	10:55 - 11:00 PM	Nixon
9/12/68	CBS	11:55 - 12:00 N	Nixon-Agnew
9/13/68	CBS	10:55 - 11:00 PM	Nixon-Agnew
9/17/68	NBC	10:55 - 11:00 PM	Nixon-Political
9/19/68	CBS	12:55 - 1:00 PM	Nixon-Agnew
9/19/68	CBS	10:55 - 11:00 PM	Nixon-Agnew
9/25/68	ABC	10:50 - 10:55 PM	Nixon-Agnew
9/26/68	CBS	3:55 - 4:00 PM	Nixon-Agnew
9/29/68	CBS	9:55 - 10:00 PM	Nixon-Agnew
9/30/68	NBC	7:30 - 8:00 PM	Humphrey-Muskie
10/ 1/68	CBS	10:00 - 10:30 PM	George Wallace
10/ 1/68	NBC	10:55 - 11:00 PM	Nixon-Political
10/ 2/68	CBS	10:55 - 11:00 PM	Nixon-Agnew
10/ 6/68	CBS	10:55 - 11:00 PM	Nixon-Agnew
10/ 7/68	CBS	3:25 - 3:30 PM	Nixon-Agnew
10/ 8/68	CBS	1:55 - 2:00 PM	Humphrey-Muskie
10/ 8/68	CBS	8:25 - 8:30 PM	Humphrey-Muskie
10/ 9/68	CBS	9:30 - 10:00 PM	Nixon-Agnew
10/ 9/68	ABC	10:55 - 11:00 PM	Humphrey for Pres.
10/ 9/68	CBS	10:55 - 11:00 PM	Humphrey-Muskie
10/11/68	CBS	12:55 - 1:00 PM	Humphrey-Muskie
10/11/68	CBS	8:25 - 8:30 PM	Nixon-Agnew
10/12/68	CBS	9:30 - 10:00 PM	Humphrey-Muskie
10/13/68	CBS	9:55 - 10:00 PM	Humphrey-Muskie
10/13/68	CBS	10:55 - 11:00 PM	Humphrey-Muskie
10/14/68	CBS	2:25 - 2:30 PM	Nixon-Agnew
10/14/68	CBS	10:55 - 11:00 PM	Humphrey-Muskie
10/15/68	CBS	12:55 - 1:00 PM	Humphrey-Muskie
10/15/68	CBS	8:25 - 8:30 PM	Nixon-Agnew
10/16/68	CBS	3:55 - 4:00 PM	Nixon-Agnew
10/16/68	CBS	8:25 - 8:30 PM	Humphrey-Muskie
10/17/68	CBS	1:55 - 2:00 PM	Nixon-Agnew
10/17/68	CBS	8:55 - 9:00 PM	Humphrey-Muskie
10/18/68	CBS	8:25 - 8:30 PM	Humphrey-Muskie
10/19/68	CBS	8:25 - 8:30 PM	Nixon-Agnew

§ Average of two spots.

Sponsor	Type	Average Audience % Total U.S.	Homes Reached	% Share of Audience
Ctzns. for Nixon-Agnew	Spot	3.6	2,020	30
Ctzns. for Nixon-Agnew	30 Min. Speech	10.4	5,820	26
Ctzns. for Nixon-Agnew	Spot	3.6	2,020	30
Ctzns. for Nixon-Agnew	30 Min. Speech	5.5	3,080	12
Wallace Campaign	30 Min. Speech	12.1	6,900	26
Ctzns. for Nixon-Agnew	Spot	13.9	7,920	24
Wallace Campaign	30 Min. Speech	8.5	4,850	14
Citizens for Nixon	Spot	10.8	6,160	25
Ctzns. for Nixon-Agnew	Spot	7.4	4,220	39
Ctzns. for Nixon-Agnew	Spot	15.4	8,780	34
Ctzns. for Nixon-Agnew	Spot	17.9	10,200	37
Ctzns. for Nixon-Agnew	Spot	8.7	4,960	40
Ctzns. for Nixon-Agnew	Spot	10.1	5,760	20
Ctzns. for Nixon-Agnew	Spot	10.0	5,700	21
Ctzns. for Nixon-Agnew	Spot	6.8	3,880	29
Ctzns. for Nixon-Agnew	Spot	17.5	9,980	27
Ctzns. for Humphrey-Muskie	30 Min. Speech	12.6	7,180	23
Wallace Campaign	30 Min. Speech	9.3	5,300	19
Nixon-Agnew Victory Commit.	Spot	13.3	7,580	33
Ctzns. for Nixon-Agnew	Spot	9.1	5,190	20
Ctzns. for Nixon-Agnew	Spot	17.3	9,860	36
Ctzns. for Nixon-Agnew	Spot	6.5	3,710	19
Ctzns. for Humphrey-Muskie	Spot	9.5	5,420	35
Ctzns. for Humphrey-Muskie	Spot	16.3	9,290	26
Ctzns. for Nixon-Agnew	30 Min. Speech	10.3	5,870	18
Ctzns. for Humphrey	Spot	8.2	4,670	20
Ctzns. for Humphrey-Muskie	Spot	9.7	5,530	24
Ctzns. for Humphrey-Muskie	Spot	9.0	5,130	38
Ctzns. for Nixon-Agnew	Spot	14.4	8,210	26
Ctzns. for Humphrey-Muskie	30 Min. Speech	10.4	5,930	18
Ctzns. for Humphrey-Muskie	Spot	18.5	10,550	30
Ctzns. for Humphrey-Muskie	Spot	14.1	8,040	29
Ctzns. for Nixon-Agnew	Spot	6.7	3,820	27
Ctzns. for Humphrey-Muskie	Spot	15.0	8,550	30
Ctzns. for Humphrey-Muskie	Spot	8.3	4,730	37
Ctzns. for Nixon-Agnew	Spot	18.3	10,430	28
Ctzns. for Nixon-Agnew	Spot	8.6	4,900	34
Ctzns. for Humphrey-Muskie	Spot	12.3	7,010	21
Ctzns. for Nixon-Agnew	Spot	8.8	5,020	32
Ctzns. for Humphrey-Muskie	Spot	14.3	8,150	23
Ctzns. for Humphrey-Muskie	Spot	14.6	8,320	25
Ctzns. for Nixon-Agnew	Spot	14.3	8,150	24

PRESIDENTIAL CAMPAIGN MEDIA EXPOSURE

Network Television Programs and Spot Announcements: 1968
(continued)

Date	Network	Time	Person Appearing
10/19/68	ABC	9:25 – 9:30 PM	George Wallace
10/20/68	CBS	8:55 – 9:00 PM	George Wallace
10/20/68	CBS	10:00 – 11:00 PM	Humphrey-Muskie
10/21/68	CBS	8:25 – 8:30 PM	George Wallace
10/21/68	CBS	10:55 – 11:00 PM	George Wallace
10/22/68	CBS	3:25 – 3:30 PM	Humphrey-Muskie
10/22/68	CBS	9:25 – 9:30 PM	Humphrey-Muskie
10/23/68	CBS	12:55 – 1:00 PM	Nixon-Agnew
10/24/68	CBS	2:25 – 2:30 PM	Nixon-Agnew
10/24/68	CBS	10:55 – 11:00 PM	George Wallace
10/25/68	CBS	3:55 – 4:00 PM	Humphrey-Muskie
10/25/68	ABC	8:30 – 9:00 PM	Humphrey-Muskie
10/25/68	CBS	10:55 – 11:00 PM	Nixon-Agnew
10/26/68	ABC	9:25 – 9:30 PM	Nixon-Agnew
10/26/68	ABC	10:25 – 10:30 PM	Humphrey for Pres.
10/27/68	CBS	8:55 – 9:00 PM	Nixon-Agnew
10/27/68	CBS	9:55 – 10:00 PM	Nixon-Agnew
10/27/68	NBC	10:00 – 10:30 PM	Nixon-Agnew
10/28/68	CBS	1:55 – 2:00 PM	Humphrey-Muskie
10/28/68	NBC	7:30 – 8:00 PM	George Wallace
10/28/68	CBS	8:25 – 8:30 PM	Nixon-Agnew
10/28/68	ABC	10:55 – 11:00 PM	George Wallace
10/29/68	NBC§	8:55 – 9:00 AM	Humphrey-Muskie
10/29/68	CBS	9:25 – 9:30 PM	Nixon-Agnew
10/29/68	NBC	10:55 – 11:00 PM	Humphrey-Muskie
10/30/68	NBC§	8:55 – 9:00 AM	Humphrey-Muskie
10/30/68	CBS	11:00 – 11:30 AM	Humphrey-Muskie
10/30/68	CBS	2:25 – 2:30 PM	Humphrey-Muskie
10/30/68	NBC	3:30 – 4:00 PM	Nixon-Agnew
10/30/68	CBS	8:25 – 8:30 PM	Nixon-Agnew
10/30/68	CBS	8:30 – 9:00 PM	Humphrey-Muskie
10/30/68	NBC	9:00 – 9:30 PM	Humphrey-Muskie
10/30/68	ABC	10:55 – 11:00 PM	George Wallace
10/31/68	NBC	8:55 – 9:00 AM	Nixon-Agnew
10/31/68	CBS	11:30 – 12:00 N	Nixon-Agnew
10/31/68	CBS	3:55 – 4:00 PM	Nixon-Agnew
10/31/68	ABC	9:30 – 10:30 PM	Nixon-Agnew
10/31/68	NBC	9:30 – 10:00 PM	Humphrey-Muskie
10/31/68	CBS	10:55 – 11:00 PM	Humphrey-Muskie
11/ 1/68	NBC	8:55 – 9:00 AM	Humphrey-Muskie
11/ 1/68	CBS	3:25 – 3:30 PM	Nixon-Agnew

§ Average of three spots.

Sponsor	Type	% Total U.S.	Average Audience Homes Reached	% Share of Audience
Wallace Campaign	Spot	15.6	8,890	26
Wallace Campaign	Spot	20.4	11,630	37
Ctzns. for Humphrey-Muskie	60 Min. Speech	11.4	6,500	19
Wallace Campaign	Spot	19.6	11,170	29
Wallace Campaign	Spot	15.0	8,550	30
Ctzns. for Humphrey-Muskie	Spot	7.7	4,390	30
Ctzns. for Humphrey-Muskie	Spot	19.4	11,060	31
Ctzns. for Nixon-Agnew	Spot	9.6	5,470	44
Ctzns. for Nixon-Agnew	Spot	7.0	3,990	27
Wallace Campaign	Spot	11.6	6,610	24
Ctzns. for Humphrey-Muskie	Spot	7.4	4,220	27
Ctzns. for Humphrey-Muskie	30 Min. Speech	7.6	4,330	14
Ctzns. for Nixon-Agnew	Spot	11.9	6,780	25
Ctzns. for Nixon-Agnew	Spot	17.7	10,090	30
Ctzns. for Humphrey	Spot	13.6	7,750	25
Ctzns. for Nixon-Agnew	Spot	19.8	11,290	30
Ctzns. for Nixon-Agnew	Spot	17.8	10,150	31
Ctzns. for Nixon-Agnew	30 Min. Speech	9.6	5,470	19
Ctzns. for Humphrey-Muskie	Spot	10.8	6,160	37
Wallace for President	30 Min. Speech	12.5	7,130	19
Ctzns. for Nixon-Agnew	Spot	19.7	11,230	31
Wallace Campaign	Spot	9.6	5,470	19
Ctzns. for Humphrey-Muskie	Spot	4.2	2,390	30
Ctzns. for Nixon-Agnew	Spot	22.7	12,940	35
Ctzns. for Humphrey-Muskie	Spot	15.0	8,550	37
Ctzns. for Humphrey-Muskie	Spot	4.2	2,390	30
Ctzns. for Humphrey-Muskie	30 Min. Speech	5.0	2,850	34
Ctzns. for Humphrey-Muskie	Spot	7.3	4,160	28
Nixon-Agnew Victory Comm.	30 Min. Speech	4.2	2,390	16
Nixon-Agnew Victory Comm.	Spot	12.8	7,300	21
Ctzns. for Humphrey-Muskie	30 Min. Speech	11.3	6,440	19
Ctzns. for Humphrey-Muskie	30 Min. Speech	13.1	7,470	22
Wallace Campaign	Spot	10.1	5,760	26
Ctzns. for Nixon-Agnew	Spot	4.4	2,510	31
Ctzns. for Nixon-Agnew	30 Min. Speech	4.7	2,680	28
Ctzns. for Nixon-Agnew	Spot	7.2	4,100	29
Ctzns. for Nixon-Agnew	60 Min. Speech	8.7	4,960	15
Ctzns. for Humphrey-Muskie	30 Min. Speech	10.1	5,760	17
Ctzns. for Humphrey-Muskie	Spot	16.7	9,520	37
Ctzns. for Humphrey-Muskie	Spot	4.2	2,390	30
Ctzns. for Nixon-Agnew	Spot	8.3	4,730	33

PRESIDENTIAL CAMPAIGN MEDIA EXPOSURE

Network Television Programs and Spot Announcements: 1968
(continued)

Date	Network	Time	Person Appearing
11/ 1/68	NBC	3:30 - 4:00 PM	Humphrey-Muskie
11/ 1/68	CBS	8:30 - 9:00 PM	Humphrey-Muskie
11/ 1/68	CBS	10:55 - 11:00 PM	George Wallace
11/ 2/68	NBC	8:00 - 8:30 PM	Nixon-Agnew
11/ 2/68	CBS	8:25 - 8:30 PM	Humphrey-Muskie
11/ 2/68	CBS	8:30 - 9:00 PM	Nixon-Agnew
11/ 2/68	NBC	9:00 - 9:30 PM	Humphrey-Muskie
11/ 2/68	ABC	10:25 - 10:30 PM	Nixon-Agnew
11/ 3/68	CBS	7:30 - 8:00 PM	Nixon-Agnew
11/ 3/68	NBC	8:30 - 9:00 PM	Humphrey-Muskie
11/ 3/68	CBS	8:55 - 9:00 PM	Humphrey-Muskie
11/ 4/68	CBS	12:55 - 1:00 PM	Nixon-Agnew
11/ 4/68	NBC	1:30 - 2:00 PM	Humphrey-Muskie
11/ 4/68	CBS	1:55 - 2:00 PM	Nixon-Agnew
11/ 4/68	NBC	3:30 - 4:00 PM	Nixon-Agnew
11/ 4/68	CBS	7:30 - 8:00 PM	Humphrey-Muskie
11/ 4/68	NBC	8:00 - 8:30 PM	Wallace for Pres.
11/ 4/68	ABC	8:30 - 10:30 PM	Humphrey-Political
11/ 4/68	CBS	8:30 - 9:00 PM	Nixon-Agnew
11/ 4/68	NBC	8:30 - 9:00 PM	Humphrey-Muskie
11/ 4/68	NBC	8:55 - 9:00 PM	Nixon-Agnew
11/ 4/68	CBS	9:00 - 9:30 PM	George Wallace
11/ 4/68	NBC	9:00 - 11:00 PM	Nixon-Agnew
11/ 4/68	ABC	10:30 - 11:00 PM	George Wallace
11/ 4/68	NBC	11:30 - 12:00 PM	Humphrey-Muskie

Sponsor	Type	% Total U.S.	Average Audience Homes Reached	% Share of Audience
Ctzns. for Humphrey-Muskie 30 Min. Speech		4.7	2,680	18
Ctzns. for Humphrey-Muskie 30 Min. Speech		13.4	7,640	24
Wallace Campaign	Spot	11.0	6,270	24
Ctzns. for Nixon-Agnew	30 Min. Speech	8.0	4,560	13
Ctzns. for Humphrey-Muskie	Spot	23.0	13,110	37
Ctzns. for Nixon-Agnew	30 Min. Speech	11.3	6,440	18
Ctzns. for Humphrey-Muskie 30 Min. Speech		9.5	5,420	16
Nixon-Agnew Victory Comm.	Spot	10.9	6,210	20
Nixon-Agnew Victory Comm.	30 Min. Speech	9.9	5,640	16
Ctzns. for Humphrey-Muskie 30 Min. Speech		11.6	6,610	18
Ctzns. for Humphrey-Muskie	Spot	23.3	13,280	36
Ctzns. for Nixon-Agnew	Spot	10.8	6,160	45
Ctzns. for Humphrey-Muskie 30 Min. Speech		5.7	3,250	21
Ctzns. for Nixon-Agnew	Spot	11.1	6,330	39
Ctzns. for Nixon-Agnew	30 Min. Speech	4.2	2,390	16
Ctzns. for Humphrey-Muskie 30 Min. Speech		16.0	9,120	26
Wallace for President	30 Min. Speech	13.9	7,920	21
Ctzns. for Humphrey-Muskie 120 Min. Speech		12.6	7,180	22
Ctzns. for Nixon-Agnew	30 Min. Speech	17.7	10,090	29
Ctzns. for Humphrey-Muskie 30 Min. Speech		12.3	7,010	20
Nixon-Agnew Victory Comm.	Spot	3.6	2,050	28
Wallace Campaign	30 Min. Speech	14.9	8,490	25
Ctzns. for Nixon-Agnew	120 Min. Speech	14.4	8,210	26
Wallace Campaign	30 Min. Speech	5.9	3,360	12
Ctzns. for Humphrey-Muskie 30 Min. Speech		5.3	3,020	22

263

Public Opinion Polls

The Gallup Polls are used exclusively in this section because they are the only Public Opinion Polls that not only span the entire 1948–1968 period but also are available in toto. Although there have been slight variations in wording and procedure since 1948, the following are the basic questions asked of the Gallup sample. The data included in Part VII is derived from these questions.

Preconvention, Party Member Preference

"Here is a list of men who have been mentioned as possible Presidential candidates for the Republican (or Democratic) party in (year). Which one would you like to see nominated as the Republican (or Democratic) candidate in (year)?"

Preconvention, Public Preference Among Major Party Candidates

"Suppose the Presidential election were being held today. If (candidate's name) were the Republican candidate and (candidate's name) were the Democratic candidate, which would you like to see win?" (Often within the same poll, this "trial heat" question tests one candidate against all the leading contenders of the opposition party so that there may be more than one entry for a candidate under a single date.)

Postconvention, Public Preference Between Major Party Candidates

"Suppose you were voting today for President of the United States. Here is a Gallup Poll Ballot listing the candidates for this office. Will you please mark the ballot for the candidates you favor as you would in a real election if it were being held today—and then drop the folded ballot in this box."

SOURCE

Public Opinion Polls

American Institute of Public Opinion, Princeton, New Jersey (Gallup Polls, 1948–1968).

PUBLIC OPINION POLLS: PRESIDENTIAL CANDIDATES 1948

Public Preference Among Major Party Candidates

Candidates	Date Poll Released				
	January 4	January 21	January 21	January 21	February 15
Democrats					
Truman	55	46	40	51	45
Republicans					
Dewey		41			
Eisenhower			47		
Stassen					41
Taft	33			31	
Other Party Candidates					
Wallace (Progressive)		7	6	8	6
Undecided, No Opinion, Other	12	6	7	10	8

Candidates	Date Poll Released					
	April 11	May 9	May 19	July 3	July 19	August 22
Democrats						
Truman	39	33	39	37	38	37
Republicans						
Dewey				48	49	48
Stassen	44	56				
Vandenberg			45			
Other Party Candidates						
Wallace (Progressive)	7	5	5	5	6	4
Thurmond (States Rights)						2
Undecided, No Opinion, Other	10	6	11	10	7	9

PUBLIC OPINION POLLS: PRESIDENTIAL CANDIDATES 1948

Public Preference Among Major Party Candidates
(continued)

Candidates	September 8	Date Poll Released September 24	November 1
Democrats			
Truman	36.5	39	44.5
Republicans			
Dewey	48.5	46.5	49.5
Other Party Candidates			
Wallace (Progressive)	5	3.5	4
Thurmond (States Rights)		2	2
Undecided, No Opinion, Other	10	10	

PUBLIC OPINION POLLS: PRESIDENTIAL CANDIDATES 1948

Party Member Preference Among Republicans

Candidates	Date Poll Released			
	March 14	April 25	May 14	June 14
Dewey	32	29	24	33
Stassen	15	31	37	26
Taft	14	9	8	10
Vandenberg	13	10	13	13
MacArthur	12	16	12	11
Warren	6	2	2	2
Martin	1	1	1	1
Saltonstall	1			
No Opinion, Other	1	2	3	4

Party Member Preference Among Democrats

Candidates	Date Poll Released	
	June 4	July 7
Truman	76	67
Marshall	10	12
Byrnes	3	4
Byrd	2	4
Farley	1	3
Douglas	1	2
Pepper		2
Forrestal	1	1
No Opinion, Other	6	5

Public Preference Among Major Party Candidates

Candidates	Date Poll Released				
	February 3	February 3	February 3	February 3	March 5
Democrats					
Kefauver					47
Truman	31	33	28	42	
Republicans					
Eisenhower			64		
Stassen	49				
Taft				45	41
Warren		55			
Undecided, No Opinion, Other	20	12	8	13	12

Candidates	Date Poll Released				
	March 7	April 18	April 20	May 16	May 21	June 11
Democrats						
Kefauver	32	49	30	49	36	35
Republicans						
Eisenhower	57		60		56	55
Taft		40		41		
Undecided, No Opinion, Other	11	11	10	10	8	10

PUBLIC OPINION POLLS: PRESIDENTIAL CANDIDATES 1952

Public Preference Among Major Party Candidates
(continued)

Candidates	June 16	August 10	Date Poll Released September 21	October 10	October 31	November 3
Democrats						
Stevenson	31	41	40	38	39.5	40
Republicans						
Eisenhower	59	47	55	50	47.5	47
Undecided, No Opinion, Other	10	12	5	12	13	13

PUBLIC OPINION POLLS: PRESIDENTIAL CANDIDATES 1952

Party Member Preference Among Republicans

| Candidates | Date Poll Released | | | | |
	February 13	March 2	April 9	May 2	June 4
Eisenhower	33	33	37	44	43
Taft	33	34	34	33	36
MacArthur	14	14	12	10	9
Warren	8	6	9	6	6
Stassen	5	6	4	3	3
Dewey	5	5	3	3	2
No Opinion, Other	2	2	1	1	1

Party Member Preference Among Democrats

| Candidates | Date Poll Released | | | | |
	February 15	April 7	May 9	June 8	July 14
Truman	36	32			
Kefauver	21	33	41	45	45
Barkley	17	8	9	17	18
Russell		7	8	10	10
Stevenson		2	11	10	12
Paul Douglas	8	5			
Vinson	6	4			
Byrd	7				
Harriman				5	5
Kerr				3	2
McMahen				1	1
No Opinion, Other		9	31	9	7

PUBLIC OPINION POLLS: PRESIDENTIAL CANDIDATES 1956

Public Preference Among Major Party Candidates

Candidates	Date Poll Released					
	February 11	February 13	March 7	April 16	April 18	May 23
Democrats						
Kefauver				38		
Stevenson	55	35	33		37	35
Republicans						
Eisenhower		61	63	59	61	62
Nixon	38					
Undecided, No Opinion, Other	7	4	4	3	2	3

Candidates	Date Poll Released						
	July 2	July 11	July 13	July 15	August 1	August 1	September 10
Democrats							
Harriman		46	32			32	
Stevenson	51			35	37		41
Republicans							
Eisenhower			64	62	61	65	52
Nixon	44	47					
Undecided, No Opinion, Other	5	7	4	3	2	3	7

PUBLIC OPINION POLLS: PRESIDENTIAL CANDIDATES 1956

Public Preference Among Major Party Candidates
(continued)

Candidates	Date Poll Released			
	September 26	October 10	October 26	November 4
Democrats				
Stevenson	41	40	41	39
Republicans				
Eisenhower	52	52	51	57
Undecided, No Opinion, Other	7	8	8	3

PUBLIC OPINION POLLS: PRESIDENTIAL CANDIDATES 1956

Party Member Preference Among Republicans

Eisenhower was the choice of 82% of Republican voters
on January 30, 1956 for their party's nomination.
When asked who their choice would be if Eisenhower did
not run, they responded: Warren 30%; Nixon 23%; Stassen
9%; Dewey 8%; Milton Eisenhower 5%; Knowland 5%; Lodge
4%; Dulles 3%; Dirksen 2%; No Opinion 11%.

Party Member Preference Among Democrats

Candidates	February 6	March 5	Date Poll Released April 11	May 21	June 29
Stevenson	48	51	39	41	45
Kefauver	17	18	33	29	16
Harriman	8	8	6	6	12
Russell	4	4	4	3	5
Rayburn	4	4			2
Lausche	3	2	2	3	3
Johnson	3	2	3	4	4
Williams		2	3		
Douglas		2			
Symington			2	2	4
No Opinion, Other	12	7	8	12	9

PUBLIC OPINION POLLS: PRESIDENTIAL CANDIDATES 1960

Public Preference Among Major Party Candidates

| Candidates | Date Poll Released | | | | | |
	January 24	January 27	March 4	March 6	March 30	April 1
Democrats						
Johnson					46	
Kennedy	47		50			53
Stevenson		45		45		
Republicans						
Nixon	53	55	50	55	54	47

| Candidates | Date Poll Released | | | | | | |
	April 29	May 1	May 4	May 15	May 18	May 20	May 25
Democrats							
Johnson	46						
Kennedy			54			51	57
Stevenson		48			47		
Symington				44			
Republicans							
Nixon	54	52	46	56	53	49	
Rockefeller							43

| Candidates | Date Poll Released | | | | | |
	June 12	June 15	June 15	June 15	July 6	July 17
Democrats						
Johnson			44			
Kennedy	49				52	52
Stevenson		44				
Symington				43		
Republicans						
Nixon	51	56	56	57	48	48

PUBLIC OPINION POLLS: PRESIDENTIAL CANDIDATES 1960

Public Preference Among Major Party Candidates
(continued)

Candidates	Date Poll Released			
	August 17	August 31	September 14	October 12
Democrats				
Kennedy	44	47	48	49
Republicans				
Nixon	50	47	47	46
Undecided, No Opinion, Other	6	6	5	5

Candidates	Date Poll Released		
	October 26	November 4	November 7
Democrats			
Kennedy	49	51	49
Republicans			
Nixon	45	45	48
Undecided, No Opinion, Other	6	4	3

PUBLIC OPINION POLLS: PRESIDENTIAL CANDIDATES 1960

Party Member Preference Among Republicans

Candidates	Date Poll Released			
	January 20	May 22	June 17	July 24
Nixon	84	75	72	75
Lodge	6	2	5	4
Herter	2			2
Mitchell	2			
Goldwater	1			
Halleck	1			
Rockefeller		13	14	12
Milton Eisenhower		4	4	2
No Opinion, Other	4	6	5	5

Party Member Preference Among Democrats

Candidates	Date Poll Released						
	January 29	February 26	March 27	April 20	May 27	June 17	July 10
Kennedy	32	35	34	39	41	42	41
Stevenson	28	23	23	21	21	24	25
Johnson	12	13	15	11	11	14	16
Kefauver	6	6					
Symington	6	5	6	6	7	8	7
Humphrey	5	6	5	7	7		
Brown	2		3	3			
Williams	2						
Meyner	1	2					
No Opinion, Other	6	10	14	13	13	12	11

PUBLIC OPINION POLLS: PRESIDENTIAL CANDIDATES 1964

Public Preference Among Major Party Candidates

Candidates	Date Poll Released				
	January 1	January 3	January 24	January 24	January 24
Democrats					
Johnson	69	75	68	71	77
Republicans					
Lodge			25		
Nixon	24	20		24	
Rockefeller					16
Undecided, No Opinion, Other	7	5	7	5	7

Candidates	Date Poll Released				
	January 24	February 28	February 28	March 18	March 18
Democrats					
Johnson	75	69	68	68	68
Republicans					
Goldwater	18				
Lodge			27		27
Nixon		27		27	
Undecided, No Opinion, Other	7	4	5	5	5

PUBLIC OPINION POLLS: PRESIDENTIAL CANDIDATES 1964

Public Preference Among Major Party Candidates
(continued)

Candidates	Date Poll Released						
	April 19	July 1	July 1	July 1	July 10	July 10	August 9
Democrats							
Johnson	65	70	69	77	67	76	59
Republicans							
Goldwater						20	31
Lodge	30						
Nixon		27					
Scranton			26	18	27		
Undecided, No Opinion, Other	5	3	5	5	6	4	10

Candidates	Date Poll Released				
	August 23	September 16	October 4	October 12	November 2
Democrats					
Johnson	65	65	62	64	61
Republicans					
Goldwater	29	29	32	29	32
Undecided, No Opinion, Other	6	6	6	7	7

PUBLIC OPINION POLLS: PRESIDENTIAL CANDIDATES 1964

Party Member Preference Among Republicans

Candidates	Date Poll Released							
	Jan. 5	Feb. 16	March 20	April 17	May 3	May 17	June 21	July 12
Nixon	29	31	34	26	28	27	25	
Goldwater	23	20	17	14	14	15	21	34
Lodge	19	12	16	42	37	36	26	
Rockefeller	12	16	13	6	9	7	10	
Romney	8	5	6	4	3	4	5	
Scranton	4	7	5	4	4	5	9	60
No Opinion, Other	5	9	9	4	5	6	4	6

PUBLIC OPINION POLLS: PRESIDENTIAL CANDIDATES 1968

Public Preference Among Major Party Candidates

Candidates	Date Poll Released				
	January 7	January 7	February 25	February 25	February 25
Democrats					
Johnson	46	39	39	41	37
Republicans					
Nixon	41	30	39		
Rockefeller				46	40
Other Party Candidates					
Wallace		11	11		13
McCarthy		12			
Undecided, No Opinion, Other	13	8	11	13	10

Candidates	Date Poll Released						
	February 25	March 27	April 20	April 20	April 20	May 12	May 12
Democrats							
Humphrey			34				33
Johnson	42	39					
Kennedy				38			
McCarthy					38	31	
Republicans							
Nixon	42	41	43	41	41		
Rockefeller						40	40
Other Party Candidates							
Wallace		14	9	10	10	17	16
Undecided, No Opinion, Other	16	6	14	11	11	12	11

PUBLIC OPINION POLLS: PRESIDENTIAL CANDIDATES 1968

Public Preference Among Major Party Candidates
(continued)

Candidates	Date Poll Released						
	May 12	May 12	May 12	May 12	June 12	June 12	June 12
Democrats							
Humphrey	36				42	40	
Kennedy		32	28				
McCarthy				37			38
Republicans							
Nixon	39	42		39	36		40
Rockefeller			42			35	
Other Party Candidates							
Wallace	14	15	18	14	14	17	13
Undecided, No Opinion, Other	11	11	12	10	8	8	9

Candidates	Date Poll Released					
	June 12	June 23	June 23	June 23	June 23	July 11
Democrats						
Humphrey		42	38			36
McCarthy	34			41	39	
Republicans						
Nixon		37		39		
Rockefeller	40		39		38	36
Other Party Candidates						
Wallace	17	14	17	14	16	21
Undecided, No Opinion, Other	9	7	6	6	7	7

PUBLIC OPINION POLLS: PRESIDENTIAL CANDIDATES 1968

Public Preference Among Major Party Candidates
(continued)

Candidates	Date Poll Released					
	July 11	July 12	July 12	July 31	July 31	July 31
Democrats						
Humphrey	40					36
McCarthy		37	39	36	35	
Republicans						
Nixon	35		36	41		
Rockefeller		35			36	36
Other Party Candidates						
Wallace	16	20	18	16	20	21
Undecided, No Opinion, Other	9	8	7	7	9	7

Candidates	Date Poll Released				
	July 31	August 21	August 21	September 15	September 29
Democrats					
Humphrey	38		29	31	28
McCarthy		37			
Republicans					
Nixon	40	42	45	43	43
Other Party Candidates					
Wallace	16	16	18	19	21
Undecided, No Opinion, Other	6	5	8	7	8

PUBLIC OPINION POLLS: PRESIDENTIAL CANDIDATES 1968

Public Preference Among Major Party Candidates
(continued)

Candidates	October 10	October 22	Date Poll Released October 27	November 4	Final
Democrats					
Humphrey	29	31	36	40	42
Republicans					
Nixon	44	43	44	42	43
Other Party Candidates					
Wallace	20	20	15	14	15
Undecided, No Opinion, Other	7	6	5	4	

PUBLIC OPINION POLLS: PRESIDENTIAL CANDIDATES 1968

Party Member Preference Among Republicans

Candidates	January	February 21	March 4	March 27	July 28
			Date Poll Released		
Nixon	42	51	49	60	60
Rockefeller	27	25	22	24	23
Reagan	8	8	11	6	7
Romney	12	7	7		
Percy	5	3	4	5	2
Hatfield	2	2	1		1
Lindsay	1	2	3		4
Gavin	1	1			
Stassen			1		1
No Opinion, Other	2	1	2	5	2

Party Member Preference Among Democrats

Candidates	March 17	March 24	March 24	April 14	April 28
			Date Poll Released		
Kennedy	44	44		35	28
Johnson	45	41	59		
McCarthy			29	23	33
Humphrey				31	25
No Opinion, Other	11	15	12		14

285

PUBLIC OPINION POLLS: PRESIDENTIAL CANDIDATES 1968

Party Member Preference Among Democrats
(continued)

| Candidates | Date Poll Released | | | | |
	May 15	June 23	July 10	August 7	August 21
Kennedy	31				
McCarthy	19	37	39	39	42
Humphrey	40	56	52	53	46
No Opinion, Other	10	7	9	8	12

PART VIII

Voting Participation in Presidential Elections

NOTE

Registration data for the years 1948, 1952, and 1956 was in some cases impossible to obtain, simply because records were not kept. Reliable estimates were used when available. West Virginia in 1960 and Indiana in 1968 had total registrations that exceeded the voting age population of the state as reported by the U.S. Census Bureau. This may be a result of the fact that both states have permanent registration, which would mean some delay in clearing the registration lists of those not eligible due to moving, death, etc. In any case, the figures as reported are used as best estimates.

SOURCES

Registration Data

Compiled from the records of the various Secretaries of State.

Voting Age Population

U.S. Bureau of the Census. STATISTICAL ABSTRACT OF THE UNITED STATES: 1969 (90th Edition). Washington, D.C., 1969.

Actual Vote Cast for President

Scammon, Richard M. (ed.). AMERICA AT THE POLLS: A HANDBOOK OF AMERICAN PRESIDENTIAL ELECTION STATISTICS: 1920–1964. Pittsburgh: University of Pittsburgh Press, 1965.

VOTING PARTICIPATION IN PRESIDENTIAL ELECTIONS

Number and Percentage of Potential and Registered Voters Who Voted in
the Presidential Election of 1948

States	Voting Age Population (Thousands)	Registered Voters	Votes Cast	Percent Voting Age Voting	Percent Registered Voting
Alabama	1,698	A	214,980	12.7	
Arizona	404	240,998	177,065	43.8	73.5
Arkansas	1,070	463,411	242,475	22.7	52.3
California	6,856	5,061,997	4,021,538	58.7	79.4
Colorado	804	641,747	515,237	64.1	80.3
Connecticut	1,394	1,033,901	883,518	63.4	85.5
Delaware	209	A	139,073	66.5	
Florida	1,679	1,003,503	577,643	34.4	57.6
Georgia	2,059	F	418,844	20.3	
Idaho	331	A	214,816	64.9	
Illinois	5,873	F	3,984,046	67.8	
Indiana	2,547	2,236,591	1,656,212	65.0	74.1
Iowa	1,661	B	1,038,264	62.5	
Kansas	1,235	B	788,819	63.9	
Kentucky	1,660	A	822,658	49.6	
Louisiana	1,541	F	416,336	27.0	
Maine	558	F	264,787	47.5	
Maryland	1,472	F	596,748	40.5	
Massachusetts	3,209	2,484,938	2,107,146	65.7	84.8
Michigan	4,041	A	2,109,609	52.2	
Minnesota	1,858	B	1,212,226	65.2	

VOTING PARTICIPATION IN PRESIDENTIAL ELECTIONS

Number and Percentage of Potential and Registered Voters Who Voted in
the Presidential Election of 1948
(continued)

States	Voting Age Population (Thousands)	Registered Voters	Votes Cast	Percent Voting Age Voting	Percent Registered Voting
Mississippi	1,156	A	192,190	16.6	
Missouri	2,590	B	1,578,628	61.0	
Montana	344	269,779	224,278	65.2	83.1
Nebraska	824	B	488,940	59.3	
Nevada	106	F	62,117	58.6	
New Hampshire	346	312,644	231,440	66.9	74.0
New Jersey	3,309	2,380,295	1,949,555	58.9	81.9
New Mexico	329	F	187,063	56.9	
New York	10,210	7,044,676	6,177,337	60.5	87.7
North Carolina	2,162	F	791,209	36.6	
North Dakota	346	C	220,716	63.8	
Ohio	5,281	B	2,936,071	55.6	
Oklahoma	1,288	A	721,599	56.0	
Oregon	941	694,635	524,080	55.7	75.4
Pennsylvania	6,874	4,452,131	3,735,348	54.3	83.9
Rhode Island	528	382,340	327,702	62.1	85.7
South Carolina	1,069	F	142,571	13.3	
South Dakota	377	A	250,105	66.3	
Tennessee	1,940	C	550,283	28.4	
Texas	4,665	1,720,093	1,249,577	26.8	72.6
Utah	372	F	276,306	74.3	

VOTING PARTICIPATION IN PRESIDENTIAL ELECTIONS

Number and Percentage of Potential and Registered Voters Who Voted in
the Presidential Election of 1948
(continued)

States	Voting Age Population (Thousands)	Registered Voters	Votes Cast	Percent Voting Age Voting	Percent Registered Voting
Vermont	229	191,521	123,382	53.9	64.4
Virginia	1,901	A	419,256	22.1	
Washington	1,480	1,304,406	905,058	61.2	69.4
West Virginia	1,115	1,103,928	748,750	67.2	67.8
Wisconsin	2,165	B	1,276,800	59.0	
Wyoming	164	A	101,425	61.8	
District of Columbia	610	D			
Totals	94,877		48,793,826	51.4	

A Registration required but no central records maintained
B Registration required only in cities and counties over a certain size
C Registration not required
D Not eligible to cast ballots for President
E Estimate
F Registration, but no information available

VOTING PARTICIPATION IN PRESIDENTIAL ELECTIONS

Number and Percentage of Potential and Registered Voters Who Voted in
the Presidential Election of 1952

States	Voting Age Population (Thousands)	Registered Voters	Votes Cast	Percent Voting Age Voting	Percent Registered Voting
Alabama	1,742	A	426,120	24.4	
Arizona	481	330,083	260,570	54.2	78.9
Arkansas	1,081	555,470	404,800	37.4	72.9
California	7,591	5,998,300	5,141,849	67.7	85.7
Colorado	843	752,030	630,103	74.7	83.8
Connecticut	1,385	1,185,234	1,096,911	79.2	92.5
Delaware	219	A	174,025	79.5	
Florida	1,975	1,213,472	989,337	50.1	81.5
Georgia	2,191	1,313,788	655,785	29.9	49.9
Idaho	338	A	276,254	81.7	
Illinois	5,927	5,303,521	4,481,058	75.6	84.5
Indiana	2,641	2,616,091	1,955,049	74.0	74.7
Iowa	1,683	B	1,268,773	75.4	
Kansas	1,250	B	896,166	71.7	
Kentucky	1,687	A	993,148	58.9	
Louisiana	1,639	1,056,511	651,952	39.8	64.5
Maine	565	520,000E	351,786	62.3	67.7
Maryland	1,542	1,084,138	902,074	58.5	83.2
Massachusetts	3,079	2,666,025	2,383,398	77.4	89.4
Michigan	4,193	A	2,798,592	66.7	
Minnesota	1,917	B	1,379,483	72.0	

291

VOTING PARTICIPATION IN PRESIDENTIAL ELECTIONS

Number and Percentage of Potential and Registered Voters Who Voted in
the Presidential Election of 1952
(continued)

States	Voting Age Population (Thousands)	Registered Voters	Votes Cast	Percent Voting Age Voting	Percent Registered Voting
Mississippi	1,189	A	258,532	21.7	
Missouri	2,633	B	1,892,062	71.9	
Montana	367	304,053	265,037	72.2	87.2
Nebraska	835	B	609,660	73.0	
Nevada	115	101,248	82,190	71.5	81.2
New Hampshire	348	338,204	272,950	78.4	80.7
New Jersey	3,418	2,744,165	2,418,554	70.8	88.1
New Mexico	393	360,000E	238,608	60.7	66.3
New York	10,492	7,841,613	7,128,239	67.9	90.9
North Carolina	2,302	1,804,238	1,210,910	52.6	67.1
North Dakota	360	C	270,127	75.0	
Ohio	5,310	B	3,700,758	69.7	
Oklahoma	1,328	A	948,984	71.5	
Oregon	1,034	851,516	695,059	67.2	81.6
Pennsylvania	6,941	5,341,970	4,580,969	66.0	85.8
Rhode Island	510	447,249	414,498	81.3	92.7
South Carolina	1,164	625,000	341,087	29.3	54.6
South Dakota	394	A	294,283	74.7	
Tennessee	2,001	A	892,553	44.6	
Texas	4,930	2,338,261	2,075,946	42.1	88.8

VOTING PARTICIPATION IN PRESIDENTIAL ELECTIONS

Number and Percentage of Potential and Registered Voters Who Voted in
the Presidential Election of 1952
(continued)

States	Voting Age Population (Thousands)	Registered Voters	Votes Cast	Percent Voting Age Voting	Percent Registered Voting
Utah	406	375,000E	329,554	81.2	87.9
Vermont	233	201,000	153,557	65.9	76.4
Virginia	1,964	A	619,689	31.6	
Washington	1,540	1,392,594	1,102,708	71.6	79.2
West Virginia	1,191	1,176,428	873,548	73.3	74.3
Wisconsin	2,204	B	1,607,370	72.9	
Wyoming	173	A	129,253	74.7	
District of Columbia	572	D			
Totals	98,279		61,550,918	62.6	

A Registration required but no central records maintained
B Registration required only in cities and counties over a certain size
C Registration not required
D Not eligible to cast ballots for President
E Estimate

VOTING PARTICIPATION IN PRESIDENTIAL ELECTIONS

Number and Percentage of Potential and Registered Voters Who Voted in
the Presidential Election of 1956

States	Voting Age Population (Thousands)	Registered Voters	Votes Cast	Percent Voting Age Voting	Percent Registered Voting
Alabama	1,760	A	496,861	28.2	
Arizona	573	367,661	290,173	50.6	78.9
Arkansas	1,023	580,645	406,572	39.7	70.0
California	8,593	6,408,821	5,466,355	63.6	85.3
Colorado	975	789,204	657,074	67.4	83.3
Connecticut	1,464	1,242,267	1,117,121	76.3	89.9
Delaware	248	188,062	177,988	71.8	94.6
Florida	2,460	1,606,750	1,125,762	45.8	70.1
Georgia	2,261	1,310,586	669,655	29.6	51.1
Idaho	353	A	272,989	77.3	
Illinois	6,046	5,217,858	4,407,407	72.9	84.5
Indiana	2,761	2,467,459	1,974,607	71.5	80.0
Iowa	1,693	B	1,234,564	72.9	
Kansas	1,294	B	866,243	66.9	
Kentucky	1,799	A	1,053,805	58.6	
Louisiana	1,704	1,057,687	617,544	36.2	58.4
Maine	562	F	351,706	62.6	
Maryland	1,717	1,185,098	932,827	54.3	78.7
Massachusetts	3,113	2,671,369	2,348,506	75.4	87.9
Michigan	4,538	3,128,572	3,080,468	67.9	98.5
Minnesota	1,986	B	1,340,005	67.5	

VOTING PARTICIPATION IN PRESIDENTIAL ELECTIONS

Number and Percentage of Potential and Registered Voters Who Voted in
the Presidential Election of 1956
(continued)

States	Voting Age Population (Thousands)	Registered Voters	Votes Cast	Percent Voting Age Voting	Percent Registered Voting
Mississippi	1,146	A	248,104	21.6	
Missouri	2,712	B	1,832,562	67.6	
Montana	384	316,444	271,171	70.6	85.7
Nebraska	863	B	577,137	66.9	
Nevada	154	120,984	96,689	62.8	79.9
New Hampshire	356	337,591	266,994	75.0	79.1
New Jersey	3,613	2,846,794	2,484,312	68.8	87.3
New Mexico	427	F	253,926	59.5	
New York	10,786	7,715,154	7,095,971	65.8	92.0
North Carolina	2,429	2,000,000E	1,165,592	48.0	58.3
North Dakota	361	C	253,991	70.4	
Ohio	5,720	B	3,702,265	64.7	
Oklahoma	1,356	A	859,350	63.4	
Oregon	1,084	877,952	736,132	67.9	83.8
Pennsylvania	6,991	5,422,150	4,576,503	65.5	84.4
Rhode Island	528	439,575	387,609	73.4	88.2
South Carolina	1,199	761,162	300,583	25.1	39.5
South Dakota	401	A	293,857	73.3	
Tennessee	2,037	A	939,404	46.1	
Texas	5,170	2,410,188	1,955,168	37.8	81.1
Utah	445	379,903	333,995	75.1	87.9

VOTING PARTICIPATION IN PRESIDENTIAL ELECTIONS

Number and Percentage of Potential and Registered Voters Who Voted in
the Presidential Election of 1956
(continued)

States	Voting Age Population (Thousands)	Registered Voters	Votes Cast	Percent Voting Age Voting	Percent Registered Voting
Vermont	228	200,381	152,978	67.1	76.3
Virginia	2,093	A	697,978	33.3	
Washington	1,631	1,451,375	1,150,889	71.0	79.3
West Virginia	1,109	1,107,453	830,831	75.0	75.0
Wisconsin	2,310	B	1,550,558	67.1	
Wyoming	183	A	124,127	67.8	
District of Columbia	525	D			
Totals	103,166		62,026,908	60.1	

A Registration required but no central records maintained
B Registration required only in cities and counties over a certain size
C Registration not required
D Not eligible to cast ballots for President
E Estimate
F Registration but no information available

VOTING PARTICIPATION IN PRESIDENTIAL ELECTIONS

Number and Percentage of Potential and Registered Voters Who Voted in
the Presidential Election of 1960

States	Voting Age Population (Thousands)	Registered Voters	Votes Cast	Percent Voting Age Voting	Percent Registered Voting
Alabama	1,828	A	570,225	31.1	
Alaska	103	C	60,762	58.9	
Arizona	741	474,124	398,491	53.7	84.0
Arkansas	1,041	603,795	428,509	41.1	70.9
California	9,583	7,464,626	6,506,578	67.8	87.1
Colorado	1,027	882,422	736,236	71.6	83.4
Connecticut	1,587	1,320,954	1,222,883	77.0	92.5
Delaware	263	232,333	196,683	74.7	84.6
Florida	3,086	2,016,586	1,544,176	50.0	76.5
Georgia	2,354	1,302,139	733,349	31.1	56.3
Hawaii	313	202,059	184,705	59.0	91.4
Idaho	373	362,704	300,450	80.5	82.8
Illinois	6,220	5,499,469	4,757,409	76.4	86.5
Indiana	2,776	2,268,420	2,135,360	76.9	94.1
Iowa	1,658	B	1,273,810	76.8	
Kansas	1,294	B	928,825	71.7	
Kentucky	1,859	A	1,124,462	60.4	
Louisiana	1,790	1,152,398	807,891	45.1	70.1
Maine	570	537,922	421,767	73.9	78.4
Maryland	1,810	1,329,279	1,055,349	58.3	79.3
Massachusetts	3,212	2,720,359	2,469,480	76.8	90.7

VOTING PARTICIPATION IN PRESIDENTIAL ELECTIONS

Number and Percentage of Potential and Registered Voters Who Voted in
the Presidential Election of 1960
(continued)

States	Voting Age Population (Thousands)	Registered Voters	Votes Cast	Percent Voting Age Voting	Percent Registered Voting
Michigan	4,564	3,454,804	3,318,097	72.7	96.0
Minnesota	2,001	B	1,541,887	77.0	
Mississippi	1,162	A	298,171	25.6	
Missouri	2,665	B	1,934,422	72.5	
Montana	387	322,876	277,579	71.7	85.9
Nebraska	851	B	613,095	72.0	
Nevada	176	128,898	107,267	60.9	83.2
New Hampshire	369	353,717	295,761	80.1	83.6
New Jersey	3,860	3,073,894	2,773,111	71.8	90.2
New Mexico	482	423,265	311,107	64.5	73.5
New York	10,897	8,359,947	7,291,079	66.9	87.2
North Carolina	2,528	2,071,780	1,368,556	54.1	66.0
North Dakota	352	C	278,431	79.0	
Ohio	5,837	B	4,161,859	71.3	
Oklahoma	1,404	1,019,759	903,150	64.3	88.5
Oregon	1,072	900,616	776,421	72.4	86.2
Pennsylvania	7,085	5,687,837	5,006,541	70.6	88.0
Rhode Island	524	471,114	405,535	77.3	86.0
South Carolina	1,230	595,989	386,688	31.4	64.8
South Dakota	389	A	306,487	78.7	
Tennessee	2,086	1,718,168	1,051,792	50.4	61.2

VOTING PARTICIPATION IN PRESIDENTIAL ELECTIONS

Number and Percentage of Potential and Registered Voters Who Voted in
the Presidential Election of 1960
(continued)

States	Voting Age Population (Thousands)	Registered Voters	Votes Cast	Percent Voting Age Voting	Percent Registered Voting
Texas	5,452	2,594,254	2,311,084	42.3	89.0
Utah	475	419,095	374,709	78.8	89.4
Vermont	230	206,034	167,324	72.7	81.2
Virginia	2,241	978,307	771,449	34.4	78.8
Washington	1,676	1,527,516	1,241,572	74.0	81.2
West Virginia	1,076	1,090,042	837,781	77.8	76.8
Wisconsin	2,352	B	1,729,082	73.5	
Wyoming	189	B	140,782	74.4	
District of Columbia	501	D			
Totals	107,597		68,838,219	64.0	

A Registration required but no central records maintained
B Registration required only in cities and counties over a certain size
C Registration not required
D Not eligible to cast ballots for President

VOTING PARTICIPATION IN PRESIDENTIAL ELECTIONS

Number and Percentage of Potential and Registered Voters Who Voted in
the Presidential Election of 1964

States	Voting Age Population (Thousands)	Registered Voters	Votes Cast	Percent Voting Age Voting	Percent Registered Voting
Alabama	1,906	1,057,477	689,818	36.2	65.2
Alaska	106	C	67,259	63.5	
Arizona	846	584,337	480,770	56.8	82.3
Arkansas	1,112	715,528	560,426	50.4	78.3
California	10,671	8,184,143	7,057,586	66.1	86.2
Colorado	1,091	933,312	776,986	71.2	83.3
Connecticut	1,698	1,373,443	1,218,578	71.8	88.7
Delaware	279	245,494	201,320	72.2	82.0
Florida	3,406	2,501,546	1,854,481	54.4	74.1
Georgia	2,538	1,669,778	1,139,335	44.9	68.2
Hawaii	338	239,361	207,271	61.3	86.6
Idaho	378	364,925	292,477	77.4	80.1
Illinois	6,348	5,534,676	4,702,841	74.1	85.0
Indiana	2,827	2,628,627	2,091,606	74.0	79.6
Iowa	1,636	B	1,184,539	72.4	
Kansas	1,295	B	857,901	61.5	
Kentucky	1,934	A	1,046,105	54.1	
Louisiana	1,874	1,201,785	896,293	47.8	74.6
Maine	565	522,236	380,965	67.4	72.9
Maryland	1,960	1,410,281	1,116,457	57.0	79.2
Massachusetts	3,239	2,723,598	2,344,798	72.4	86.1

VOTING PARTICIPATION IN PRESIDENTIAL ELECTIONS

Number and Percentage of Potential and Registered Voters Who Voted in
the Presidential Election of 1964
(continued)

States	Voting Age Population (Thousands)	Registered Voters	Votes Cast	Percent Voting Age Voting	Percent Registered Voting
Michigan	4,658	3,351,730	3,203,102	68.8	95.6
Minnesota	2,018	B	1,554,462	77.0	
Mississippi	1,214	A	409,146	33.7	
Missouri	2,705	B	1,817,879	67.2	
Montana	388	327,477	278,628	71.8	85.1
Nebraska	855	B	584,154	68.3	
Nevada	243	163,475	135,433	55.7	82.8
New Hampshire	392	365,224	288,093	73.5	78.9
New Jersey	4,094	3,253,603	2,847,663	69.6	87.5
New Mexico	500	464,911	328,645	65.7	70.7
New York	11,253	8,443,430	7,166,275	63.7	84.9
North Carolina	2,680	1,933,763	1,424,983	53.2	73.7
North Dakota	352	C	258,389	73.4	
Ohio	5,966	B	3,969,196	66.5	
Oklahoma	1,459	1,058,465	932,499	63.9	88.1
Oregon	1,129	932,461	786,305	69.6	84.3
Pennsylvania	7,075	5,728,359	4,822,690	68.2	84.2
Rhode Island	532	472,659	390,091	73.3	82.5
South Carolina	1,311	772,572	524,779	40.0	67.9
South Dakota	389	A	293,118	75.4	
Tennessee	2,213	1,628,825	1,144,046	51.7	70.2

VOTING PARTICIPATION IN PRESIDENTIAL ELECTIONS

Number and Percentage of Potential and Registered Voters Who Voted in
the Presidential Election of 1964
(continued)

States	Voting Age Population (Thousands)	Registered Voters	Votes Cast	Percent Voting Age Voting	Percent Registered Voting
Texas	5,783	2,984,766	2,626,811	45.4	88.0
Utah	506	448,463	401,413	79.3	89.5
Vermont	232	209,225	163,089	70.3	77.9
Virginia	2,418	1,305,383	1,042,267	43.1	79.8
Washington	1,705	1,582,046	1,258,374	73.8	79.5
West Virginia	1,064	1,055,429	792,040	74.4	75.0
Wisconsin	2,387	B	1,691,815	70.9	
Wyoming	188	B	142,716	75.9	
District of Columbia	497	219,000E	198,597	40.0	90.7
Totals	112,250		70,644,510	62.9	

A Registration required but no central records maintained
B Registration required only in cities and counties over a certain size
C Registration not required
E Estimate

VOTING PARTICIPATION IN PRESIDENTIAL ELECTIONS

Number and Percentage of Potential and Registered Voters Who Voted in
the Presidential Election of 1968

States	Voting Age Population (Thousands)	Registered Voters	Votes Cast	Percent Voting Age Voting	Percent Registered Voting
Alabama	2,034	1,389,198	1,049,909	51.6	75.6
Alaska	123	C	83,035	67.5	
Arizona	932	614,763	486,936	52.2	79.2
Arkansas	1,169	769,704	619,969	53.0	80.5
California	11,645	8,587,673	7,251,587	62.3	84.4
Colorado	1,153	970,575	810,251	70.3	83.5
Connecticut	1,817	1,435,298	1,254,932	69.1	87.4
Delaware	300	262,032	214,367	71.5	81.8
Florida	3,772	2,765,316	2,187,805	58.0	79.1
Georgia	2,776	1,960,436	1,250,101	45.0	63.8
Hawaii	376	274,164	236,218	62.8	86.2
Idaho	398	366,532	291,183	73.2	79.4
Illinois	6,565	5,676,131	4,619,424	70.4	81.4
Indiana	2,952	3,044,186	2,123,561	71.9	69.8
Iowa	1,650	B	1,167,679	70.8	
Kansas	1,350	B	872,783	64.7	
Kentucky	2,021	A	1,055,893	52.2	
Louisiana	2,012	1,451,836	1,097,450	54.3	75.6
Maine	570	529,137	392,936	68.9	74.3
Maryland	2,137	1,595,436	1,235,039	57.8	77.4
Massachusetts	3,344	2,725,058	2,331,699	69.9	85.6

VOTING PARTICIPATION IN PRESIDENTIAL ELECTIONS

Number and Percentage of Potential and Registered Voters Who Voted in
the Presidential Election of 1968
(continued)

States	Voting Age Population (Thousands)	Registered Voters	Votes Cast	Percent Voting Age Voting	Percent Registered Voting
Michigan	4,953	3,336,677	3,306,221	66.8	99.1
Minnesota	2,089	B	1,588,510	76.0	
Mississippi	1,274	A	654,509	51.4	
Missouri	2,792	B	1,809,502	64.8	
Montana	398	331,078	274,404	68.9	82.9
Nebraska	854	668,512	536,851	62.9	80.3
Nevada	276	188,811	154,218	55.9	81.7
New Hampshire	421	378,706	297,298	70.6	78.5
New Jersey	4,376	3,310,043	2,875,395	65.7	86.9
New Mexico	519	445,776	327,281	63.1	73.4
New York	11,702	8,109,259	6,790,066	58.0	83.7
North Carolina	2,873	2,077,538	1,587,493	55.3	76.4
North Dakota	357	C	247,882	69.4	
Ohio	6,225	B	3,959,698	63.6	
Oklahoma	1,504	1,273,008	943,086	62.7	74.1
Oregon	1,237	971,851	818,547	66.2	84.2
Pennsylvania	7,252	5,599,364	4,747,928	65.5	84.8
Rhode Island	545	471,122	384,938	70.6	81.7
South Carolina	1,400	853,014	666,978	47.6	78.2
South Dakota	382	348,254	281,264	73.6	80.8
Tennessee	2,345	1,676,000E	1,248,617	53.2	74.5

VOTING PARTICIPATION IN PRESIDENTIAL ELECTIONS

Number and Percentage of Potential and Registered Voters Who Voted in
the Presidential Election of 1968
(continued)

States	Voting Age Population (Thousands)	Registered Voters	Votes Cast	Percent Voting Age Voting	Percent Registered Voting
Texas	6,205	4,073,576	3,078,917	49.6	75.6
Utah	552	542,793	422,568	76.6	77.9
Vermont	246	222,024	161,375	65.6	72.7
Virginia	2,579	1,737,214	1,358,930	52.7	78.2
Washington	1,794	1,646,831	1,304,281	72.7	79.2
West Virginia	1,079	993,024	754,206	69.9	76.0
Wisconsin	2,468	B	1,689,196	68.4	
Wyoming	183	B	127,205	69.5	
District of Columbia	497	201,937	170,578	34.3	84.5
Totals	118,465		73,203,260	61.8	

A Registration required but no central records maintained
B Registration required only in cities and counties over a certain size
C Registration not required
E Estimate

Presidential Election Results

NOTE

The following abbreviations are used in Part IX:

D—Democratic
R—Republican
SR—States' Rights
U—Unpledged Electors
AIP—American Independent Party

SOURCES

1948–1964 Presidential Election Results

Scammon, Richard M. (ed.). AMERICA AT THE POLLS: A HANDBOOK OF AMERICAN PRESIDENTIAL ELECTION STATISTICS: 1920–1964. Pittsburgh: University of Pittsburgh Press, 1965.

1968 Presidential Election Results

Compiled from the records of the various Secretaries of State.

PRESIDENTIAL ELECTION RESULTS

POPULAR VOTE: 1948

State	Republican	Democratic	All Others	Total Vote Cast
Alabama	40,930		174,050	214,980
Alaska				
Arizona	77,597	95,251	4,217	177,065
Arkansas	50,959	149,659	41,857	242,475
California	1,895,269	1,913,134	213,135	4,021,538
Colorado	239,714	267,288	8,235	515,237
Connecticut	437,754	423,297	22,467	883,518
Delaware	69,588	67,813	1,672	139,073
Florida	194,280	281,988	101,375	577,643
Georgia	76,691	254,646	87,507	418,844
Hawaii				
Idaho	101,514	107,370	5,932	214,816
Illinois	1,961,103	1,994,715	28,228	3,984,046
Indiana	821,079	807,831	27,302	1,656,212
Iowa	494,018	522,380	21,866	1,038,264
Kansas	423,039	351,902	13,878	788,819
Kentucky	341,210	466,756	14,692	822,658
Louisiana	72,657	136,344	207,335	416,336
Maine	150,234	111,916	2,637	264,787
Maryland	294,814	286,521	15,413	596,748
Massachusetts	909,370	1,151,788	45,988	2,107,146
Michigan	1,038,595	1,003,448	67,566	2,109,609
Minnesota	483,617	692,966	35,643	1,212,226

POPULAR VOTE: 1948
(continued)

State	Republican	Democratic	All Others	Total Vote Cast
Mississippi	5,043	19,384	167,763	192,190
Missouri	655,039	917,315	6,274	1,578,628
Montana	96,770	119,071	8,437	224,278
Nebraska	264,774	224,165	1	488,940
Nevada	29,357	31,291	1,469	62,117
New Hampshire	121,299	107,995	2,146	231,440
New Jersey	981,124	895,455	72,976	1,949,555
New Mexico	80,303	105,464	1,296	187,063
New York	2,841,163	2,780,204	555,970	6,177,337
North Carolina	258,572	459,070	73,567	791,209
North Dakota	115,139	95,812	9,765	220,716
Ohio	1,445,684	1,452,791	37,596	2,936,071
Oklahoma	268,817	452,782		721,599
Oregon	260,904	243,147	20,029	524,080
Pennsylvania	1,902,197	1,752,426	80,725	3,735,348
Rhode Island	135,787	188,736	3,179	327,702
South Carolina	5,386	34,423	102,762	142,571
South Dakota	129,651	117,653	2,801	250,105
Tennessee	202,914	270,402	76,967	550,283
Texas	303,467	824,235	121,875	1,249,577
Utah	124,402	149,151	2,753	276,306
Vermont	75,926	45,557	1,899	123,382
Virginia	172,070	200,786	46,400	419,256

PRESIDENTIAL ELECTION RESULTS

POPULAR VOTE: 1948
(continued)

State	Republican	Democratic	All Others	Total Vote Cast
Washington	386,314	476,165	42,579	905,058
West Virginia	316,251	429,188	3,311	748,750
Wisconsin	590,959	647,310	38,531	1,276,800
Wyoming	47,947	52,354	1,124	101,425
Total	21,991,291	24,179,345	2,623,190	48,793,826

PRESIDENTIAL ELECTION RESULTS

ELECTION OF 1948:
PARTY PERCENTAGES, PLURALITY AND ELECTORAL VOTE

State	Republican	Democratic	Plurality		Electoral Vote	
Alabama	19.0		SR	130,513	SR	11
Alaska						
Arizona	43.8	53.8	D	17,654	D	4
Arkansas	21.0	61.7	D	98,700	D	9
California	47.1	47.6	D	17,865	D	25
Colorado	46.5	51.9	D	27,574	D	6
Connecticut	49.5	47.9	R	14,457	R	8
Delaware	50.0	48.8	R	1,775	R	3
Florida	33.6	48.8	D	87,708	D	8
Georgia	18.3	60.8	D	169,511	D	12
Hawaii						
Idaho	47.3	50.0	D	5,856	D	4
Illinois	49.2	50.1	D	33,612	D	28
Indiana	49.6	48.8	R	13,248	R	13
Iowa	47.6	50.3	D	28,362	D	10
Kansas	53.6	44.6	R	71,137	R	8
Kentucky	41.5	56.7	D	125,546	D	11
Louisiana	17.5	32.7	SR	67,946	SR	10
Maine	56.7	42.3	R	38,318	R	5
Maryland	49.4	48.0	R	8,293	R	8
Massachusetts	43.2	54.7	D	242,418	D	16
Michigan	49.2	47.6	R	35,147	R	19

ELECTION OF 1948:
PARTY PERCENTAGES, PLURALITY AND ELECTORAL VOTE
(continued)

State	Republican	Democratic	Plurality		Electoral Vote	
Minnesota	39.9	57.2	D	209,349	D	11
Mississippi	2.6	10.1	SR	148,154	SR	9
Missouri	41.5	58.1	D	262,276	D	15
Montana	43.1	53.1	D	22,301	D	4
Nebraska	54.2	45.8	R	40,609	R	6
Nevada	47.3	50.4	D	1,934	D	3
New Hampshire	52.4	46.7	R	13,304	R	4
New Jersey	50.3	45.9	R	85,669	R	16
New Mexico	42.9	56.4	D	25,161	D	4
New York	46.0	45.0	R	60,959	R	47
North Carolina	32.7	58.0	D	200,498	D	14
North Dakota	52.2	43.4	R	19,327	R	4
Ohio	49.2	49.5	D	7,107	D	25
Oklahoma	37.3	62.7	D	183,965	D	10
Oregon	49.8	46.4	R	17,757	R	6
Pennsylvania	50.9	46.9	R	149,771	R	35
Rhode Island	41.4	57.6	D	52,949	D	4
South Carolina	3.8	24.1	SR	68,184	SR	8
South Dakota	51.8	47.0	R	11,998	R	4
Tennessee	36.9	49.1	D	67,488	D	11
					SR	1
Texas	24.3	66.0	D	520,768	D	23

ELECTION OF 1948:
PARTY PERCENTAGES, PLURALITY AND ELECTORAL VOTE
(continued)

State	Republican	Democratic	Plurality		Electoral Vote	
Utah	45.0	54.0	D	24,749	D	4
Vermont	61.5	36.9	R	30,369	R	3
Virginia	41.0	47.9	D	28,716	D	11
Washington	42.7	52.6	D	89,851	D	8
West Virginia	42.2	57.3	D	112,937	D	8
Wisconsin	46.3	50.7	D	56,351	D	12
Wyoming	47.3	51.6	D	4,407	D	3
Total	45.1	49.6	D 2,188,054		SR	39
					R	189
					D	303
						531

PRESIDENTIAL ELECTION RESULTS

POPULAR VOTE: 1952

State	Republican	Democratic	All Others	Total Vote Cast
Alabama	149,231	275,075	1,814	426,120
Alaska				
Arizona	152,042	108,528		260,570
Arkansas	177,155	226,300	1,345	404,800
California	2,897,310	2,197,548	46,991	5,141,849
Colorado	379,782	245,504	4,817	630,103
Connecticut	611,012	481,649	4,250	1,096,911
Delaware	90,059	83,315	651	174,025
Florida	544,036	444,950	351	989,337
Georgia	198,961	456,823	1	655,785
Hawaii				
Idaho	180,707	95,081	466	276,254
Illinois	2,457,327	2,013,920	9,811	4,481,058
Indiana	1,136,259	801,530	17,260	1,955,049
Iowa	808,906	451,513	8,354	1,268,773
Kansas	616,302	273,296	6,568	896,166
Kentucky	495,029	495,729	2,390	993,148
Louisiana	306,925	345,027		651,952
Maine	232,353	118,806	627	351,786
Maryland	499,424	395,337	7,313	902,074
Massachusetts	1,292,325	1,083,525	7,548	2,383,398
Michigan	1,551,529	1,230,657	16,406	2,798,592
Minnesota	763,211	608,458	7,814	1,379,483

POPULAR VOTE: 1952
(continued)

State	Republican	Democratic	All Others	Total Vote Cast
Mississippi	112,966	172,566		285,532
Missouri	959,429	929,830	2,803	1,892,062
Montana	157,394	106,213	1,430	265,037
Nebraska	421,603	188,057		609,660
Nevada	50,502	31,688		82,190
New Hampshire	166,287	106,663		272,950
New Jersey	1,373,613	1,015,902	29,039	2,418,554
New Mexico	132,170	105,661	777	238,608
New York	3,952,813	3,104,601	70,825	7,128,239
North Carolina	558,107	652,803		1,210,910
North Dakota	191,712	76,694	1,721	270,127
Ohio	2,100,391	1,600,367		3,700,758
Oklahoma	518,045	430,939		948,984
Oregon	420,815	270,579	3,665	695,059
Pennsylvania	2,415,789	2,146,269	18,911	4,580,969
Rhode Island	210,935	203,293	270	414,498
South Carolina	168,082	173,004	1	341,087
South Dakota	203,857	90,426		294,283
Tennessee	446,147	443,710	2,696	892,553
Texas	1,102,878	969,228	3,840	2,075,946
Utah	194,190	135,364		329,554
Vermont	109,717	43,355	485	153,557
Virginia	349,037	268,677	1,975	619,689

PRESIDENTIAL ELECTION RESULTS

POPULAR VOTE: 1952
(continued)

State	Republican	Democratic	All Others	Total Vote Cast
Washington	599,107	492,845	10,756	1,102,708
West Virginia	419,970	453,578		873,548
Wisconsin	979,744	622,175	5,451	1,607,370
Wyoming	81,049	47,934	270	129,253
Total	33,936,234	27,314,992	299,692	61,550,918

PRESIDENTIAL ELECTION RESULTS

ELECTION OF 1952:
PARTY PERCENTAGES, PLURALITY AND ELECTORAL VOTE

State	Republican	Democratic	Plurality		Electoral Vote	
Alabama	35.0	64.6	D	125,844	D	11
Alaska						
Arizona	58.3	41.7	R	43,514	R	4
Arkansas	43.8	55.9	D	49,145	D	8
California	56.3	42.7	R	699,762	R	32
Colorado	60.3	39.0	R	134,278	R	6
Connecticut	55.7	43.9	R	129,363	R	8
Delaware	51.8	47.9	R	6,744	R	3
Florida	55.0	45.0	R	99,086	R	10
Georgia	30.3	69.7	D	257,862	D	12
Hawaii						
Idaho	65.4	34.4	R	85,626	R	4
Illinois	54.8	44.9	R	443,407	R	27
Indiana	58.1	41.0	R	334,729	R	13
Iowa	63.8	35.6	R	357,393	R	10
Kansas	68.8	30.5	R	343,006	R	8
Kentucky	49.8	49.9	D	700	D	10
Louisiana	47.1	52.9	D	38,102	D	10
Maine	66.0	33.8	R	113,547	R	5
Maryland	55.4	43.8	R	104,087	R	9
Massachusetts	54.2	45.5	R	208,800	R	16
Michigan	55.4	44.0	R	320,872	R	20

PRESIDENTIAL ELECTION RESULTS

ELECTION OF 1952:
PARTY PERCENTAGES, PLURALITY AND ELECTORAL VOTE
(continued)

State	Republican	Democratic	Plurality		Electoral Vote	
Minnesota	55.3	44.1	R	154,753	R	11
Mississippi	39.6	60.4	D	59,600	D	8
Missouri	50.7	49.1	R	29,599	R	13
Montana	59.4	40.1	R	51,181	R	4
Nebraska	69.2	30.8	R	233,546	R	6
Nevada	61.4	38.6	R	18,814	R	3
New Hampshire	60.9	39.1	R	59,624	R	4
New Jersey	56.8	42.0	R	357,711	R	16
New Mexico	55.4	44.3	R	26,509	R	4
New York	55.5	43.6	R	848,212	R	45
North Carolina	46.1	53.9	D	94,696	D	14
North Dakota	71.0	28.4	R	115,018	R	4
Ohio	56.8	43.2	R	500,024	R	25
Oklahoma	54.6	45.4	R	87,106	R	8
Oregon	60.5	38.9	R	150,236	R	6
Pennsylvania	52.7	46.9	R	269,520	R	32
Rhode Island	50.9	49.0	R	7,642	R	4
South Carolina	49.3	50.7	D	4,922	D	8
South Dakota	69.3	30.7	R	113,431	R	4
Tennessee	50.0	49.7	R	2,437	R	11
Texas	53.1	46.7	R	133,650	R	24
Utah	58.9	41.1	R	58,826	R	4

PRESIDENTIAL ELECTION RESULTS

ELECTION OF 1952:
PARTY PERCENTAGES, PLURALITY AND ELECTORAL VOTE
(continued)

State	Republican	Democratic	Plurality		Electoral Vote	
Vermont	71.5	28.2	R	66,362	R	3
Virginia	56.3	43.4	R	80,360	R	12
Washington	54.3	44.7	R	106,262	R	9
West Virginia	48.1	51.9	D	33,608	D	8
Wisconsin	61.0	38.7	R	357,569	R	12
Wyoming	62.7	37.1	R	33,115	R	3
Total	55.1	44.4	R	6,621,242	R	89
					D	442
						531

POPULAR VOTE: 1956

State	Republican	Democratic	All Others	Total Vote Cast
Alabama	195,694	280,844	20,323	496,861
Alaska				
Arizona	176,990	112,880	303	290,173
Arkansas	186,287	213,277	7,008	406,572
California	3,027,668	2,420,135	18,552	5,466,355
Colorado	394,479	257,997	4,598	657,074
Connecticut	711,837	405,079	205	1,117,121
Delaware	98,057	79,421	510	177,988
Florida	643,849	480,371	1,542	1,125,762
Georgia	222,778	444,688	2,189	669,655
Hawaii				
Idaho	166,979	105,868	142	272,989
Illinois	2,623,327	1,775,682	8,398	4,407,407
Indiana	1,182,811	783,908	7,888	1,974,607
Iowa	729,187	501,858	3,519	1,234,564
Kansas	566,878	296,317	3,048	866,243
Kentucky	572,192	476,453	5,160	1,053,805
Louisiana	329,047	243,977	44,520	617,544
Maine	249,238	102,468		351,706
Maryland	559,738	372,613	476	932,827
Massachusetts	1,393,197	948,190	7,119	2,348,506
Michigan	1,713,647	1,359,898	6,923	3,080,468
Minnesota	719,302	617,525	3,178	1,340,005

PRESIDENTIAL ELECTION RESULTS

POPULAR VOTE: 1956
(continued)

State	Republican	Democratic	All Others	Total Vote Cast
Mississippi	60,685	144,453	42,966	248,104
Missouri	914,289	918,273		1,832,562
Montana	154,933	116,238		271,171
Nebraska	378,108	199,029		577,137
Nevada	56,049	40,640		96,689
New Hampshire	176,519	90,364	111	266,994
New Jersey	1,606,942	850,337	27,033	2,484,312
New Mexico	146,788	106,098	1,040	253,926
New York	4,345,506	2,747,944	2,521	7,095,971
North Carolina	575,062	590,530		1,165,592
North Dakota	156,766	96,742	483	253,991
Ohio	2,262,610	1,439,655		3,702,265
Oklahoma	473,769	385,581		859,350
Oregon	406,393	329,204	535	736,132
Pennsylvania	2,585,252	1,981,769	9,482	4,576,503
Rhode Island	225,819	161,790		387,609
South Carolina	75,700	136,372	88,511	300,583
South Dakota	171,569	122,288		293,857
Tennessee	462,288	456,507	20,609	939,404
Texas	1,080,619	859,958	14,591	1,955,168
Utah	215,631	118,364		333,995
Vermont	110,390	42,549	39	152,978
Virginia	386,459	267,760	43,759	697,978

POPULAR VOTE: 1956
(continued)

State	Republican	Democratic	All Others	Total Vote Cast
Washington	620,430	523,002	7,457	1,150,889
West Virginia	449,297	381,534		830,831
Wisconsin	954,844	586,768	8,946	1,550,558
Wyoming	74,573	49,554		124,127
Total	35,590,472	26,022,752	413,684	62,026,908

PRESIDENTIAL ELECTION RESULTS

ELECTION OF 1956:
PARTY PERCENTAGES, PLURALITY AND ELECTORAL VOTE

State	Republican	Democratic	Plurality		Electoral Vote	
Alabama	39.4	56.5	D	85,150	D	10
Alaska					§	1
Arizona	61.0	38.9	R	64,110	R	4
Arkansas	45.8	52.5	D	26,990	D	8
California	55.4	44.3	R	607,533	R	32
Colorado	60.0	39.3	R	136,482	R	6
Connecticut	63.7	36.3	R	306,758	R	8
Delaware	55.1	44.6	R	18,636	R	3
Florida	57.2	42.7	R	163,478	R	10
Georgia	33.3	66.4	D	221,910	D	12
Hawaii						
Idaho	61.2	38.8	R	61,111	R	4
Illinois	59.5	40.3	R	847,645	R	27
Indiana	59.9	39.7	R	398,903	R	13
Iowa	59.1	40.7	R	227,329	R	10
Kansas	65.4	34.2	R	270,561	R	8
Kentucky	54.3	45.2	R	95,739	R	10
Louisiana	53.3	39.5	R	85,070	R	10
Maine	70.9	29.1	R	146,770	R	5
Maryland	60.0	39.9	R	187,125	R	9
Massachusetts	59.3	40.4	R	445,007	R	16
Michigan	55.6	44.1	R	353,749	R	20

ELECTION OF 1956:
PARTY PERCENTAGES, PLURALITY AND ELECTORAL VOTE
(continued)

State	Republican	Democratic	Plurality		Electoral Vote	
Minnesota	53.7	46.1	R	101,777	R	11
Mississippi	24.5	58.2	D	83,768	D	8
Missouri	49.9	50.1	D	3,984	D	13
Montana	57.1	42.9	R	38,695	R	4
Nebraska	65.5	34.5	R	179,079	R	6
Nevada	58.0	42.0	R	15,409	R	3
New Hampshire	66.1	33.8	R	86,155	R	4
New Jersey	64.7	34.2	R	756,605	R	16
New Mexico	57.8	41.8	R	40,690	R	4
New York	61.2	38.7	R	1,597,562	R	45
North Carolina	49.3	50.7	D	15,468	D	14
North Dakota	61.7	38.1	R	60,024	R	4
Ohio	61.1	38.9	R	822,955	R	25
Oklahoma	55.1	44.9	R	88,188	R	8
Oregon	55.2	44.7	R	77,189	R	6
Pennsylvania	56.5	43.3	R	603,483	R	32
Rhode Island	58.3	41.7	R	64,029	R	4
South Carolina	25.2	45.4	D	47,863	D	8
South Dakota	58.4	41.6	R	49,281	D	4
Tennessee	49.2	48.6	R	5,781	R	11
Texas	55.3	44.0	R	220,661	R	24
Utah	64.6	35.4	R	97,267	R	4

ELECTION OF 1956:
PARTY PERCENTAGES, PLURALITY AND ELECTORAL VOTE
(continued)

State	Republican	Democratic	Plurality		Electoral Vote	
Vermont	72.2	27.8	R	67,841	R	3
Virginia	55.4	38.4	R	118,699	R	12
Washington	53.9	45.4	R	97,428	R	9
West Virginia	54.1	45.9	R	67,763	R	8
Wisconsin	61.6	37.8	R	368,076	R	12
Wyoming	60.1	39.9	R	25,019	R	3
Total	57.4	42.0	R	9,567,720	§	1
					D	73
					R	457
						531

§ Vote for Walter B. Jones and Herman Talmadge.

PRESIDENTIAL ELECTION RESULTS

POPULAR VOTE: 1960

State	Republican	Democratic	All Others	Total Vote Cast
Alabama	237,981	324,050	8,194	570,225
Alaska	30,953	29,809		60,762
Arizona	221,241	176,781	469	398,491
Arkansas	184,508	215,049	28,952	428,509
California	3,259,722	3,224,099	22,757	6,506,578
Colorado	402,242	330,629	3,365	736,236
Connecticut	565,813	657,055	15	1,222,883
Delaware	96,373	99,590	720	196,683
Florida	795,476	748,700		1,544,176
Georgia	274,472	458,638	239	733,349
Hawaii	92,295	92,410		184,705
Idaho	161,597	138,853		300,450
Illinois	2,368,988	2,377,846	10,575	4,757,409
Indiana	1,175,120	952,358	7,882	2,135,360
Iowa	722,381	550,565	864	1,273,810
Kansas	561,474	363,213	4,138	928,825
Kentucky	602,607	521,855		1,124,462
Louisiana	230,980	407,339	169,572	807,891
Maine	240,608	181,159		421,767
Maryland	489,538	565,808	3	1,055,349
Massachusetts	976,750	1,487,174	5,556	2,469,480
Michigan	1,620,428	1,687,269	10,400	3,318,097
Minnesota	757,915	779,933	4,039	1,541,887

POPULAR VOTE: 1960
(continued)

State	Republican	Democratic	All Others	Total Vote Cast
Mississippi	73,561	108,362	116,248	298,171
Missouri	962,221	972,201		1,934,422
Montana	141,841	134,891	847	277,579
Nebraska	380,553	232,542		613,095
Nevada	52,387	54,880		107,267
New Hampshire	157,989	137,772		295,761
New Jersey	1,363,324	1,385,415	24,372	2,773,111
New Mexico	153,733	156,027	1,347	311,107
New York	3,446,419	3,830,085	14,575	7,291,079
North Carolina	655,420	713,136		1,368,556
North Dakota	154,310	123,963	158	278,431
Ohio	2,217,611	1,944,248		4,161,859
Oklahoma	533,039	370,111		903,150
Oregon	408,060	367,402	959	776,421
Pennsylvania	2,439,956	2,556,282	10,303	5,006,541
Rhode Island	147,502	258,032	1	405,535
South Carolina	188,558	198,129	1	386,688
South Dakota	178,417	128,070		306,487
Tennessee	556,577	481,453	13,762	1,051,792
Texas	1,121,310	1,167,567	22,207	2,311,084
Utah	205,361	169,248	100	374,709
Vermont	98,131	69,186	7	167,324

PRESIDENTIAL ELECTION RESULTS

POPULAR VOTE: 1960
(continued)

State	Republican	Democratic	All Others	Total Vote Cast
Virginia	404,521	362,327	4,601	771,449
Washington	629,273	599,298	13,001	1,241,572
West Virginia	395,995	441,786		837,781
Wisconsin	895,175	830,805	3,102	1,729,082
Wyoming	77,451	63,331		140,782
Total	34,108,157	34,226,731	503,331	68,838,219

PRESIDENTIAL ELECTION RESULTS

ELECTION OF 1960:
PARTY PERCENTAGES, PLURALITY AND ELECTORAL VOTE

State	Republican	Democratic	Plurality		Electoral Vote	
Alabama	41.7	56:8	D	86,069	D	5
					§	6
Alaska	50.9	49.1	R	1,144	R	3
Arizona	55.5	44.4	R	44,460	R	4
Arkansas	43.1	50.2	D	30,541	D	8
California	50.1	49.6	R	35,623	R	32
Colorado	54.6	44.9	R	71,613	R	6
Connecticut	46.3	53.7	D	91,242	D	8
Delaware	49.0	50.6	D	3,217	D	3
Florida	51.5	48.5	R	46,776	R	10
Georgia	37.4	62.5	D	181,166	D	12
Hawaii	50.0	50.0	D	115	D	3
Idaho	53.8	46.2	R	22,744	R	4
Illinois	49.8	50.0	D	8,858	D	27
Indiana	55.0	44.6	R	222,762	R	13
Iowa	56.7	43.2	R	171,816	R	10
Kansas	60.4	39.1	R	198,261	R	8
Kentucky	53.6	46.4	R	80,752	R	10
Louisiana	28.6	50.4	D	176,359	D	10
Maine	57.0	43.0	R	59,449	R	5
Maryland	46.4	53.6	D	76,270	D	9
Massachusetts	39.6	60.2	D	510,424	D	16
Michigan	48.8	50.9	D	66,841	D	20

PRESIDENTIAL ELECTION RESULTS

ELECTION OF 1960:
PARTY PERCENTAGES, PLURALITY AND ELECTORAL VOTE
(continued)

State	Republican	Democratic	Plurality		Electoral Vote	
Minnesota	49.2	50.6	D	22,018	D	11
Mississippi	24.7	36.3	U	7,886	§	8
Missouri	49.7	50.3	D	9,980	D	13
Montana	51.1	48.6	R	6,950	R	4
Nebraska	62.1	37.9	R	148,011	R	6
Nevada	48.8	51.2	D	2,493	D	3
New Hampshire	53.4	46.6	R	20,217	R	4
New Jersey	49.2	50.0	D	22,091	D	16
New Mexico	49.4	50.2	D	2,294	D	4
New York	47.3	52.5	D	383,666	D	45
North Carolina	47.9	52.1	D	57,716	D	14
North Dakota	55.4	44.5	R	30,347	R	4
Ohio	53.3	46.7	R	273,363	R	25
Oklahoma	59.0	41.0	R	162,928	R	7
					§	1
Oregon	52.6	47.3	R	40,658	R	6
Pennsylvania	48.7	51.1	D	116,326	D	32
Rhode Island	36.4	63.6	D	110,330	D	4
South Carolina	48.8	51.2	D	9,571	D	8
South Dakota	58.2	41.8	R	50,347	R	4
Tennessee	52.9	45.8	R	75,124	R	11
Texas	48.5	50.5	D	46,257	D	24

ELECTION OF 1960:
PARTY PERCENTAGES, PLURALITY AND ELECTORAL VOTE
(continued)

State	Republican	Democratic	Plurality		Electoral Vote	
Utah	54.8	45.2	R	36,113	R	4
Vermont	58.6	41.3	R	28,945	R	3
Virginia	52.4	47.0	R	42,194	R	12
Washington	50.7	48.3	R	29,975	R	9
West Virginia	47.3	52.7	D	45,791	D	8
Wisconsin	51.8	48.0	R	64,370	R	12
Wyoming	55.0	45.0	R	14,120	R	3
Total	49.5	49.7	D	118,574	§	15
					R	219
					D	303
						537

§ Vote for Senator Harry Flood Byrd.

PRESIDENTIAL ELECTION RESULTS

POPULAR VOTE: 1964

State	Republican	Democratic	All Others	Total Vote Cast
Alabama	479,085		210,733	689,818
Alaska	22,930	44,329		67,259
Arizona	242,535	237,753	482	480,770
Arkansas	243,264	314,197	2,965	560,426
California	2,879,108	4,171,877	6,601	7,057,586
Colorado	296,767	476,024	4,195	776,986
Connecticut	390,996	826,269	1,313	1,218,578
Delaware	78,078	122,704	538	201,320
Florida	905,941	948,540		1,854,481
Georgia	616,584	522,556	195	1,139,335
Hawaii	44,022	163,249		207,271
Idaho	143,557	148,920		292,477
Illinois	1,905,946	2,796,833	62	4,702,841
Indiana	911,118	1,170,848	9,640	2,091,606
Iowa	449,148	733,030	2,361	1,184,539
Kansas	386,579	464,028	7,294	857,901
Kentucky	372,977	669,659	3,469	1,046,105
Louisiana	509,225	387,068		896,293
Maine	118,701	262,264		380,965
Maryland	385,495	730,912	50	1,116,457
Massachusetts	549,727	1,786,422	8,649	2,344,798
Michigan	1,060,152	2,136,615	6,335	3,203,102
Minnesota	559,624	991,117	3,721	1,554,462

POPULAR VOTE: 1964
(continued)

State	Republican	Democratic	All Others	Total Vote Cast
Mississippi	356,528	52,618		409,146
Missouri	653,535	1,164,344		1,817,879
Montana	113,032	164,246	1,350	278,628
Nebraska	276,847	307,307		584,154
Nevada	56,094	79,339		135,433
New Hampshire	104,029	184,064		288,093
New Jersey	964,174	1,868,231	15,258	2,847,663
New Mexico	132,838	194,015	1,792	328,645
New York	2,243,559	4,913,102	9,614	7,166,275
North Carolina	624,844	800,139		1,424,983
North Dakota	108,207	149,784	398	258,389
Ohio	1,470,865	2,498,331		3,969,196
Oklahoma	412,665	519,834		932,499
Oregon	282,779	501,017	2,509	786,305
Pennsylvania	1,673,657	3,130,954	18,079	4,822,690
Rhode Island	74,615	315,463	13	390,091
South Carolina	309,048	215,723	8	524,779
South Dakota	130,108	163,010		293,118
Tennessee	508,965	635,047	34	1,144,046
Texas	958,566	1,663,185	5,060	2,626,811
Utah	181,785	219,628		401,413
Vermont	54,942	108,127	20	163,089

POPULAR VOTE: 1964
(continued)

State	Republican	Democratic	All Others	Total Vote Cast
Virginia	481,334	558,038	2,895	1,042,267
Washington	470,366	779,699	8,309	1,258,374
West Virginia	253,953	538,087		792,040
Wisconsin	638,495	1,050,424	2,896	1,691,815
Wyoming	61,998	80,718		142,716
District of Columbia	28,801	169,796		198,597
Total	27,178,188	43,129,484	336,838	70,644,510

PRESIDENTIAL ELECTION RESULTS

ELECTION OF 1964:
PARTY PERCENTAGES, PLURALITY AND ELECTORAL VOTE

State	Republican	Democratic	Plurality	Electoral Vote
Alabama	69.5		R 268,353	R 10
Alaska	34.1	65.9	D 21,399	D 3
Arizona	50.4	49.5	R 4,782	R 5
Arkansas	43.4	56.1	D 70,933	D 6
California	40.8	59.1	D 1,292,769	D 40
Colorado	38.2	61.3	D 179,257	D 6
Connecticut	32.1	67.8	D 435,273	D 8
Delaware	38.8	60.9	D 44,626	D 3
Florida	48.9	51.1	D 42,599	D 14
Georgia	54.1	45.9	R 94,028	R 12
Hawaii	21.2	78.8	D 119,227	D 4
Idaho	49.1	50.9	D 5,363	D 4
Illinois	40.5	59.5	D 890,887	D 26
Indiana	43.6	56.0	D 259,730	D 13
Iowa	37.9	61.9	D 283,882	D 9
Kansas	45.1	54.1	D 77,449	D 7
Kentucky	35.7	64.0	D 296,682	D 9
Louisiana	56.8	43.2	R 122,157	R 10
Maine	31.2	68.8	D 143,563	D 4
Maryland	34.5	65.5	D 345,417	D 10
Massachusetts	23.4	76.2	D 1,236,695	D 14
Michigan	33.1	66.7	D 1,076,463	D 21

PRESIDENTIAL ELECTION RESULTS

ELECTION OF 1964:
PARTY PERCENTAGES, PLURALITY AND ELECTORAL VOTE
(continued)

State	Republican	Democratic	Plurality		Electoral Vote	
Minnesota	36.0	63.8	D	431,493	D	10
Mississippi	87.1	12.9	R	303,910	R	7
Missouri	36.0	64.0	D	510,809	D	12
Montana	40.6	58.9	D	51,214	D	4
Nebraska	47.6	52.6	D	30,460	D	5
Nevada	41.4	58.6	D	23,245	D	3
New Hampshire	36.1	63.9	D	80,035	D	4
New Jersey	33.9	65.6	D	904,057	D	17
New Mexico	40.4	59.0	D	61,177	D	4
New York	31.3	68.6	D	2,669,543	D	43
North Carolina	43.8	56.2	D	175,295	D	13
North Dakota	41.9	58.0	D	41,577	D	4
Ohio	37.1	62.9	D	1,027,466	D	26
Oklahoma	44.3	55.7	D	107,169	D	8
Oregon	36.0	63.7	D	218,238	D	6
Pennsylvania	34.7	64.9	D	1,457,297	D	29
Rhode Island	19.1	80.9	D	240,848	D	4
South Carolina	58.9	41.1	R	93,325	R	8
South Dakota	44.4	55.6	D	32,902	D	4
Tennessee	44.5	55.5	D	126,082	D	11
Texas	36.5	63.3	D	704,619	D	25
Utah	45.3	54.7	D	37,843	D	4

PRESIDENTIAL ELECTION RESULTS

ELECTION OF 1964:
PARTY PERCENTAGES, PLURALITY AND ELECTORAL VOTE
(continued)

State	Republican	Democratic	Plurality		Electoral Vote	
Vermont	33.7	66.3	D	53,185	D	3
Virginia	46.2	53.5	D	76,704	D	12
Washington	37.4	62.0	D	309,333	D	9
West Virginia	32.1	67.9	D	284,134	D	7
Wisconsin	37.7	62.1	D	411,929	D	12
Wyoming	43.4	56.6	D	18,720	D	3
District of Columbia	14.5	85.5	D	140,995	D	3
Total	38.5	61.1	D15,951,296		R	52
					D	486
						538

PRESIDENTIAL ELECTION RESULTS

POPULAR VOTE: 1968

State	Republican	Democratic	All Others	Total Vote Cast
Alabama	146,923	196,579	706,407	1,049,909
Alaska	37,600	35,411	10,024	83,035
Arizona	266,721	170,514	49,701	486,936
Arkansas	190,759	188,228	240,982	619,969
California	3,467,664	3,244,318	539,605	7,251,587
Colorado	409,345	335,174	65,732	810,251
Connecticut	556,721	621,561	76,650	1,254,932
Delaware	96,714	89,194	28,459	214,367
Florida	886,804	676,794	624,207	2,187,805
Georgia	380,111	334,440	535,550	1,250,101
Hawaii	91,425	141,324	3,469	236,218
Idaho	165,369	89,273	36,541	291,183
Illinois	2,174,774	2,039,814	404,836	4,619,424
Indiana	1,067,885	806,659	249,017	2,123,561
Iowa	619,106	476,699	71,874	1,167,679
Kansas	478,674	302,996	91,113	872,783
Kentucky	462,411	397,541	195,941	1,055,893
Louisiana	257,535	309,615	530,300	1,097,450
Maine	169,254	217,312	6,370	392,936
Maryland	517,995	538,310	178,734	1,235,039
Massachusetts	766,844	1,469,218	95,637	2,331,699
Michigan	1,370,665	1,593,082	342,474	3,306,221
Minnesota	658,643	857,738	72,129	1,588,510

PRESIDENTIAL ELECTION RESULTS

POPULAR VOTE: 1968
(continued)

State	Republican	Democratic	All Others	Total Vote Cast
Mississippi	88,516	150,644	415,349	654,509
Missouri	811,932	791,444	206,126	1,809,502
Montana	138,835	114,117	21,452	274,404
Nebraska	321,163	170,784	44,904	536,851
Nevada	73,188	60,598	20,432	154,218
New Hampshire	154,903	130,589	11,806	297,298
New Jersey	1,325,467	1,264,206	285,722	2,875,395
New Mexico	169,692	130,081	27,508	327,281
New York	3,007,932	3,378,470	403,664	6,790,066
North Carolina	627,192	464,113	496,188	1,587,493
North Dakota	138,669	94,769	14,444	247,882
Ohio	1,791,014	1,700,586	468,098	3,959,698
Oklahoma	449,697	301,658	191,731	943,086
Oregon	408,433	358,866	51,248	818,547
Pennsylvania	2,090,017	2,259,405	398,506	4,747,928
Rhode Island	122,359	246,518	16,061	384,938
South Carolina	254,062	197,486	215,430	666,978
South Dakota	149,841	118,023	13,400	281,264
Tennessee	472,592	351,233	424,792	1,248,617
Texas	1,227,844	1,266,804	584,269	3,078,917
Utah	238,728	156,665	27,175	422,568
Vermont	85,142	70,255	5,978	161,375

POPULAR VOTE: 1968
(continued)

State	Republican	Democratic	All Others	Total Vote Cast
Virginia	590,319	442,387	328,785	1,361,491
Washington	588,510	616,037	99,734	1,304,281
West Virginia	307,555	374,091	72,560	754,206
Wisconsin	809,997	748,804	130,395	1,689,196
Wyoming	70,927	45,173	11,105	127,205
District of Columbia	31,012	139,566		170,578
Total	31,785,480	31,275,166	10,142,614	73,203,260

PRESIDENTIAL ELECTION RESULTS

ELECTION OF 1968:
PARTY PERCENTAGES, PLURALITY AND ELECTORAL VOTE

State	Republican	Democratic	Plurality		Electoral Vote	
Alabama	14.0	18.7	AIP	494,846	AIP	10
Alaska	45.3	42.6	R	2,189	R	3
Arizona	54.8	35.0	R	96,207	R	5
Arkansas	30.8	30.4	AIP	50,223	AIP	6
California	47.8	44.7	R	223,346	R	40
Colorado	50.5	41.4	R	74,171	R	6
Connecticut	44.4	49.5	D	64,840	D	8
Delaware	45.1	41.6	R	7,520	R	3
Florida	40.5	30.9	R	210,010	R	14
Georgia	30.4	26.8	AIP	155,439	AIP	12
Hawaii	38.7	59.8	D	49,899	D	4
Idaho	56.8	30.7	R	76,096	R	4
Illinois	47.1	44.2	R	134,960	R	26
Indiana	50.3	38.0	R	261,226	R	13
Iowa	53.0	40.8	R	142,407	R	9
Kansas	54.8	34.7	R	175,678	R	7
Kentucky	43.8	37.6	R	64,870	R	9
Louisiana	23.5	28.2	AIP	220,685	AIP	10
Maine	43.1	55.3	D	48,058	D	4
Maryland	41.9	43.6	D	20,315	D	10
Massachusetts	32.9	63.0	D	720,374	D	14
Michigan	41.5	48.2	D	222,417	D	12

ELECTION OF 1968:
PARTY PERCENTAGES, PLURALITY AND ELECTORAL VOTE
(continued)

State	Republican	Democratic	Plurality		Electoral Vote	
Minnesota	41.5	54.0	D	199,095	D	10
Mississippi	13.5	23.0	AIP	264,705	AIP	7
Missouri	44.9	43.7	R	20,488	R	12
Montana	50.6	41.6	R	24,718	R	4
Nebraska	59.8	31.8	R	150,379	R	5
Nevada	47.5	39.3	R	12,590	R	3
New Hampshire	52.1	43.9	R	24,314	R	4
New Jersey	46.1	43.4	R	61,261	R	17
New Mexico	51.8	39.7	R	39,611	R	4
New York	44.3	49.8	D	370,538	D	43
North Carolina	39.5	29.2	R	131,004	R	12
					AIP	1
North Dakota	55.9	38.2	R	43,900	R	4
Ohio	45.2	42.9	R	90,428	R	26
Oklahoma	47.7	32.0	R	148,039	R	8
Oregon	49.9	43.8	R	49,567	R	6
Pennsylvania	44.0	47.6	D	169,388	D	29
Rhode Island	31.8	64.0	D	124,159	D	4
South Carolina	38.1	29.6	R	38,632	R	8
South Dakota	53.3	42.0	R	31,818	R	4
Tennessee	37.8	28.1	R	47,800	R	11
Texas	39.9	41.1	D	38,960	D	25

ELECTION OF 1968:
PARTY PERCENTAGES, PLURALITY AND ELECTORAL VOTE
(continued)

State	Republican	Democratic		Plurality		Electoral Vote
Utah	56.5	37.1	R	82,063	R	4
Vermont	52.8	43.5	R	14,887	R	3
Virginia	43.4	32.5	R	147,932	R	12
Washington	45.1	47.2	D	27,527	D	9
West Virginia	40.8	49.6	D	66,536	D	7
Wisconsin	48.0	44.3	R	61,193	R	12
Wyoming	55.8	35.5	R	25,754	R	3
District of Columbia	18.2	81.8	D	108,554	D	3
Total	43.4	42.7	R	510,314§	AIP	46
					D	191
					R	301
						538

§ Republican total vote minus Democratic total vote

PART X

Minor Party Voting

NOTE

Where no data appears following a state as listed, no vote was cast there for minor party candidates in that election year.

SOURCES

1948–1960

Data for popular vote totals and percentages for minor parties for the election of 1948 through 1960 are taken from A STATISTICAL HISTORY OF THE AMERICAN PRESIDENTIAL ELECTIONS by Svend Petersen by permission of Frederick Ungar Publishing Co.

1964–1968

Compiled from the records of the various Secretaries of State.

MINOR PARTY VOTING

NATIONAL TOTALS: ELECTION OF 1948

Party	Candidates	Vote	Percentage of Total Vote Cast	Electoral Vote
States Rights	Strom Thurmond Fielding L. Wright	1,169,032	2.40	39
Progressive	Henry A. Wallace Glen H. Taylor	1,157,063	2.38	0
Socialist	Norman Thomas Tucker P. Smith	139,523	.29	0
Prohibition	Claude A. Watson Dale H. Learn	103,343	.21	0
Socialist Labor	Edward A. Teichert Stephen Emery	29,240	.06	0
Socialist Workers	Farrell Dobbs Grace Carlson	13,611	.03	0
Total		2,611,812	5.37	39

MINOR PARTY VOTING

STATE TOTALS: ELECTION OF 1948

State	Party	Vote	Percentage of Total Vote Cast	Electoral Vote
Alabama	States Rights	171,443	79.75	11
	Progressive	1,522	.71	
	Prohibition	1,085	.50	
Alaska				
Arizona	Progressive	3,310	1.87	
	Prohibition	786	.44	
	Socialist Labor	121	.07	
Arkansas	States Rights	40,068	16.52	
	Socialist	1,037	.43	
	Progressive	751	.31	
	Prohibition	1	.00	
California	Progressive	190,381	4.73	
	Prohibition	16,926	.42	
	Socialist	3,459	.09	
	States Rights	1,228	.03	
	Socialist Labor	195	.00	
	Socialist Workers	133	.00	
Colorado	Progressive	6,115	1.19	
	Socialist	1,678	.33	
	Socialist Workers	228	.04	
	Socialist Labor	214	.04	
Connecticut	Progressive	13,713	1.55	
	Socialist	6,964	.79	
	Socialist Labor	1,184	.13	
	Socialist Workers	606	.07	
Delaware	Progressive	1,050	.75	
	Prohibition	343	.25	
	Socialist	250	.18	
	Socialist Labor	29	.02	
Florida	States Rights	89,755	15.54	
	Progressive	11,620	2.01	
Georgia	States Rights	85,055	20.31	
	Progressive	1,636	.39	
	Prohibition	732	.17	

STATE TOTALS: ELECTION OF 1948
(continued)

State	Party	Vote	Percentage of Total Vote Cast	Electoral Vote
Idaho	Progressive	4,972	2.31	
	Prohibition	628	.29	
	Socialist	332	.15	
Illinois	Prohibition	11,959	.30	
	Socialist	11,522	.29	
	Socialist Labor	3,118	.08	
Indiana	Prohibition	14,711	.89	
	Progressive	9,649	.58	
	Socialist	2,179	.13	
	Socialist Labor	763	.05	
Iowa	Progressive	12,125	1.17	
	Socialist Labor	4,274	.41	
	Prohibition	3,382	.33	
	Socialist	1,829	.18	
	Socialist Workers	256	.02	
Kansas	Prohibition	6,468	.82	
	Progressive	4,603	.58	
	Socialist	2,807	.36	
Kentucky	States Rights	10,411	1.27	
	Progressive	1,567	.19	
	Socialist	1,284	.16	
	Prohibition	1,245	.15	
	Socialist Labor	185	.02	
Louisiana	States Rights	204,290	49.07	10
	Progressive	3,035	.73	
Maine	Progressive	1,884	.71	
	Socialist	547	.21	
	Socialist Labor	206	.08	
Maryland	Progressive	9,983	1.67	
	Socialist	2,941	.49	
	States Rights	2,476	.41	

STATE TOTALS: ELECTION OF 1948
(continued)

State	Party	Vote	Percentage of Total Vote Cast	Electoral Vote
Massachusetts	Progressive	38,157	1.81	
	Socialist Labor	5,535	.26	
	Prohibition	1,663	.08	
Michigan	Progressive	46,515	2.20	
	Prohibition	13,052	.62	
	Socialist	6,063	.29	
	Socialist Labor	1,263	.06	
	Socialist Workers	672	.03	
Minnesota	Progressive	27,866	2.30	
	Socialist	4,646	.38	
	Socialist Labor	2,525	.21	
	Socialist Workers	606	.05	
Mississippi	States Rights	167,538	87.17	9
	Progressive	225	.12	
Missouri	Progressive	3,998	.25	
	Socialist	2,222	.14	
Montana	Progressive	7,313	3.26	
	Socialist	695	.31	
	Prohibition	429	.19	
Nebraska				
Nevada	Progressive	1,469	2.36	
New Hampshire	Progressive	1,970	.85	
	Socialist	86	.04	
	States Rights	7	.00	
New Jersey	Progressive	42,683	2.19	
	Prohibition	10,593	.54	
	Socialist	10,521	.54	
	Socialist Workers	5,825	.30	
	Socialist Labor	3,354	.17	
New Mexico	Progressive	1,037	.55	
	Prohibition	127	.07	
	Socialist	83	.04	
	Socialist Labor	49	.03	

STATE TOTALS: ELECTION OF 1948
(continued)

State	Party	Vote	Percentage of Total Vote Cast	Electoral Vote
New York	Progressive	509,559	8.25	
	Socialist	40,879	.66	
	Socialist Labor	2,729	.04	
	Socialist Workers	2,675	.04	
North Carolina	States Rights	69,652	8.80	
	Progressive	3,915	.49	
North Dakota	Progressive	8,391	3.80	
	Socialist	1,000	.45	
	States Rights	374	.17	
Ohio	Progressive	37,596	1.28	
Oklahoma				
Oregon	Progressive	14,978	2.86	
	Socialist	5,051	.96	
Pennsylvania	Progressive	55,161	1.48	
	Socialist	11,325	.30	
	Prohibition	10,338	.28	
	Socialist Workers	2,133	.06	
	Socialist Labor	1,461	.04	
Rhode Island	Progressive	2,605	.79	
	Socialist	428	.13	
	Socialist Labor	130	.04	
South Carolina	States Rights	102,607	71.97	8
	Progressive	154	.11	
	Socialist	1	.00	
South Dakota	Progressive	2,801	1.12	
Tennessee	States Rights	73,826	13.42	1
	Progressive	1,866	.34	
	Socialist	1,291	.23	
Texas	States Rights	106,909	9.32	
	Progressive	3,764	.33	
	Prohibition	2,758	.24	

STATE TOTALS: ELECTION OF 1948
(continued)

State	Party	Vote	Percentage of Total Vote Cast	Electoral Vote
Utah	Progressive	2,582	.94	
	Socialist Workers	71	.03	
Vermont	Progressive	1,279	1.04	
	Socialist	585	.47	
Virginia	States Rights	43,393	10.35	
	Progressive	2,047	.49	
	Socialist	726	.17	
	Socialist Labor	234	.06	
Washington	Progressive	31,692	3.50	
	Prohibition	6,117	.68	
	Socialist	3,534	.39	
	Socialist Labor	1,133	.13	
	Socialist Workers	103	.01	
West Virginia	Progressive	3,311	1.44	
Wisconsin	Progressive	25,282	1.98	
	Socialist	12,547	.98	
	Socialist Labor	399	.03	
	Socialist Workers	303	.02	
Wyoming	Progressive	931	.92	
	Socialist	137	.14	
	Socialist Labor	56	.06	

MINOR PARTY VOTING

NATIONAL TOTALS: ELECTION OF 1952

Party	Candidates	Vote	Percentage of Total Vote Cast	Electoral Vote
Progressive	Vincent Hallinan Charlotta Bass	140,178	.23	0
Prohibition	Stuart Hamblen Enock A. Holtwick	72,778	.12	0
Socialist Labor	Eric Hass Stephen Emery	30,376	.05	0
Socialists	Darlington Hoopes Samuel H. Friedman	20,189	.03	0
Socialist Workers	Farrell Dobbs Myra Tanner Weiss	10,306	.02	0
Constitution	Douglas MacArthur	17,205	.03	0
Poor Man's	Henry B. Krajewski Frank Jenkins	4,203	.01	0
Total		295,235	.49	0

MINOR PARTY VOTING

STATE TOTALS: ELECTION OF 1952

State	Party	Vote	Percentage of Total Vote Cast	Electoral Vote
Alabama	Prohibition	1,814	.43	
Alaska				
Arizona				
Arkansas	Prohibition	886	.22	
	Constitution	458	.11	
	Socialist Labor	1	.00	
California	Progressive	24,106	.47	
	Prohibition	15,653	.30	
	Constitution	3,504	.07	
	Socialist Labor	273	.01	
	Socialist	206	.00	
Colorado	Constitution	2,181	.35	
	Progressive	1,919	.30	
	Socialist	365	.06	
	Socialist Labor	352	.06	
Connecticut	Socialist	2,244	.22	
	Progressive	1,466	.13	
	Socialist Labor	535	.05	
Delaware	Socialist Labor	242	.14	
	Prohibition	234	.13	
	Progressive	155	.09	
	Socialist	20	.01	
Florida				
Georgia				
Idaho	Progressive	443	.16	
Illinois	Socialist Labor	9,363	.19	
Indiana	Prohibition	15,335	.78	
	Progressive	1,222	.06	
	Socialist Labor	979	.05	
Kansas	Prohibition	6,038	.67	
	Socialist	530	.06	

STATE TOTALS: ELECTION OF 1952
(continued)

State	Party	Vote	Percentage of Total Vote Cast	Electoral Vote
Iowa	Progressive	5,085	.40	
	Prohibition	2,882	.23	
	Socialist	219	.02	
	Socialist Labor	139	.01	
Kentucky	Prohibition	1,161	.12	
	Socialist Labor	893	.09	
	Progressive	336	.03	
Louisiana				
Maine	Progressive	332	.09	
	Socialist Labor	156	.04	
	Socialist	138	.04	
Maryland	Progressive	7,313	.81	
Massachusetts	Progressive	4,636	.19	
	Socialist Labor	1,957	.08	
	Prohibition	886	.04	
Michigan	Prohibition	10,331	.37	
	Progressive	3,922	.14	
	Socialist Labor	1,495	.05	
	Socialist Workers	655	.02	
Minnesota	Progressive	2,666	.19	
	Socialist Labor	2,383	.17	
	Prohibition	2,147	.16	
	Socialist Workers	618	.04	
Mississippi				
Missouri	Progressive	987	.05	
	Prohibition	885	.05	
	Constitution	535	.03	
	Socialist	227	.01	
	Socialist Labor	169	.01	
Montana	Progressive	723	.27	
	Prohibition	548	.21	
	Socialist	159	.06	
Nebraska				

STATE TOTALS: ELECTION OF 1952
(continued)

State	Party	Vote	Percentage of Total Vote Cast	Electoral Vote
New Hampshire				
New Jersey	Socialist	8,593	.36	
	Socialist Labor	5,815	.24	
	Progressive	5,589	.23	
	Poor Man's	4,203	.17	
	Socialist Workers	3,850	.16	
	Prohibition	989	.04	
New Mexico	Prohibition	297	.12	
	Progressive	225	.09	
	Constitution	220	.09	
	Socialist Labor	35	.01	
New York	Progressive	64,211	.90	
	Socialist	2,664	.04	
	Socialist Workers	2,212	.03	
	Socialist Labor	1,560	.02	
North Carolina				
North Dakota	Constitution	1,075	.40	
	Progressive	344	.13	
	Prohibition	302	.11	
Ohio				
Oklahoma				
Oregon	Progressive	3,665	.53	
Pennsylvania	Prohibition	8,771	.19	
	Progressive	4,200	.09	
	Socialist	2,684	.06	
	Socialist Workers	1,502	.03	
	Socialist Labor	1,347	.03	
Rhode Island	Progressive	187	.05	
	Socialist Labor	83	.02	
South Carolina	Prohibition	1	.00	
South Dakota				

STATE TOTALS: ELECTION OF 1952
(continued)

State	Party	Vote	Percentage of Total Vote Cast	Electoral Vote
Tennessee	Prohibition	1,441	.16	
	Progressive	925	.10	
	Constitution	379	.04	
Texas	Prohibition	1,983	.10	
	Constitution	1,563	.08	
	Progressive	294	.01	
Utah				
Vermont	Progressive	282	.18	
	Socialist	185	.12	
Virginia	Socialist Labor	1,160	.19	
	Socialist	504	.08	
	Progressive	311	.05	
Washington	Constitution	7,290	.66	
	Progressive	2,460	.22	
	Socialist Labor	633	.06	
	Socialist	254	.02	
	Socialist Workers	119	.01	
West Virginia				
Wisconsin	Progressive	2,174	.14	
	Socialist Workers	1,350	.08	
	Socialist	1,157	.07	
	Socialist Labor	770	.05	
Wyoming	Prohibition	194	.15	
	Socialist	40	.03	
	Socialist Labor	36	.03	

MINOR PARTY VOTING

NATIONAL TOTALS: ELECTION OF 1956

Party	Candidates	Vote	Percentage of Total Vote Cast	Electoral Vote
Constitution	T. Coleman Andrews Thomas H. Werdel	176,887	.29	0
States Rights	Harry Flood Byrd William E. Jenner	134,132	.21	0
Socialist Labor	Eric Hass Georgia Cozzini	44,443	.07	0
Prohibition	Enock H. Holtwick Edwin M. Cooper	41,937	.07	0
Socialist Workers	Farrell Dobbs Myra Tanner Weiss	7,795	.01	0
Socialist	Darlington Hoopes Samuel H. Friedman	2,121	.00	0
American Third Party	Henry B. Krajewski Anne Marie Yezo	1,829	.00	0
Christian Nationalist	Gerald L.K. Smith Charles F. Robertson	8	.00	0
Total		409,152	.65	0

MINOR PARTY VOTING

STATE TOTALS: ELECTION OF 1956

State	Party	Vote	Percentage of Total Vote Cast	Electoral Vote
Alabama	Constitution	20,323	4.09	
Alaska				
Arizona	Constitution	303	.10	
Arkansas	Constitution	7,008	1.72	
California	Prohibition	11,119	.20	
	Constitution	6,087	.10	
	Socialist Labor	300	.01	
	Socialist	123	.00	
	Socialist Workers	96	.00	
	Christian National	8	.00	
Colorado	Socialist Labor	3,308	.50	
	Constitution	759	.11	
	Socialist	531	.08	
Connecticut				
Delaware	Prohibition	400	.22	
	Socialist Labor	110	.06	
Florida	Constitution	1,348	.12	
Georgia	Constitution	2,096	.31	
Idaho	Constitution	126	.05	
Illinois	Socialist Labor	8,342	.19	
Indiana	Prohibition	6,554	.33	
	Socialist Labor	1,334	.07	
Iowa	Constitution	3,202	.26	
	Socialist	192	.02	
	Socialist Labor	125	.01	
Kansas	Prohibition	3,048	.35	
Kentucky	States Rights	2,657	.25	
	Prohibition	2,145	.20	
	Socialist Labor	358	.03	

STATE TOTALS: ELECTION OF 1956
(continued)

State	Party	Vote	Percentage of Total Vote Cast	Electoral Vote
Louisiana	Constitution	44,520	7.21	
Maine				
Maryland				
Massachusetts	Socialist Labor	5,573	.25	
	Prohibition	1,205	.05	
Michigan	Prohibition	6,923	.22	
Minnesota	Socialist Labor	2,080	.16	
	Socialist Workers	1,098	.08	
Mississippi	States Rights	42,966	17.31	
Missouri				
Montana				
Nebraska				
New Hampshire	Constitution	111	.04	
New Jersey	Prohibition	9,147	.37	
	Socialist Labor	6,736	.27	
	Constitution	5,317	.21	
	Socialist Workers	4,004	.16	
	American Third	1,829	.07	
New Mexico	Prohibition	607	.24	
	Constitution	364	.14	
	Socialist Labor	69	.03	
New York	Constitution	1,027	.01	
	Socialist Labor	150	.00	
	Socialist	82	.00	
North Carolina				
North Dakota	Constitution	483	.19	
Ohio				

STATE TOTALS: ELECTION OF 1956
(continued)

State	Party	Vote	Percentage of Total Vote Cast	Electoral Vote
Oklahoma				
Oregon				
Pennsylvania	Socialist Labor	7,447	.16	
	Socialist Workers	2,035	.04	
Rhode Island				
South Carolina	States Rights	88,509	29.45	
	Constitution	2	.00	
South Dakota				
Tennessee	Constitution	19,886	2.12	
	Prohibition	789	.08	
Texas	Constitution	14,591	.75	
Utah				
Vermont				
Virginia	Constitution	42,964	6.16	
	Socialist	444	.06	
	Socialist Labor	351	.05	
Washington	Socialist Labor	7,457	.65	
West Virginia				
Wisconsin	Constitution	6,918	.45	
	Socialist	754	.05	
	Socialist Labor	710	.05	
	Socialist Workers	564	.04	
Wyoming	Constitution	72	.06	

NATIONAL TOTALS: ELECTION OF 1960

Party	Candidates	Vote	Percentage of Total Vote Cast	Electoral Vote
States Rights	Unpledged	169,572 (440,298)§	.25 (.64)§	0 (14)§
Socialist Labor	Eric Hass Georgia Cozzini	47,522	.07	0
Prohibition	Rutherford L. Decker E. Harold Munn	46,220	.07	0
National States Rights	Orval E. Faubus John G. Crammelin	44,967	.07	0
Socialist Workers	Farrell Dobbs Myra Tanner Weiss	40,175	.06	0
Constitution	Charles L. Sullivan Merrett B. Curtis	18,169	.03	0
Conservative	J. Bracken Lee Kent H. Courtney	8,708	.01	0
Conservative	C. Benton Coiner Edward J. Silverman	4,204	.01	0
Tax Cut	Lar Daly B.M. Miller	1,767	.00	0
Independent Afro-American	Clennon King Reginald Carter	1,485	.00	0
Constitution	Merrett B. Curtis B.M. Miller	1,401	.00	0
Independent American		539	.00	0
Total		384,729 (825,027)§§	.57 (1.21)§§	0 (14)§§§

§ Vote for Unpledged Electors in Mississippi and Alabama.
§§ Including Alabama and Mississippi Unpledged Elector Vote.
§§§ One additional vote was cast by a Republican Elector from Oklahoma for Harry Byrd.

MINOR PARTY VOTING

STATE TOTALS: ELECTION OF 1960

State	Party	Vote	Percentage of Total Vote Cast	Electoral Vote
Alabama	Unpledged Democrats	324,050	56.80	
	National States Rights	4,367	.73	
	Prohibition	2,106	.37	
	Independent Afro-American	1,485	.26	
	Other	236	.00	
Alaska				
Arizona	Socialist Labor	469	.12	
Arkansas	National States Rights	28,952	6.67	
California	Prohibition	21,706	.33	
	Socialist Labor	1,051	.02	
Colorado	Socialist Labor	2,803	.38	
	Socialist Workers	572	.08	
Connecticut				
Delaware	National States Rights	354	.18	
	Prohibition	284	.14	
	Socialist Labor	82	.04	
Florida				
Georgia				
Hawaii				
Idaho				
Illinois	Socialist Labor	10,560	.22	
Indiana	Prohibition	6,746	.32	
	Socialist Labor	1,136	.05	
Iowa	Socialist Workers	634	.05	
	Socialist Labor	230	.02	
Kansas	Prohibition	4,138	.45	
Kentucky				

STATE TOTALS: ELECTION OF 1960
(continued)

State	Party	Vote	Percentage of Total Vote Cast	Electoral Vote
Louisiana	States Rights	169,572	20.99	
Maine				
Maryland				
Massachusetts	Socialist Labor	3,892	.16	
	Prohibition	1,633	.07	
Michigan	Socialist Workers	4,347	.13	
	Prohibition	2,029	.06	
	Tax Cut	1,767	.05	
	Socialist Labor	1,718	.05	
	Independent American	539	.02	
Minnesota	Socialist Workers	3,077	.20	
	Socialist Labor	962	.06	
Mississippi	Unpledged Democrats	116,248	38.99	
Missouri				
Montana	Prohibition	456	.16	
	Socialist Workers	391	.14	
Nebraska				
New Hampshire				
New Jersey	Socialist Workers	11,402	.41	
	Conservative	8,708	.31	
	Socialist Labor	4,262	.15	
New Mexico	Prohibition	777	.25	
	Socialist Labor	570	.18	
New York	Socialist Workers	14,319	.20	
North Carolina				
North Dakota	Socialist Workers	158	.06	
Ohio				

STATE TOTALS: ELECTION OF 1960
(continued)

State	Party	Vote	Percentage of Total Vote Cast	Electoral Vote
Oklahoma				
Oregon				
Pennsylvania	Socialist Labor	7,185	.14	
	Socialist Workers	2,678	.05	
Rhode Island				
South Carolina				
South Dakota				
Tennessee	National States Rights	11,304	1.07	
	Prohibition	2,475	.24	
Texas	Constitution	18,169	.79	
	Prohibition	3,870	.17	
Utah	Socialist Workers	100	.03	
Vermont				
Virginia	Virginia Conservative	4,204	.54	
	Socialist Labor	397	.05	
Washington	Socialist Labor	10,895	.88	
	Constitution	1,401	.11	
	Socialist Workers	705	.06	
West Virginia				
Wisconsin	Socialist Workers	1,792	.10	
	Socialist Labor	1,310	.08	
Wyoming				

MINOR PARTY VOTING

NATIONAL TOTALS: ELECTION OF 1964

Party	Candidates	Vote	Percentage of Total Vote Cast	Electoral Vote
States Rights	Unpledged	210,732	.29	0
Socialist Labor	Eric Hass Henning H. Blomen	45,219	.06	0
Socialist Workers	Clifton DeBarry Edward Shaw	32,720	.05	0
Prohibition	E. Harold Munn Mark R. Shaw	23,267	.03	0
National States Rights	John Kasper J.B. Stoner	6,953	.01	0
Constitution	Joseph B. Lightburn T.C. Billings	5,060	.01	0
Universal	James Hensley John O. Hopkins	19	.00	0
Total		323,970	.45	0

MINOR PARTY VOTING

STATE TOTALS: ELECTION OF 1964

State	Party	Vote	Percentage of Total Vote Cast	Electoral Vote
Alabama	Unpledged Democrats	210,732	30.50	
Arizona	Socialist Labor	482	.10	
Arkansas	National States Rights	2,965	.53	
California	Socialist Labor	489	.01	
	Socialist Workers	378	.00	
	Prohibition	305	.00	
	Universal	19	.00	
Colorado	Socialist Workers	2,537	.33	
	Prohibition	1,356	.17	
	Socialist Labor	302	.04	
Connecticut				
Delaware	Prohibition	425	.21	
	Socialist Labor	113	.06	
Florida				
Georgia				
Hawaii				
Idaho				
Illinois				
Indiana	Prohibition	8,266	.40	
	Socialist Labor	1,374	.07	
Iowa	Prohibition	1,902	.16	
	Socialist Labor	182	.02	
	Socialist Workers	159	.01	
Kansas	Prohibition	5,393	.63	
	Socialist Labor	1,901	.22	
Kentucky	National States Rights	3,469	.33	
Louisiana				
Maine				

366

STATE TOTALS: ELECTION OF 1964
(continued)

State	Party	Vote	Percentage of Total Vote Cast	Electoral Vote
Maryland				
Massachusetts	Socialist Labor	4,755	.20	
	Prohibition	3,735	.16	
Michigan	Socialist Workers	3,817	.12	
	Socialist Labor	1,704	.05	
	Prohibition	669	.02	
Minnesota	Socialist Labor	2,544	.16	
	Socialist Workers	1,177	.08	
Mississippi				
Missouri				
Montana	National States Rights	519	.19	
	Prohibition	499	.18	
	Socialist Workers	332	.12	
Nebraska				
Nevada				
New Hampshire				
New Jersey	Socialist Workers	8,183	.29	
	Socialist Labor	7,075	.25	
New Mexico	Socialist Labor	1,217	.37	
	Prohibition	542	.16	
New York	Socialist Labor	6,118	.08	
	Socialist Workers	3,228	.05	
North Carolina				
North Dakota	Socialist Workers	224	.09	
	Prohibition	174	.07	
Ohio				
Oklahoma				

STATE TOTALS: ELECTION OF 1964
(continued)

State	Party	Vote	Percentage of Total Vote Cast	Electoral Vote
Oregon				
Pennsylvania	Socialist Workers	10,456	.22	
	Socialist Labor	5,092	.11	
Rhode Island				
South Carolina				
South Dakota				
Tennessee				
Texas	Constitution	5,060	.19	
Utah				
Vermont				
Virginia	Socialist Labor	2,895	.28	
Washington	Socialist Labor	7,772	.62	
	Socialist Workers	537	.04	
West Virginia				
Wisconsin	Socialist Workers	1,692	.10	
	Socialist Labor	1,204	.07	
Wyoming				

MINOR PARTY VOTING

NATIONAL TOTALS: ELECTION OF 1968

Party	Candidates	Vote	Percentage of Total Vote Cast	Electoral Vote
American Independent	George C. Wallace S. Marvin Griffin Curtis E. LeMay	9,906,473	13.53	46
Socialist Workers	Fred Halstead Paul Boutelle	41,389	.06	
Socialist Labor	Henning A. Blomen George S. Taylor	52,594	.07	
Prohibition	Earle Harold Munn Rolland E. Fisher	11,101	.02	
Peace and Freedom	Dick Gregory (G) Eldridge Cleaver (C) Other (O) Peggy Terry Larry Hockman Corky Gonzales Mark Lane David Frost (Total)	47,097 8,678 27,887 (83,662)	.06 .01 .04 (.11)	
New Party	Eugene McCarthy	25,067	.03	
Communist	Charlene Mitchell Michael Zagarell	1,075	.00	
Miscellaneous Parties		2,182	.00	
Total		10,123,543	13.82	46

MINOR PARTY VOTING

STATE TOTALS: ELECTION OF 1968

State	Party	Vote	Percentage of Total Vote Cast	Electoral Vote
Alabama	American Independent	691,425	65.86	10
	Other	14,982	1.43	
Alaska	American Independent	10,024	12.07	
Arizona	American Independent	46,573	9.56	
	New Party	2,751	.56	
	Peace and Freedom (C)	217	.04	
	Socialist Workers	85	.02	
	Socialist Labor	75	.02	
Arkansas	American Independent	240,982	38.87	6
California	American Independent	487,270	6.72	
	Peace and Freedom (O)	27,707	.38	
	New Party	20,721	.29	
	Peace and Freedom (G)	3,230	.04	
	Socialist Labor	341	.00	
	Communist	260	.00	
	Prohibition	59	.00	
	Berkeley Defense	17	.00	
Colorado	American Independent	60,813	7.51	
	Socialist Labor	3,016	.37	
	Peace and Freedom (G)	1,393	.17	
	Prohibition	275	.03	
	Socialist Workers	235	.03	
Connecticut	American Independent	76,650	6.11	
Delaware	American Independent	28,459	13.28	
Florida	American Independent	624,207	28.53	
Georgia	American Independent	535,550	42.84	12
Hawaii	American Independent	3,469	1.47	
Idaho	American Independent	36,541	12.55	
Illinois	American Independent	390,958	8.46	
	Socialist Labor	13,878	.30	

STATE TOTALS: ELECTION OF 1968
(continued)

State	Party	Vote	Percentage of Total Vote Cast	Electoral Vote
Indiana	American Independent	243,108	11.45	
	Prohibition	4,616	.22	
	Socialist Workers	1,293	.06	
Iowa	American Independent	66,422	5.69	
	Socialist Workers	3,377	.29	
	Peace and Freedom (C)	1,332	.11	
	Prohibition	362	.03	
	Socialist Labor	241	.02	
	Universal	142	.01	
Kansas	American Independent	88,921	10.19	
	Prohibition	2,192	.25	
Kentucky	American Independent	193,098	18.29	
	Socialist Workers	2,843	.27	
Louisiana	American Independent	530,300	48.32	10
Maine	American Independent	6,370	1.62	
Maryland	American Independent	178,734	14.47	
Massachusetts	American Independent	87,088	3.74	
	Socialist Labor	6,180	.27	
	Prohibition	2,369	.10	
Michigan	American Independent	331,968	10.04	
	Peace and Freedom (C)	4,585	.14	
	Socialist Workers	4,099	.12	
	Socialist Labor	1,762	.05	
	Prohibition	60	.00	
Minnesota	American Independent	68,931	4.34	
	Peace and Freedom (C)	935	.06	
	Socialist Workers	808	.05	
	New Party	585	.04	
	Communist	415	.03	
	Socialist Labor	285	.02	
Mississippi	American Independent	415,349	63.46	7

STATE TOTALS: ELECTION OF 1968
(continued)

State	Party	Vote	Percentage of Total Vote Cast	Electoral Vote
Missouri	American Independent	206,126	11.39	
Montana	American Independent	20,015	7.29	
	Prohibition	510	.19	
	New Reform	470	.17	
	Socialist Workers	457	.17	
Nebraska	American Independent	44,904	8.36	
Nevada	American Independent	20,432	13.25	
New Hampshire	American Independent	11,173	3.76	
	New Party	421	.11	
	Socialist Workers	104	.03	
New Jersey	American Independent	262,187	9.12	
	Socialist Workers	8,667	.30	
	Peace and Freedom (G)	8,084	.28	
	Socialist Labor	6,784	.24	
New Mexico	American Independent	25,737	7.86	
	Chavey	1,519	.46	
	Socialist Workers	252	.08	
New York	American Independent	358,864	5.29	
	Peace and Freedom (G)	24,517	.36	
	Socialist Workers	11,851	.17	
	Socialist Labor	8,438	.12	
North Carolina	American Independent	496,188	31.26	1
North Dakota	American Independent	14,244	5.75	
	Socialist Workers	128	.05	
	Prohibition	38	.02	
	Constitution	34	.01	
Ohio	American Independent	467,495	11.81	
	Peace and Freedom (G)	372	.01	
	Socialist Labor	120	.00	
	Socialist Workers	69	.00	
	Communist	23	.00	
	Prohibition	19	.00	

STATE TOTALS: ELECTION OF 1968
(continued)

State	Party	Vote	Percentage of Total Vote Cast	Electoral Vote
Oklahoma	American Independent	191,731	20.33	
Oregon	American Independent	49,683	6.07	
	Scattered	1,565	.19	
Pennsylvania	American Independent	378,582	7.97	
	Peace and Freedom (G)	7,821	.16	
	Socialist Labor	4,977	.10	
	Socialist Workers	4,862	.10	
	Scattered	2,264	.05	
Rhode Island	American Independent	15,678	4.07	
	Socialist Workers	383	.10	
South Carolina	American Independent	215,430	32.30	
South Dakota	American Independent	13,400	4.76	
Tennessee	American Independent	424,792	34.02	
Texas	American Independent	584,269	18.98	
Utah	American Independent	26,906	6.37	
	Peace and Freedom (O)	180	.04	
	Socialist Workers	89	.02	
Vermont	American Independent	5,104	3.16	
	New Party	579	.36	
	Socialist Workers	295	.18	
Virginia	American Independent	321,833	23.64	
	Socialist Labor	4,671	.34	
	Peace and Freedom (G)	1,680	.12	
	Prohibition	601	.04	
Washington	American Independent	96,990	7.44	
	Peace and Freedom (C)	1,609	.12	
	Socialist Labor	488	.04	
	Communist	377	.03	
	Socialist Workers	270	.02	
West Virginia	American Independent	72,560	9.62	

STATE TOTALS: ELECTION OF 1968
(continued)

State	Party	Vote	Percentage of Total Vote Cast	Electoral Vote
Wisconsin	American Independent	127,835	7.57	
	Socialist Labor	1,338	.08	
	Socialist Workers	1,222	.07	
Wyoming	American Independent	11,105	8.73	

SELECTED BIBLIOGRAPHY

Presidential Politics and Campaigns

Abels, Jules. OUT OF THE JAWS OF VICTORY. New York: Holt, Rinehart, and Winston, 1959.

Almond, G., and Verba, S. THE CIVIC CULTURE. Princeton: Princeton University Press, 1963.

Anderson, Walt. CAMPAIGNS: CASES IN POLITICAL CONFLICT. California: Goodyear Publishing Co., 1970.

David, Paul T. (ed.). THE PRESIDENTIAL ELECTION AND TRANSITION, 1960–1961. Washington: Brookings Institution, 1961.

Davis, James W. PRESIDENTIAL PRIMARIES: ROAD TO THE WHITE HOUSE. New York: Thomas Y. Crowell Co., 1967.

Eisenstein, Virginia and James. PRESIDENTIAL PRIMARIES OF 1968. Washington: Center for Information on America, 1968.

Ernst, Harry. THE PRIMARY THAT MADE A PRESIDENT: WEST VIRGINIA, 1960. New York: McGraw-Hill Book Co., 1962.

Ewing, Cortez A. M. PRESIDENTIAL ELECTIONS. Norman: University of Oklahoma Press, 1940.

Gilder, George, and Chapman, Bruce K. THE PARTY THAT LOST ITS HEAD. New York: Knopf, 1966.

Johnson, Walter. HOW WE DRAFTED ADLAI STEVENSON. New York: Knopf, 1955.

Kelley, Stanley, Jr. POLITICAL CAMPAIGNING. Washington: Brookings Institution, 1960.

Kraus, Sidney (ed.). THE GREAT DEBATES. Bloomington: University of Indiana Press, 1962.

Lamb, Karl A., and Smith, Paul A. CAMPAIGN DECISION-MAKING: THE PRESIDENTIAL ELECTION OF 1964. Belmont, California: Wadsworth Publishing Co., 1968.

Leuthold, David A. ELECTIONEERING IN A DEMOCRACY: CAMPAIGNS FOR CONGRESS. New York: John Wiley and Sons, Inc., 1968.

Levin, Murray B. KENNEDY CAMPAIGNING. Boston: Beacon Press, 1966.

Martin, Joseph W., Jr. MY FIRST FIFTY YEARS IN POLITICS. New York: McGraw-Hill Book Co., 1960.

Mazo, Earl. THE GREAT DEBATES. Santa Barbara: Center for the Study of Democratic Institutions, 1962.

Moos, Malcolm. THE REPUBLICANS. New York: Random House, 1956.

———. POLITICS, PRESIDENTS AND COATTAILS. Baltimore, Johns Hopkins Press, 1952.

Nash, Howard P., Jr. THIRD PARTIES IN AMERICAN POLITICS. Washington: Public Affairs Press, 1959.

Nimmo, Dan. THE POLITICAL PERSUADERS. Englewood Cliffs: Prentice Hall, 1970.

Novak, Robert D. THE AGONY OF THE GOP 1964. New York: Macmillan, 1965.

Ogden, Daniel M., Jr., and Peterson, Arthur L. ELECTING THE PRESIDENT: 1964. San Francisco: Chandler Publishing Co., 1964.

Petersen, Svend. A STATISTICAL HISTORY OF THE AMERICAN PRESIDENTIAL ELECTIONS. New York: Frederick Ungar Publishing Co., 1963.

Polsby, Nelson W., and Wildavsky, Aaron B. PRESIDENTIAL ELECTIONS. New York: Charles Scribner's Sons, 1964.

Pomper, Gerald. ELECTIONS IN AMERICA. New York: Dodd, Mead & Co., 1970.

Pusey, Merlo J. EISENHOWER THE PRESIDENT. New York: The Macmillan Co., 1956.

Ranney, Austin, and Dendall, Willmoore. DEMOCRACY AND THE AMERICAN PARTY SYSTEM. New York: Harcourt, 1956.

Redding, Jack. INSIDE THE DEMOCRATIC PARTY. New York: Bobbs-Merrill, 1958.

Roseboom, Eugene H. A HISTORY OF PRESIDENTIAL ELECTIONS. New York: Macmillan, 1957.

Rovere, Richard. THE EISENHOWER YEARS. New York: Farrar, Straus and Cudahy, Inc., 1956.

————. THE GOLDWATER CAPER. New York: Harcourt, Brace & World, 1965.

Schattschneider, E. E. PARTY GOVERNMENT. New York: Farrar and Rinehart, 1942.

Sevareid, Eric (ed.). CANDIDATES, 1960. New York: Basic Books, 1959.

Shadess, Stephen C. HOW TO WIN AN ELECTION: THE ART OF POLITICAL VICTORY. New York: Taplinger Publishing Co., 1964.

Steinberg, Alfred. THE MAN FROM MISSOURI. New York: G. P. Putnam's Sons, 1962.

Thomson, Charles A. H., and Shattuck, Francis M. THE 1956 PRESIDENTIAL CAMPAIGN. Washington: The Brookings Institution, 1960.

U.S. Senate. Committee on Commerce. THE SPEECHES, REMARKS, PRESS CONFERENCES, AND STUDY PAPERS OF VICE PRESIDENT RICHARD M. NIXON, AUGUST 25 THROUGH NOVEMBER 7, 1960. Report 994, Part 2, 87th Congress, 1st Session, 1961.

————. THE SPEECHES, REMARKS, PRESS CONFERENCES, AND STATEMENTS OF JOHN F. KENNEDY, AUGUST 17 THROUGH NOVEMBER 7, 1960. Report 994, Part 1, 87th Congress, 1st Session, 1961.

————. THE JOINT APPEARANCE OF SENATOR JOHN F. KENNEDY AND VICE PRESIDENT RICHARD M. NIXON AND OTHER 1960 CAMPAIGN PRESENTATIONS. Report 994, Part 3, 87th Congress, 1st Session, 1961.

White, F. Clifton. SUITE 3505. New Rochelle, New York: Arlington House, 1967.

White, Theodore H. THE MAKING OF THE PRESIDENT, 1960. New York: Atheneum, 1961.

———. THE MAKING OF THE PRESIDENT, 1964. New York: Atheneum, 1965.

———. THE MAKING OF THE PRESIDENT, 1968. New York: Atheneum, 1969.

Conventions

Bain, Richard C. CONVENTION DECISIONS AND VOTING RECORDS. Washington: Brookings Institution, 1960.

Cummings, Milton C. THE NATIONAL ELECTION OF 1964. Washington: Brookings Institution, 1966.

David, P. T.; Goldman, R. M.; and Bain, R. C. THE POLITICS OF NATIONAL PARTY CONVENTIONS. Washington: Brookings Institution, 1960.

David, Paul T.; Moos, Malcolm; and Goldman, Ralph M. (eds.). PRESIDENTIAL NOMINATING POLITICS IN 1952. 5 Vols. Baltimore: Johns Hopkins, 1954.

Democratic National Committee. OFFICIAL REPORTS OF THE PROCEEDINGS OF THE DEMOCRATIC NATIONAL CONVENTIONS, 1948–1968. Washington: Democratic National Committee.

Eaton, Herbert. PRESIDENTIAL TIMBER. New York: The Free Press of Glencoe, 1964.

Hupman, Richard D., and Rarnholt, Eiler C. NOMINATION AND ELECTION OF THE PRESIDENT AND VICE PRESIDENT OF THE UNITED STATES. Washington: Government Printing Office, 1964.

Pomper, Gerald. NOMINATING THE PRESIDENT. Evanston: Northwestern University, 1963.

Porter, Kirk Harold, and Johnson, Donald Bruce. NATIONAL PARTY PLATFORMS, 1940–1960. 2nd ed. Urbana, Illinois: University of Illinois Press, 1961.

Republican National Committee. OFFICIAL REPORTS OF THE PROCEEDINGS OF THE REPUBLICAN NATIONAL CONVENTIONS, 1948–1968. Washington: Republican National Committee.

Stone, Irving. THEY ALSO RAN. New York: Pyramid Books, 1964.

Tillett, Paul (ed.). INSIDE POLITICS: THE NATIONAL CONVENTIONS, 1960. Dobbs Ferry, New York: Oceana Publications, Inc., 1962.

Politics and the Media

Blumler, Jay G., and McQuail, Denis. TELEVISION IN POLITICS: ITS USES AND INFLUENCE. Illinois: University of Chicago Press, 1969.

Bogart, Leo. THE AGE OF TELEVISION: A STUDY OF VIEWING HABITS AND THE IMPACT OF TELEVISION ON AMERICAN LIFE. New York: Frederick Ungar, 1958.

Boorstin, Daniel J. THE IMAGE OR WHAT HAPPENED TO THE AMERICAN DREAM. New York: Atheneum, 1962.

Clausen, Aage R. POLITICAL PREDICTIONS AND PROJECTIONS: DO

THEY INFLUENCE THE OUTCOME OF ELECTIONS? Washington: Center for Information on America, 1966.

Federal Communications Commission. SURVEY OF POLITICAL BROADCASTING, SEPTEMBER 1–NOVEMBER 8, 1960. Washington: FCC, 1961.

———. SURVEY OF POLITICAL BROADCASTING: PRIMARY AND GENERAL ELECTION CAMPAIGNS OF 1964. Washington: FCC, 1965.

———. SURVEY OF POLITICAL BROADCASTING: PRIMARY AND GENERAL ELECTIONS OF 1968. Washington: FCC, 1969.

Klapper, Joseph T. THE EFFECTS OF MASS COMMUNICATION. Glencoe, Illinois: Free Press, 1960.

Lang, Kurt, and Lang, Gladys E. POLITICS AND TELEVISION. Chicago: Quadrangle Books, 1968.

MacNeil, Robert. THE PEOPLE MACHINE: THE INFLUENCE OF TELEVISION ON AMERICAN POLITICS. New York: Harper and Row, 1968.

McGinnis, Joe. THE SELLING OF THE PRESIDENT 1968. New York: Trident Press, 1969.

Minow, Newton N. EQUAL TIME: THE PRIVATE BROADCASTER AND THE PUBLIC INTEREST. Edited by Lawrence Laurent. New York: Atheneum, 1964.

Roper, Burns W. EMERGING PROFILES OF TELEVISION AND OTHER MASS MEDIA: PUBLIC ATTITUDES 1959–1967. New York: Television Information Office, 1967.

Rubin, Bernard. POLITICAL TELEVISION. Belmont, California: Wadsworth Publishing Co., 1967.

Salinger, Pierre. WITH KENNEDY. New York: Doubleday, 1966.

Simonson, Solomon. CRISIS IN TELEVISION: A STUDY OF THE PRIVATE JUDGMENT AND THE PUBLIC INTEREST. New York: Living Books, 1966.

Thomson, Charles A. H. TELEVISION AND PRESIDENTIAL POLITICS. Washington: The Brookings Institution, 1956.

Wyckoff, Gene. THE IMAGE CANDIDATES: AMERICAN POLITICS IN THE AGE OF TELEVISION. New York: Macmillan Co., 1968.

Campaign Finance

Alexander, Herbert E. FINANCING THE 1960 ELECTION. Princeton: Citizens' Research Foundation, 1961.

———. FINANCING THE 1964 ELECTION. Princeton: Citizens' Research Foundation, 1966.

——— (ed.). STUDIES IN MONEY AND POLITICS: A SERIES OF SEVEN MONOGRAPHS. Princeton: Citizens' Research Foundation, 1965.

Davis, Ellen. MONEY FOR POLITICS. Washington: Center for Information on America, 1964.

Heard, Alexander. THE COSTS OF DEMOCRACY. Chapel Hill: University of North Carolina Press, 1960.

Owens, John R. MONEY AND POLITICS IN CALIFORNIA: DEMOCRATIC

SENATORIAL PRIMARY, 1964. Princeton: Citizens' Research Foundation, 1966.

Shannon, Jasper B. MONEY AND POLITICS. New York: Random House, 1959.

U.S. President's Commission on Campaign Costs. FINANCING PRESIDENTIAL CAMPAIGNS. U.S. Government Printing Office, April 1962.

U.S. Senate Subcommittee on Privileges and Elections. REPORT, 1956 GENERAL ELECTION CAMPAIGNS. 85th Congress, 1st Session, 1957.

The Electorate

Berelson, Bernard R.; Lazarsfeld, Paul E.; and McPhee, William N. VOTING: A STUDY OF OPINION FORMATION IN A PRESIDENTIAL CAMPAIGN. Chicago: Chicago University Press, 1954.

Burdick, Eugene, and Broderick, Arthur J. (eds.). AMERICAN VOTING BEHAVIOR. Glencoe, Illinois: Free Press, 1959.

Campbell, Angus, and Kahn, Robert L. THE PEOPLE ELECT A PRESIDENT. Ann Arbor: University of Michigan Survey Research Center, 1952.

Campbell, Angus; Gurin, Gerald; and Miller, Warren E. THE VOTER DECIDES. Evanston: Row Petersen and Co., 1954.

Campbell, Angus; Converse, Philip E.; Miller, Warren E.; and Stokes, Donald E. THE AMERICAN VOTER. New York: Wiley, 1960.

Dawidowicz, Lucy S., and Goldstein, Leon J. POLITICS IN A PLURALIST DEMOCRACY. New York: Institute of Human Relations Press, 1963.

Gallup, George (ed.). THE POLITICAL ALMANAC 1952. New York: Forbes, 1952.

Greenstein, Fred I. THE AMERICAN PARTY SYSTEM AND THE AMERICAN PEOPLE. Englewood Cliffs, New Jersey: Prentice-Hall, 1964.

Hennessy, Bernard C. PUBLIC OPINION. California: Wadsworth Publishing Co., 1965.

Jennings, M. Kent, and Zeider, Harmon L. (eds.). THE ELECTORAL PROCESS. Englewood Cliffs, New Jersey: Prentice-Hall, 1966.

Key, V. O., Jr. PUBLIC OPINION AND AMERICAN DEMOCRACY. New York: Knopf, 1961.

————. THE RESPONSIBLE ELECTORATE. Cambridge: Harvard University Press, 1966.

Knight, Robert P. POLLS, SAMPLING, AND THE VOTER. Columbia, Missouri: School of Journalism, University of Missouri, 1966.

Lane, Robert E. POLITICAL LIFE. Glencoe, Illinois: Free Press, 1959.

Lang, Kurt, and Lang, Gladys E. VOTING AND NONVOTING. Waltham, Massachusetts: Blaisdell, 1968.

Lazarsfeld, Paul F.; Berelson, Bernard; and Gaudet, Hazel. THE PEOPLE'S CHOICE: HOW THE VOTER MAKES UP HIS MIND IN A PRESIDENTIAL CAMPAIGN. New York: Columbia University Press, 1948.

Lippmann, Walter. PUBLIC OPINION. New York: Macmillan, 1953.

Milbrath, Lester W. POLITICAL PARTICIPATION. Chicago: Rand McNally, 1965.

Scammon, Richard M. (ed.). AMERICA VOTES, Volumes I–VIII (1952–1968). Washington, D.C.: Congressional Quarterly.

———. AMERICA AT THE POLLS: A HANDBOOK OF AMERICAN PRESIDENTIAL ELECTION STATISTICS 1920–1964. Pittsburgh: University of Pittsburgh Press, 1965.

Scammon, Richard M., and Wattenberg, Ben J. THE REAL MAJORITY. New York: Coward-McCann, 1970.

Election Laws and Electoral Reform

Eisenstein, Virginia and James. THE ELECTORAL COLLEGE: HOW DOES IT WORK? Washington: Center for Information on America, 1965.

Herzberg, Donald G. THE RIGHT TO VOTE: HOW OUR LAWS RESTRICT IT. Washington: Center for Information on America, 1967.

League of Women Voters of the United States. WHO SHOULD ELECT THE PRESIDENT? Washington: League of Women Voters of the United States, 1969.

NOMINATION AND ELECTION OF THE PRESIDENT AND VICE PRESIDENT OF THE UNITED STATES, INCLUDING THE MANNER OF SELECTING DELEGATES TO NATIONAL POLITICAL CONVENTIONS. House Document No. 332. Washington, D.C.: 1960.

NOMINATION AND ELECTION OF THE PRESIDENT AND VICE PRESIDENT OF THE UNITED STATES, INCLUDING THE MANNER OF SELECTING DELEGATES TO NATIONAL POLITICAL CONVENTIONS. Senate Item No. 998. Washington, D.C.: January, 1964.

Peirce, Neal. THE PEOPLE'S PRESIDENT: THE ELECTORAL COLLEGE AND THE EMERGING CONSENSUS FOR A DIRECT VOTE. New York: Simon & Schuster, 1968.

Smith, Constance E. VOTING AND ELECTION LAWS. New York: Oceana Publications, Inc., 1960.